D1015073

Web 2.0:
A Strategy Guide

Web 2.0:
A Strategy Guide

Amy Shuen

O'REILLY®

Beijing • Cambridge • Farnham • Köln • Paris • Sebastopol • Taipei • Tokyo

Web 2.0: A Strategy Guide
by Amy Shuen

Copyright © 2008 Amy Shuen. All rights reserved. Printed in Canada.

Published by O'Reilly Media, Inc. 1005 Gravenstein Highway North, Sebastopol, CA 95472.

O'Reilly books may be purchased for educational, business, or sales promotional use. Online editions are also available for most titles (*safari.oreilly.com*). For more information, contact our corporate/institutional sales department: (800) 998-9938 or *corporate@oreilly.com*.

Editor: Simon St.Laurent	**Proofreader:** Loranah Dimant
Production Editor: Loranah Dimant	**Indexer:** John Bickelhaupt
	Interior Designer: Ron Bilodeau
Copyeditors: Laurel R.T. Ruma and Jim Duffy	**Illustrator:** Robert Romano

Printing History:

April 2008:   First Edition.

The O'Reilly logo is a registered trademark of O'Reilly Media, Inc. *Web 2.0: A Strategy Guide* and related trade dress are trademarks of O'Reilly Media, Inc.

Many of the designations used by manufacturers and sellers to distinguish their products are claimed as trademarks. Where those designations appear in this book, and O'Reilly Media, Inc. was aware of a trademark claim, the designations have been printed in caps or initial caps.

While every precaution has been taken in the preparation of this book, the publisher and author assume no responsibility for errors or omissions, or for damages resulting from the use of the information contained herein.

```
31143007305882
658.4038 Shuen
Shuen, Amy Anne.
Web 2.0 : a strategy
guide
1st ed.
```

ISBN: 978-0-596-52996-3

[F]

*To my wonderful father and mother
for their inspiration, and to my family
for their love and encouragement.*

Contents

Foreword

In 2004, when O'Reilly Media, John Battelle, and CMP announced the Web 2.0 Conference (later renamed the Web 2.0 Summit), we had no idea that we'd be naming the next big thing in the computer industry. The original premise of the Web 2.0 name was much simpler than that. In 2001, after the dot-com bust, everyone had written off the Web. But at O'Reilly, we believed deeply that the Web was here to stay, and that it was indeed the next platform. We also noted that all of the companies that had survived the dot-com bust—and all of the exciting new startups that were gaining remarkable traction—had something in common: they understood and exploited the opportunities of the network as a platform, rather than trying to graft old business models onto that platform. We saw Web 2.0 not as a new version of the Web, but rather, as the realization of the Web's potential, its second coming, so to speak. We launched a conference to tell that story, and to reignite excitement in the industry about the transformative power of this technology.

The term Web 2.0 caught everyone's imagination, coming at just the right time to capitalize on the rise of Google, mashups, and Ajax. But to us, the term meant far more than just advertising-based business models or new types of web applications. In 2005, I wrote a paper, *What Is Web 2.0?*, to formalize our ideas about this new platform. I argued that Web 2.0 is ultimately about harnessing network effects and the collective intelligence of users to build applications that literally get better the more people use them. What's more, I argued that just as the personal computer rewrote the rules of the computer industry in ways that blindsided the giants of that era, so too, would the Internet upend all the power structures and business models of today's industry. Only companies that understood and adapted to the new rules of business would survive and prosper.

Since then, the name Web 2.0 has been widely accepted, and the concepts in that paper, and its predecessor, *The Open Source Paradigm Shift* have been the basis of many new business plans and development strategies. But with popular acceptance and enthusiasm has come a great deal of misinformation, as marketers have tried to wrap products in the mantle of Web 2.0 whether or not they fit.

It is for this reason that I'm excited to see the publication of Amy Shuen's *Web 2.0: A Strategy Guide*. It's the first book that really does justice to my ideas, explaining in plain language the business implications of the Web as a platform. Amy works through a series of practical case studies of Web 2.0 success stories to explain how the underlying principles have been applied to drive each company's growth and profitability.

There's still a lot to learn. The Web 2.0 revolution continues, and every day, entrepreneurs are finding new ways to apply the principles of Web 2.0. I expect more surprises and new success stories. But for now, this book is the best starting point for any company that wants to understand and apply Internet-era business strategy.

—Tim O'Reilly

Sebastopol, CA

March 2008

Preface

YOU ARE ALREADY AN INTEGRAL PART OF THE WEB 2.0 BUSINESS ECONOMY. Every time you click on Google, Wikipedia, eBay, or Amazon, you are sparking "network effects." If you use a Flickr-enabled cell phone or tune in to iTunes podcasts or check Yahoo! Finance for stock quotes, you are creating monetizable value for businesses—even if you don't actually buy anything.

Web 2.0 realizes and goes far beyond what Web 1.0 started. It opens tremendous opportunities as business models catch up to the technological possibilities. So many people are connected to and contribute to the Internet now that economies of scale not only lower costs, they create value.

Companies are developing business models that involve creating appealing destinations on the Web where people with shared interests can form communities. When people come together over the Web, their efforts are multiplied rather than simply added together.

Yet whether you are a seasoned business professional or a digital native, the stories about exactly how the new Web 2.0 business models work and make money may seem quite fuzzy, or even downright counterintuitive. The questions are clear:

- How is Web 2.0 different from the Web 1.0 dot-com boom and bust?

- How does Google offer "the world's knowledge" to searchers for free and still make more than $10 billion in revenue,[1] grow 68%, and have a stock market valuation of close to $200 billion?

- What could possibly make Flickr—a two-year-old photo-sharing startup—worth $40 million to Yahoo!, a video-sharing YouTube worth $1.6 billion to Google, a social networking site called Facebook worth the equivalent of $15 billion to Microsoft?

- Is Web 2.0 about corporate blogging, wikis, and podcasting, or something else entirely?

To answer these questions, you'll need some analytical tools—not just buzzwords and hype—to understand how successful Web 2.0 companies do what they do, and the economic mechanisms at work. As you walk through the real-life business stories in this book, you'll see how customers can provide value as well as cash. There are lots of ways companies can make money from that value, not just by selling goods and services directly to users. These are network effects, and you'll see them in action in almost every case.

A growing number of CEOs and executives from more traditional industries are becoming champions of Web 2.0, with hard numbers to back up their enthusiasm. Yes, Web 2.0 matters for Fortune 100s, big businesses, enterprises, multinationals, and even countries. Don Tapscott, coauthor of the Enterprise 2.0 book, *Wikinomics* (Portfolio Hardcover), states, "It's the biggest change in the organization of the corporation in a century...." In short, Web 2.0 is powering up the knowledge and network economy, starting with users, consumers, and digital natives, and accelerating as it transforms knowledge workers and businesses globally:

- Cisco chairman and CEO John Chambers is betting his company on collaboration and Web 2.0—"The next wave will be about collaboration and Web 2.0...this will drive productivity

---

[1] MarketWire, "Google Revenue to Exceed $10 Billion in 2007," March 2006, *http://www.emarketer.com/Article.aspx?id=1003885* (accessed Feb. 2008).

for the next decade...if you don't understand the power of this collaboration, you'll get left behind as a company, as a country."[2]

- A.G. Lafley, CEO of Procter & Gamble, made his consumer product company a Web 2.0 innovation success story by raising new product development success to an astounding 80%, compared to the industry average of 30%. Now more than 35% of the ideas come from outside—via collaborative web sites, such as InnoCentive, providing access to millions of contributors, not just the 9,000-person research and development staff.[3]

- "Enterprises have been ringing our phones off the hook to ask us about Web 2.0," according to Rod Smith, IBM's vice president for emerging Internet technologies.[4] IBM has a massive installed base and global Linux and open systems development ecosystem and partnership community, as well as a $50 billion services engine.

- Motorola is one of the biggest adopters of web collaboration tools with 4,400 blogs, 4,200 wiki pages, and 2,600 people actively tagging content and social bookmarking, under an initiative called Intranet 2.0. Toby Redshaw, Motorola's vice president in charge of Enterprise 2.0 technologies, says that the company is now more effective at finding people with know-how and expertise: "It actually lets people see new relationships—to see maps of what smart people and like people have done."[5]

- Enterprise 2.0 companies with success stories range from Bank of America, Wells Fargo, Boeing, FedEx, Morgan Stanley, and Pfizer. According to Forrester Research, companies

---

2 Steven Deare, "Cisco CEO sings praises of Web 2.0 future." *ZDNet Australia,* April 27, 2007, *http://www.zdnet.com.au/news/software/soa/Cisco-CEO-sings-praises-of-Web-2-0-future/0,130061733,339275139,00.htm.*

3 J. Nicholas Hoover, "At Procter & Gamble, The Good and Bad of Web 2.0 Tools," *Information Week,* June 23, 2007, *http://www.informationweek.com/story/showArticle.jhtml?articleID=200000229.*

4 Robert Hof, "Web 2.0 Has Corporate America Spinning," *BusinessWeek,* June 5, 2006, *http://www.businessweek.com/technology/content/jun2006/tc20060605_424102.htm.*

5 Ibid.

are adopting Web 2.0 technology for business productivity (74%), competitive pressure (64%), specific problem solution (53%), partner recommendation (53%), employee request (45%), and bundled service (25%).[6]

This book digs deeper and makes concrete the buzzwords that are starting to fly around. It provides the theory and practice behind *collective user value* (Chapter 1), *monetizing network effects* (Chapter 2), *capitalizing on social networks* (Chapter 3), *dynamic capabilities* (Chapter 4), and *collaborative innovation* (Chapter 5). You will understand why even managers and executives of big companies and multinationals must think differently about strategy and revenue-sharing in a Web 2.0 world. Especially in a "flat world" where "size matters not," small- and medium-size enterprises (SMEs) and even one-man local businesses or projects can use these business models to advantage.

If you feel like you missed something about Web 2.0 economics or that you somehow walked into the middle of the conversation, you're not alone.

First, the Web 2.0 business revolution has exploded in a similar way to the "tipping point" that ignited social phenomena as diverse as fashion trends and popular fads, new movies and videogames, environmental awareness, and the diffusion of literacy through Sesame Street. Critical mass matters, and the Web has reached that critical mass. Free web services, viral distribution, and active uploaders have compounded to create powerful cross-network and social network effects. These are all almost instantaneously monetizable and trackable through advertising and targeted pay-per-click marketing.

Second, even recent M.B.A.s have a hard time pulling together all the necessary pieces of the Web 2.0 business model. Business model analysis is sometimes covered in corporate strategy classes but more frequently in entrepreneurship classes. Per-user economics (originally based on subscriber economics and lifetime value) is sometimes covered in marketing classes, but again, more

---

6   R. Todd Stephens, comment on "P&G Web 2.0 Success Story," Forrester report cited on Collaborage: Enterprise 2.0 Implementation Overview blog, comment posted on Nov. 27, 2007, *http://www.rtodd.com/collaborage/2007/11pg_web_20_success_story.html.*

frequently in entrepreneurship classes. Offline advertising and television, newspaper, and print media revenue models are briefly covered in core marketing and advertising and promotion electives, but online advertising, web analytics, pay-per-click advertising, and targeted or behavioral online advertising are rarely covered.

This book brings together all of the relevant frameworks and analysis tools from several disparate disciplines to give you the overall big picture of Web 2.0 business and economics. It will give you a lens through which to see more clearly and make sense of what's transpiring right in front of us.

What Is Web 2.0?

Google this question and look at the first 10 organic search hits out of the possible 65 million web pages returned. If the results haven't changed since the time of this writing, the first-ranked entry is the Wikipedia entry. The second-ranked entry is Tim O'Reilly's article, *What Is Web 2.0?*, the online posting of his classic white paper and accompanying conference that coined the term.

The third- and fourth-ranked listed web sites are short YouTube videos that are well worth watching for two very different visual contexts and views. "What is Web 2.0?" is a techie perspective on Web 2.0, explaining how rich user experiences and the interactive, social Web are made possible by Ajax, RSS, and web services. The video account is accurate, though the presenter gives a dry mini-lecture with colored markers on a whiteboard.

The other YouTube video, "Web 2.0: The Machine is Us/ing Us," is a digital anthropology professor's perspective on Web 2.0, explaining how a shift as small as XML separating content from form so that knowledge can be exported and syndicated without complicated code could result in an explosion of uploaded user content. Billions of clicks a day contribute to the collective Web and a rethinking of ourselves—through sharing, collaborating, and trading. We visually accompany the author through a fast-paced web and blogosphere journey—keywording, hyperlinking, and clicking to the beat of techno music.

These YouTube videos provide two ends of the spectrum of Web 2.0 definitions. The technical folks tell us that techniques, architectures, and technologies have combined to trigger a phase transition—from a Web 1.0 collection of static web sites to a Web 2.0 platform for a new generation of dynamic social web applications and services. The social sciences folks show us that "we are the Web" and that right now—whether you call it Web 2.0 or not—people are shaping the Web and the world's digitized collective knowledge in unexpected directions through their uploads, content, and billions of clicks a day. By the way, the "machine" is using this super large data set, algorithmically and automatically data-mining it to aggregate and amplify its feedback.

Browsing through the Web 2.0 definitions online reminds me of the well-known story of the blind men and the elephant. Some definitions emphasize the technical aspects of Web 2.0; to me, that is like saying, "The elephant is like a column." Yes, the legs are necessary for the elephant to be able to stand and move, just like any other infrastructure or architecture, but Web 2.0 is so much more than the technology.

Other definitions emphasize the interactivity of users: Web 2.0 is read-write. Earlier versions of the Web were more passive and encouraged only downloading, whereas the new applications are more interactive and dynamic, encouraging users to be more involved and upload content onto the Web. To me, that is like saying that "the elephant is like a fan" because of the movement and shape of its large ears.

Some people argue that Web 2.0 is only Ajax and the use of this kind of "JavaScript on the Web" for applications such as Google Maps. This is like saying "an elephant is like a snake" because of its narrow, short tail. Others say that Web 2.0 is the social Web—blogging, wikis, mashups, and podcasts, defining one buzzword by several others—and it is identified by its best-known and widespread applications and web services. This is like saying "an elephant is like a turnip" because of its tusks.

Of course, the four blind men could not see the elephant in action. If they did, they would probably have observed it eating, as an elephant does almost constantly: 16 hours a day. Being a vegetarian, an elephant needs to ingest enough small leaves, branches, fruit, and bamboo to sustain itself and grow to 10–12 feet in height and nearly 4 tons of mass. Perhaps this is where Web 2.0 is most like an elephant.

Unlike the elephant, however, Web 2.0 has a long tail. This is the phenomenon whereby business can make more money by selling lower volumes of hard-to-find products than by selling larger volumes of popular items. (The "long tail" refers to the shape of the demand curve.) Monetizing the long tail—encouraging the nutritious leaves of small- and medium-size advertisers who are new to online advertising—is how Web 2.0 converts the Web into wealth. John Battelle, in his book *The Search: How Google and Its Rivals Rewrote the Rules of Business and Transformed Our Culture* (*The Search*) (Portfolio Trade), puts it eloquently: "Google made billions, one nickel at a time." He was, of course, referring to the Google AdWords advertising platform where do-it-yourself advertisers can pay a minimum of 5 cents per keyword click for paid search advertising. What's new about Web 2.0 is that both businesses and individuals can make money by providing services to customers for free.

My Executive M.B.A. students suggested that a more appropriate description and writing of Web 2.0 could be W2W or "Web to wealth." Unlike the first generation of dot-com web businesses that poured vast amounts of venture money into acquiring new customers and unsustainable market share in the hopes of an initial public offering (IPO), Web 2.0 companies have figured out a profitable path to growth and advertising-based monetization of network effects and the infinitely diverse needs of long-tail users worldwide. This is the picture of the "whole Web 2.0 elephant" and how its business models provide both customer acquisition and monetization of its considerable network effects.

Tim O'Reilly, whose eponymous Web 2.0 conferences gave the name to the phenomenon, summarized Web 2.0 as follows:

> Web 2.0 is the business revolution in the computer industry caused by the move to the internet as platform, and an attempt to understand the rules for success on that new platform. Chief among those rules is this: Build applications that harness network effects to get better the more people use them

See *http://radar.oreilly.com/archives/2006/12/web_20_compact.html*
for more.

You don't have to be a technologist to understand Web 2.0. It's
not about the underlying technology but about the new ways that
it enables large numbers of people to come together to work,
share, and build. The network effects that O'Reilly cites are at the
heart of Web 2.0 business opportunities, and most of this book
will examine the ways that network effects can help you make
money.

Who Is This Book For

If you're managing your own business, portfolio, or several groups
and projects, you need to know how the Web is changing business and your competition. You may be an executive positioning a
major strategic move or acquisition, a small-business owner
looking for ways to expand, or an entrepreneur planning your
next startup. You may be intrigued by all this Web 2.0 talk, or
ready to jump in with a new venture or project.

You don't need to know anything about programming or web
development to understand this book. A familiarity with basic
business concepts and the general structure of the Web will be
helpful, but you don't need an M.B.A. or a degree in computer science. There are some twists and turns to the story, often as old
expectations break down in the face of new approaches, but they
shouldn't be difficult to grasp if you have an open mind.

You also don't need to work for a startup, or even a Web 2.0
company. Although the details of the stories explored in this book
may not fit your situation, the broad picture applies to a wide
variety of companies and projects.

What You'll Learn

You'll learn about how to make money by monetizing the network effects the Web makes possible. Real-life business stories
will demonstrate how those pieces work.

Your tour of Web 2.0 will start with lessons from the photo-
sharing site Flickr, a classic user-driven business that created

value for itself by helping users create their own value. Flickr's early moves will demonstrate how a business or technology can build momentum and traction with online collective user value. You'll see how Flickr's six innovative collective user value strategies not only grew their community but also contributed to their bottom line and cash flow. We'll also contrast Flickr's experience with that of Netflix, a company that took advantage of many Web 2.0 community concepts but whose core business of a DVD lending library cost a lot more than Flickr to get started.

Next, we'll examine Google, the best-known Web 2.0 success, exploring the ways that it makes money with a model based on free search. We reveal a whole new set of positive network effects that you probably never thought about before and show how Google has used them to catapult itself to dominance in its field. A key deal with AOL illustrates exactly how important the growth of that user base was to Google, propelling it far ahead of its competitors. You'll also see ways that Google's services make those benefits accessible to others who want to apply Web 2.0 solutions to their problems. Google isn't merely a company to emulate. Google is a company that has changed the rules for doing business on the Web, opening up opportunities that you can take advantage of.

The next step in our guided tour takes us to Facebook and LinkedIn, where we'll examine social network effects. Ever wonder how Facebook grew to 55 million users so quickly? Or how they are monetizing social network effects, social influence, and viral distribution of applications? Why LinkedIn changed the nature of business networking? Why small numbers of hubs and connectors online can activate increased value for all users in your community or installed base?

Once you've learned to recognize and take advantage of network effects, it's time to apply that understanding to knowledge-based companies of all sizes, including the Fortune 500s and multinationals. We look at the *dynamic capabilities* and *competence syndication* of companies like Salesforce.com, IBM, and Amazon. Businesses can tap into the Web as a source of indirect revenue, using creative new approaches to monetize their investments.

Amazon, for example, lets its customers help other customers find their ways to products that they might be interested in, building a level of trust that's hard to find even in a well-done catalog. Amazon has built on that combination of community and technology to develop other services, such as its S3 and EC2 hosting services. In other cases, it may make sense to use all the community to build, well, a community. IBM has applied these lessons to its Linux evangelism, making Linux more accessible to the potential 14–16 million open systems developers emerging in China and India.

Web 2.0 isn't strictly about the Web, either. It's also about collaborative innovation and online-offline sharing. Apple's iPod and iPhone include physical, web, community, and licensing ecosystems to produce a complete experience that is proving extremely popular, and changing the nature of the music and cellular industries. Jajah's long-distance calling business is simpler, but it also takes advantage of relationships with existing companies in the "old version" of the telephone industry and the viral potential of users marketing to their friends.

Finally, you'll find out how to transform your business, examining specific practices for integrating Web 2.0. There are lots of possibilities to explore, and lots of decisions to make, but when you've finished this journey, you'll be ready to apply Web 2.0 to your own situation.

> If you want even more opportunities to learn about Web 2.0 and related business subjects, explore the Endnotes and Bibliography at the end of the book.

Implementing Web 2.0

This book examines the "why" of Web 2.0 more than the "how," focusing on strategy rather than tactics. For a more implementation-centered perspective, you might want to start with Tim O'Reilly's article *What Is Web 2.0?* at:

http://www.tim.oreilly.com/news/2005/09/30/what-is-web-20.html

If you need more detail on the tactical side of Web 2.0, John Musser's *Web 2.0: Principles and Best Practices* (O'Reilly) explores the eight patterns Tim describes in much more detail, and it includes a checklist of questions to consider while implementing a Web 2.0 strategy.

How to Contact Us

Please address comments and questions concerning this book to the publisher:

> O'Reilly Media, Inc.
> 1005 Gravenstein Highway North
> Sebastopol, CA 95472
> 800-998-9938 (in the United States or Canada)
> 707-829-0515 (international or local)
> 707-829-0104 (fax)

There is a web page for this book, where we list errata, examples, and any additional information. You can access this page at:

> *http://www.oreilly.com/catalog/9780596529963*

To comment or ask technical questions about this book, send email to:

> *bookquestions@oreilly.com*

For more information about our books, conferences, Resource Centers, and the O'Reilly Network, see our web site at:

> *http://www.oreilly.com*

Safari™ Books Online

When you see a Safari™ Books Online icon on the cover of your favorite technology book, that means the book is available online through the O'Reilly Network Safari Bookshelf.

Safari offers a solution that's better than e-books. It's a virtual library that lets you easily search thousands of top tech books, cut and paste code samples, download chapters, and find quick answers when you need the most accurate, current information. Try it for free at *http://safari.oreilly.com*.

Acknowledgments

This book was a voyage of discovery, with many adventures, fascinating views, and unexpected obstacles along the way. My thanks to:

- Tim O'Reilly and executive publisher Mike Hendrickson for championing this project and seeing its breakthrough potential
- My editor, Simon St.Laurent, for making this book readable
- Dean Rolf Cremer of China Europe International Business School (CEIBS) and former Deans Dave Hodges and Hal Varian of U.C. Berkeley
- The many executives, managers, M.B.A.s, and alums who have challenged my thinking and shaped my ideas through discussions, conversations, seminars, and workshops at Yale, Harvard, Berkeley, Wharton, CEIBS, INSEAD, Chalmers Sweden, École Polytechnique, ENPC, HEC, ETH Zurich, University of St. Gallen, University of St. Petersburg, Russia, and the World Economic Forum retreat
- IBM, Cisco, GE, Intel, Procter & Gamble, Booz Allen Hamilton, The McKenna Group, The Silicon Valley Strategy Group, WDHB, Société Générale, PPR, and Bouygues
- The Silicon Valley venture capitalists and CEOs of portfolio companies who shared their experience and insights through more than 50 M.B.A./Ph.d. entrepreneurship field projects

Despite the help, advice, and encouragement received from so many, any shortcomings or errors remain entirely my responsibility.

CHAPTER ONE

Users Create Value

WEB 2.0 TAKES A FUNDAMENTALLY DIFFERENT VIEW of how businesses, customers, and partners interact, and in doing so, it opens up a range of new business models. Back in 1980, Alvin Toffler's bestseller *The Third Wave* (Bantam) predicted a new type of "prosumer," someone who is a mix of a DIY (do-it-yourself) producer and consumer in offline marketplaces. It was a great vision, but without the recent advances in web and digital technologies, most online broadband and mobile users could not make the quantum leap from being passive viewers and readers to becoming actively participating, socially engaged, and collaborative *uploaders*—personal contributors and creators of the Web.

Web 2.0 turbocharges network effects because online users are no longer limited by how many things they can find, see, or download off the Web, but rather by how many things they can do, interact, combine, remix, upload, change, and customize for themselves. This online DIY self-expression benefits businesses and other users, not just individual uploaders.

Flickr, a Web 2.0 photo-sharing site, illustrates the business and financial impact of uploaders and their remarkable *collective user value*. We'll analyze Flickr's multiple revenue streams and cost structures, making you familiar with how to evaluate the customer profitability and financial valuation pros and cons of moving to a Web 2.0 business model.

We'll also contrast it with Netflix, an online video rental company founded during the dot-com era, which uses many of the same technologies but has a fundamentally different—and more difficult—business model.

> Most chapters in this book will lead with theory and then go into detail. To get started, though, it makes sense to see what a Web 2.0 company looks like.

Flickr and Collective User Value

Flickr, shown in Figure 1-1, is a poster child for Web 2.0. It offers users a way to share photos easily, starting with the simple stream of photos shown in Figure 1-2.

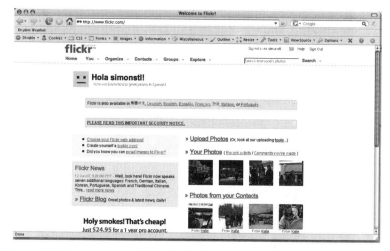

Figure 1-1. Interacting with the Flickr photo sharing service

Flickr users who accept the default mode of public photos don't have to do anything more to share their pictures. They can upload them and add captions and comments (metadata) for their own convenience, and other people can see them immediately. If users want to see the latest photos their friends have posted, they can simply visit their Flickr pages. Those photos can also be better organized (Figure 1-3), and presented as slideshows (Figure 1-4).

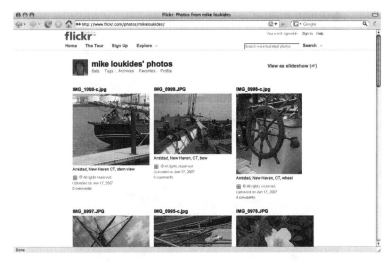

Figure 1-2. *A user's stream of photos, showing the most recent first*

This is just the beginning, of course. Flickr offers users a variety of ways to upload and manipulate their photos, several ways to organize them, a fun set of tools for connecting photos to maps, and options for printing photos in a variety of different formats. For a more detailed explanation of what Flickr offers, visit *http://flickr. com/tour/*.

Flickr's friendly and easy-to-use web interface and its free photo-management and storage service are great examples of a Web 2.0 "freemium" business model—fine-tuned to leverage collective user value, positive network effects, and community sharing.

The term "freemium"[1] was first introduced on venture capitalist Fred Wilson's blog, A VC (*http://avc.blogs.com/*). He described it this way:

> Give your service away for free, possibly ad supported but maybe not, acquire a lot of customers very efficiently through word of mouth, referral networks, organic search marketing, etc., then offer premium priced value added services or an enhanced version of your service to your customer base.

---

[1] Fred Wilson, "A VC: The Freemium Business Model," Fred Wilson's blog, comment posted on March 23, 2006, *http://avc.blogs.com/a_vc/2006/03/the_ freemium_bu.html.*

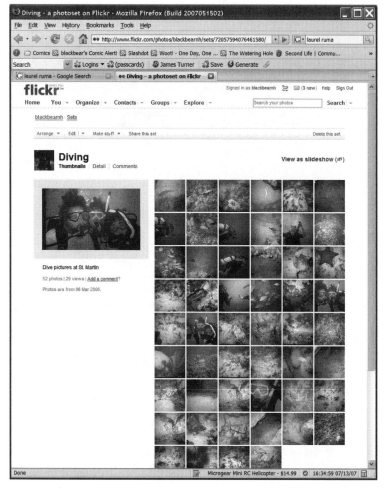

Figure 1-3. Photos organized by subject

Taking a typically Web 2.0 "collective user value" approach, Wilson asked for online suggestions about what to call this business model. Jarid Lukin, director of E-Commerce at Alacra, came up with the clear winner: Free + Premium = Freemium.

The November 2006 issue of *Business 2.0* titled its first article on the "freemium" strategy "Why It Pays to Give Away the Store."[2]

---

[2] Katherine Heires, "Why It Pays to Give Away the Store," *Business 2.0, http:// money.cnn.com/magazines/business2/business2_archive/2006/10/01/8387115/ index.htm.*

Figure 1-4. *A slideshow of related photos*

Business 2.0 later posted it online with the headline "A Business Model VCs Love," as this strategy had already been used profitably by companies as diverse as Adobe with its PDF Reader and Macromedia with its Shockwave Player, as well as Skype, Flickr, and MySpace.

In Flickr's case, practically zero marketing costs and low-cost online distribution and capital investment allow revenue from multiple streams, including value-added premium services, to very quickly cover the cost of free basic services and customer acquisition. Additionally, in Chapter 2, we will see that ad-based revenues and n-sided markets capitalize on the positive network effects of Flickr's collective user and community-generated value.

Collective User Value and Positive Network Effects

The more users, traffic, and aggregated feedback that Flickr has, the better the system performs for everyone, thanks to direct positive network effects. Flickr's system improves continuously, multiplying positive feedback, on the basis of active and passive clicks of multiple users navigating the site, sharing photos, creating user-defined tags and clusters of tags, collaboratively filtering and ranking, holding group events, syndicating photos to other sites, and blogging. Different kinds of users tend to engage different parts of the system, as shown in Figure 1-5.

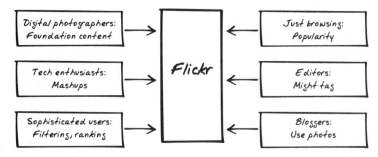

Figure 1-5. *Accumulating positive network effects*

Users can actively upload photos and contribute and collaborate on content. Even if they aren't that involved, they still passively provide clickstream feedback that can be indexed and quantified for advertisers, marketers, and complementary service and product providers. Every time someone tags a photo with keywords or metadata—e.g., Turkey, bubbles, cute—Flickr's knowledge pool increases. As the community provides keywords and conducts searches and writes captions and comments, the data becomes easier for users to find, and the database of searchable photos becomes more valuable.

Trusted Context for Interaction and Community

By default, Flickr users share their uploaded photos publicly. Many Web 2.0 companies make public sharing the "no-click" or default option, the understood norm. Those who want to keep their files private can still choose to do so.

Listening to Users

Flickr's business model depends on its users, but its connection to them goes deeper. Flickr's founders, operating under the name Ludicorp, had begun their enterprise as a site for gaming. Users actually told Flickr's founders to shift their business focus from gaming to online photo-sharing, and the company listened.

Ludicorp's management and development teams had solicited feedback through multiple channels, including forums and a blog. The feedback from its then-small but tightly knit community of users surprised its founders.

Flickr's users told it to transform into something more like a social networking site. This site would collect registered visitors and eyeballs by using digital online photo-sharing, free online storage, and amateur photography to serve a critical mass of users while organically growing a large and valuable digital photo stock and online inventory.

Web 2.0 approaches made it possible for the founders, Catarina Fake and Stewart Butterfield, to rapidly transform their core product from the game platform into a photo-sharing platform. The founders, who were techies and software developers, turned user input into rapid, sometimes daily, release cycles to develop the product features, services, and platform collaboratively with their active users.

It might seem crazy that Flickr's management listened so closely to its users, to the extent of altering its very business model. But doing so changed the company's strategic direction virtually overnight, and the photo-sharing community called Flickr was born—or more accurately, rose like a phoenix from the ashes of the former game platform.

When users find it easy to connect and open up to others, they become increasingly comfortable uploading and sharing self-generated content; frequent interaction builds community, trust, and self-policing norms. By 2006, Flickr's platform allowed more than 2 million registered users to become active uploaders of more than 100 million photos, 80% of which were publicly shared through the Flickr photo database. Flickr's online platform was quite timely in compounding the positive network effects of broadband penetration: an explosion of digital camera and cameraphone usage, blogging, social networking, and RSS (Really Simple Syndication). (Online syndication is explained further in Chapter 4.)

Why are publicly shared "open content" photos an important aspect of Flickr? Making all knowledge and images explicitly public helps the community learn to photograph, select images, build, design, or code more efficiently, thus creating better output. Not only is new knowledge produced every time users collaborate, but individual productivity increases whenever anyone joins the community and adds her knowledge and skills.

Reaching, Tagging, and Monetizing the Long Tail

Users self-select along multiple personal dimensions, categories of preference, utility, social interest, and experience. Pay-per-click (PPC), click-to-call, web analytics, and clickstreams make it easy to reach these individualized online clusters of users directly with targeted or complementary offers, or to subsidize services to these groups by interested sponsors or advertisers. As shown in Figure 1-6, Flickr's founders came up with innovative ways to reach the long tail of the online photography world: new online photo users not accustomed to photo sharing beyond their friends and family.

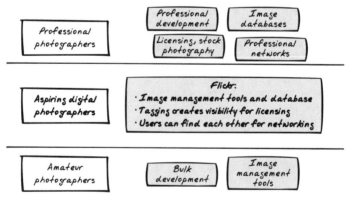

Figure 1-6. Previously underserved users' needs now met by Flickr

Millions of users became actively engaged in contributing and defining interesting categories, activities, events, and groups loosely tied to the photo-sharing community and database.

Why take the time to upload photos to Flickr and tag them? Because it serves your self-interest in three ways. First, you can store and sort your own photos, solving an immediate problem. Second, you tap into an amazingly creative photo database and knowledge pool, so you can learn about digital photography. Third, it's a great way for talented photographers to get discovered. To Steve Rubel, author of the Micro Persuasion blog (*http://www.micropersuasion.com/*), these heavily tagged databases guided by human interests are a boon for marketers, who can get real-time views of what users are really passionate about. "Where the eyeballs go, there's an opportunity to experiment with marketing."

Six Ways Flickr Created User Value Through Interaction

The core business message of Flickr is neatly summarized in a slide from its 2004 launch at the O'Reilly Emerging Technology Conference:

> *Don't build applications. Build contexts for interaction.*

In March 2005, Flickr was a *Fast Company* 50 winner for "Reinventing a category whose flashbulb burnt out." In the magazine interview,[3] founders Catarina Fake and Stewart Butterfield summed up the basis of their success—their users:

> We have quickly created the largest and best-organized online photo library in existence with 1.8 million images, of which 81% are public, and 85% have some human-added metadata. What this means is you can find photographs of anything that strikes your fancy. Flickr is infinitely shareable and easily searchable.

Open Up Digital Content to Global User Interaction

Flickr photo sharing introduces individually uploaded digital content—photos and images—to a global online community. When users upload photos to Flickr, they are usually sharing them not only with friends and family but with communities of Flickr users and the whole Internet as well. Because Flickr's default photo

---

[3] *Fast Company* 50 interview with Stewart Butterfield, "Reinventing a category whose flashbulb burnt out," *http://www.fastcompany.com/magazine/archives/2005.*

visibility setting is public rather than private, after its first year, *more than 80% of all photos were public.*

Opening up user-generated and uploaded digital content is the next stage of the open-systems movement started by Linux and followed by Google's open application programming interfaces, or APIs. Open systems and open APIs have a significant impact on hardware and software developers, products, and services. Unrestricted uploaded digital content has a much broader impact on the mass-media market, the millions of broadband and mobile users, and consumers of all media.

This type of shared digital content sets off a positive direct network effect on the breadth and variety of the image database and sparks viral marketing. Each new member adds his uploaded digital photos to the completely user-generated collective Flickr photo database rather than maintaining (or hoarding) a proprietary cache of private photos. Of course, Flickr has given users the choice of sharing their photos openly while maintaining control over licensing and ownership. Almost 130 million photos have been posted by some 3 million registered users. Open photo sharing enables Flickr to be a completely user-generated image database. Clearly, this is the same route that YouTube took a few years later but with a slightly different target: a user-generated video database and open community for online public sharing.

Create Better Search Through User-Generated Information

Ever borrowed a copy of a friend's dog-eared, underlined book and found the notes to be as interesting as the original content itself? Tags, footnotes, and annotations are forms of metadata—an interpretation, highlighting, or framing of the original data.

In Flickr, all users and observers are encouraged to become actively engaged by annotating photos—both their own and others'—with *tags* and *notes*. These actions contribute to the categorization of photo images into *tag clusters* and provide aggregated feedback, making it possible for better human-guided "fuzzy" searches of images. For example, Flickr creates tag clusters using dynamic analysis of the groups of tag words used together, such as "Turkey" with Istanbul compared to "turkey" with Thanksgiving. Figure 1-7 shows the highest-level view of these tags, called a *tag cloud*. The most popular tags are listed alphabetically; their sizes are used to differentiate popularity.

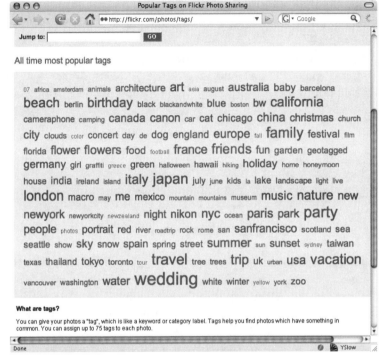

Figure 1-7. The most popular tags on Flickr, arranged in a tag cloud

Flickr has been so successful at involving users that *more than 85% of the photos on its service have human-added metadata*. As with the Google PageRank and AdWords algorithms, the quality of search and image categorization results improve as more people view, comment on, mark as a favorite, or tag photos. The system as a whole becomes more effective and valuable as a result of this direct network impact from the increased number of users. Additionally, individually generated annotations and tags provide a richer, more complex window into the metadata—a view that can be surprisingly multidimensional. For example, photos of kittens playing are more often tagged with an emotional descriptor like "cute" or "cuddly" than a more objective classification like "cats" or "felines."

As Stewart Butterfield said:[4]

> The job of tags isn't to organize all the world's information into tidy categories. It's to add value to the giant piles of data that are already out there.

User-generated tagging systems are often known as *folksonomies*,[5] a term coined by information architect Thomas Vander Wal. As he described it:

> One of the things that's nice to see is that people are actually spending time tagging and doing it in a social environment, and following the power curve and the net effect. The more people getting involved with it, the greater the value....

Discover and Explore Through Online Groups

Flickr was a leader in creating photo image metadata to make it easier to filter and search through its open photo database and also in encouraging millions of photographers to explore, and discover, through groups. Some of the collective value comes from Flickr leveraging the aggregated number of photos and tags and then dynamically analyzing usage and user behavior in its system to provide improved services, such as "search" or clusters, for users who contribute their photos to the Flickr database. Also, Flickr users gather around particular interests, many of them related to travel, and participate in groups and group events.

Catalyze and Amplify Group Social Network Effects

Flickr also has its own dynamic algorithmic means for rating, sorting, and finding photographs, which it calls *interestingness*. Rather than just running a popularity contest, using PageRanking (considering the number of links), basing traffic on Google "juice" (recent traffic or interaction), or requiring users to vote, Flickr has an undisclosed formula. Its "secret sauce" contains factors as

---

4 Daniel Terdiman, "Folksonomies Tap People Power," Wired.com, Feb. 1, 2005, *http://www.wired.com/science/discoveries/news/2005/02/66456.*
5 Ibid.

diverse as how many times a photo has been viewed, commented on, marked as a favorite, and tagged. The system also gives weight to who does each action and when.

The simple aggregation of how many times a photo has been "favorited" would be a simple popularity metric. Giving more weight to certain users than to others moves the algorithm into a whole new domain of social influence and capitalizes on key trendsetters, trendspotters, or community catalysts.

DIY Self-Service Syndication

Flickr was a first-mover in providing an integrated set of self-service tools, Web 2.0 platform services, and APIs for the exploding use of digital cameras and camera phones, high-speed broadband, and low-cost infrastructure (for digital photo storage and bandwidth). Flickr took advantage of these services to make it easy to integrate photos and visual images with blogs, social networking, and syndication via RSS. In 2006, more than 1 billion photos were taken from the more than 300 million camera phones in use. An estimated 10% of the photos on Flickr were directly uploaded from mobile devices.

Syndication was an important element of Flickr's success. It was a completely new idea to allow users to subscribe to photos as RSS feeds. By offering a basic free account and comprehensive support for the major blogging platforms, Flickr quickly became the preferred choice for a growing army of active bloggers, who became the primary subscribers to the paid Pro Account services.

Encourage Others to Become Part of Your Digital Ecosystem

Thanks to Flickr's open API, third-party individual developers, as well as companies, built image uploaders for a range of operating systems, making it easy to connect to Flickr from many different devices and applications. For example, ShoZu built tools for cameraphone users, and zipPhoto did the same for Microsoft's Smartphone.

Flickr became the center of a digital photo ecosystem of partners, third-party applications, mashup developers, and bloggers. This not only saved development costs and fostered innovation, it also built trust and long-term relationships with sophisticated and more tech-savvy users and developers.

Why Sharing Can Be Profitable

How does Flickr capture value, and how can it be measured?

- Business managers inside a company can analyze their internal business model to characterize and visually diagram a company's profit engine.

- Industry analysts or strategists evaluating a company from the outside can compare it with competitors and industry players to assess its stock market capitalization value, acquisition value, or total enterprise value. They can use industry structural analysis and consumer-focused financial valuation.

We'll use the first of these two perspectives—*the business model as a profit engine*—which is appropriate for managers and entrepreneurs who are making key business decisions and trade-offs to turn their ideas into profits and a sustainable business. We start by asking whether the business has single, multiple, or interdependent revenue streams. Then, we look at each of the sources of revenue, the revenue streams, their growth potential, and the cash flow timing for new customers.

To kick-start or fine-tune a business profit engine, let's start with identifying the inner workings of revenue sources, key cost drivers, investment size, and key success factors. Typically, companies have four choices of how to use revenue streams:

Single stream

The company relies on one predominant revenue stream stemming from one product or service.

Multiple streams

The company collects multiple revenue streams from different products or services.

Interdependent streams

> The company sells one set of products to stimulate revenue and growth from another set, for example, razors and blades.

Loss leader

> Not every revenue stream of multiple streams are independently profitable, but those that lose money drive traffic to spur other purchases and together they achieve profitability.

Rather than relying on a single stream, Flickr chose a *multiple revenue stream model*, where the company:

- Collects *subscription fees* from monthly premium account subscribers who receive unlimited storage, full-resolution images, and no advertising
- Charges *advertising transaction fees* to advertisers for contextual advertising
- Receives *sponsorship and revenue-sharing fees* from partnerships with large retail chains and complementary photo service companies

Flickr's revenue model uses the first three of the six kinds of revenue models. These models include:

Subscription/membership revenue model

> Provides a fixed amount of revenue at regular intervals based on the number of subscribers and is usually paid in advance of receiving the product or service, e.g., health club memberships or magazine subscriptions. Flickr Pro Accounts charge $24.95 per year for unlimited storage, full-resolution images, and no advertising.

Advertising-based revenue model

> Allows users to benefit from free products or services. The advertiser pays for clicks, e.g., the Google search engine, or for eyeballs, such as with network television advertising. Flickr uses contextual advertising, a revenue model that efficiently monetizes clicks into dollars for its large and fast-growing installed base of users and online usage. An additional

advantage is the ability to increase advertising spending per
customer depending on the return on investment (ROI) of an
advertising and marketing campaign.

Transaction fee revenue model

Has the customer pay the company that facilitates the transaction a fixed fee or a percentage of the total value of the
transaction. eBay, for example, charges the seller an 8%
transaction fee. Target, the department store, shares a sliver
of its Flickr clickstream photo development revenue with
Flickr.

Volume or unit-based revenue model

Has the customer or buyer pay a fixed price per unit to the
seller and receives a product or service in return. This revenue
model is common in offline, brick-and-mortar businesses and
services.

Licensing and syndication revenue model

Has the customer pay a one-time licensing or syndication fee
to use or resell the product. Often, a buyer will pay a separate licensing or royalty fee in a business-to-business transaction; for example, an enterprise pays a software company for
a certain number of site licenses, or a pharmaceutical firm
licenses a drug from a biotech startup. iStockphoto, an online
stock photo web site acquired by Getty Images (the largest
stock photography company) charges a small licensing fee for
downloading images from its site. (Several bloggers have
pointed out that it would not be difficult for Flickr to implement a licensing or syndication revenue fee that would allow
Flickr users who post photos to receive licensing royalties
from interested photo buyers with some percentage of that
revenue stream going to Flickr.)

*Sponsorship/co-marketing revenue model, also called revenue-
sharing model*

Has sponsors pay for direct marketing and branding access to
customers.

Instead of following the licensing revenue models developed by
stock photo and advertising agencies for use in the professional

photography industry, or the volume/unit-based revenue models used by the Shutterfly and Ofoto digital photo printing companies, Flickr's revenue model exploits the much larger but virtually untapped markets of amateur digital photographers and broadband, mobile, and laptop multidevice users.

The advent of low-cost, high-quality, and high-megapixel digital cameras and camera phones dramatically shifted the customer usage patterns of picture taking. Users can now take many more digital photos, delete the ones they don't like immediately, and still have lots of photos to share, keep, and organize. Unlike 35 mm film processing where customers pay a price for developing each roll they shoot—and then a per picture fee for printing onto glossy 4×6 photo paper—most amateur digital photographers need a free or low-cost, easy-to-use way to share, store, organize, manage, and access their rapidly growing personal inventories of digital photos online.

Flickr essentially gives away the services that amateur digital photographers need and want most: photo sharing; online storage; and indexing, tagging, and photo inventory. Flickr's revenue model is focused on the three revenue models—subscription, advertising, and transaction/revenue sharing—that are most attractive to the noncommercial amateur photography community. This revenue model takes into account the dramatically shifting usage patterns in digital sharing, multidevice, storage, and reuse.

Flickr's main photo-sharing community could be seen as a loss leader within interdependent streams of revenue because free services are subsidized by other more profitable revenue streams. But loss leaders are typically temporary pricing cuts intended to bring in new customers. In contrast, freemiums and n-sided strategies are actually an innovative new online business model, based on cross-network effects.

Not every revenue stream needs to be independently profitable, as long as traffic is driven to spur other purchases and achieve overall profitability and growth. In Flickr's case, maintaining a free, noncommercial (but highly trusted), interactive, and open photo database is key to the vibrancy of the user-generated activities. This free database also drives the growth of community and the partnership and third-party developer ecosystem, and it imposes relatively little cost beyond what would be needed to serve its customers' direct needs.

Flickr's Cost Drivers

To get at the inner workings of cost structures, the key questions to answer are the following:

- What are the largest cost drivers, and are they fixed, semi-variable, variable, or nonrecurring?
- How will the cost drivers change over time, by unit volume and by number of customers and usage?

From the outset, Flickr found innovative ways to avoid the four major cost drivers of the retail photo printing business and online stock photo companies. Flickr's collective user value strategies convert its significant cost savings into a competitive advantage and positive network-effects generator.

The first key cost driver is *inventory*. A typical stock photo company—online or offline—must acquire a high-quality stock photo inventory and develop a cataloging and management capability to make a large and broad inventory accessible and easily distributable to viewers, potential buyers, and image licensors.

The second key cost driver is *payroll*. A retail photo printing business has direct payroll costs for employees who are involved in the photo development and printing process, as well as indirect or support payroll for employees who are at the checkout counter or involved with the maintenance of the store equipment or supplies.

The third key cost driver is *information technology systems and developers*. Most web stores spend a large proportion of their costs on IT design, development, maintenance, and payment systems compared with offline retail stores that instead have space/rental costs (driven by real estate in square footage) for office or retail space.

The fourth key cost driver is *marketing, advertising, and customer relationship management* (CRM). Marketing and advertising costs are higher pre-sales, and customer relationship management costs are often higher post-sales. Because the barriers to entry are low in the retail photo printing business and online stock photo business, marketing, advertising, and customer relationship management are critical for differentiation, as well as for traffic and new customer acquisition.

Table 1-1 lists the seven collective user strategies on the left, and the primary cost centers for different cost structures along the top. The boxes marked "Major" indicate the areas where Flickr enjoys major cost reductions thanks to its use of collective user strategies. The boxes marked "Measurable" indicate the areas where Flickr enjoys measurable cost savings compared to more traditional approaches that do not benefit from user contributions and interactions.

One key omission in Table 1-1 is the cost of goods sold, or COGS, which isn't a factor for Flickr and is by definition a major savings.

Table 1-1. *Where Flickr's structure reduces cost*

SAVINGS TO:	DIRECT PAYROLL	SUPPORT PAYROLL	INVENTORY	IT SYSTEM	MARKETING/AD/CRM
Open photo sharing	Major		Major		Major
Self-service		Major			Major
DIY tools		Measurable		Major	Major
Tagging		Major	Major	Measurable	Major
Collaborative filtering		Measurable		Measurable	Major
Group discovery		Measurable		Measurable	Major
Syndication and blogging		Measurable	Major		Major

Flickr faced one enormous technical problem: the challenge of building a scalable and searchable image database without spending tremendous sums of money. Flickr's tag-based approach helped it on the search side and gave the database project a different set of priorites from those of many earlier image storage projects. Building the application using that approach gave Flickr the ability to capitalize on user contributions while solving a technical issue. Flickr drastically reduced the cost and risk of developing and implementing a superior (and well-connected) photo management database by creating partnerships with its users and third-party developers, rather than building all the capabilities in-house as proprietary code. Collective user value was a major competitive and strategic advantage in transforming the cost structure of Flickr and similar Web 2.0 technology companies.

Calculating Company Value

Yahoo! bought Flickr for an estimated $30 to $40 million in March 2005. Although Flickr's founders reported (*http://blog. flickr.com/en/2005/03/20/yahoo-actually-does-acquire-flickr/*) that they would "no longer have to draw straws to see who gets paid," the reality was much brighter. Flickr could bring its hypergrowth strategies to Yahoo!, and Yahoo! could provide additional publicity and infrastructure to the growing photo service.

Flickr's value, though, is a tough question. Value is clearly not just the infrastructure of the company, or even the brand. For a company growing like this, the value depends on the customers. In the past, this statement was agreed to in principle but difficult to quantify. Financial valuations of companies were calculated on earnings multiples and on forecasts of market and unit production growth. However, new forms of "customer-based" company valuation formulas and models were developed to analyze the many subscriber businesses and services such as cable and cell phone services, in which revenues are directly tied to customer fees, not unit prices.

Tracking individual customer behavior and metrics rather than unit sales volume as the actual "basis" for revenue growth and business models leads to terminology that is relatively unfamiliar to most business managers and M.B.A.s. Analysts use the terms "individual customer profitability," "average lifetime customer value," and "loyalty" to emphasize that quantitative metrics in many customer-focused industries—including the gaming and casino industries—can be aggregated to arrive at fine-grained financial enterprise valuations. These metrics can also be analyzed strategically to dramatically improve profitability at the individual customer level. Harrah's Casino is an exemplary case: quantitative individual customer analysis of its "VIPs and high-rollers" changed the company's service and business model dramatically.

Using the basic total enterprise value formula with a discounted cash flow model for lifetime values is particularly important when the average lifetime of an average subscriber can range from one month to five years. It is also important when there is a high risk that users in the installed base will "churn" or "switch" between different plans or companies, but fees are received on a regular schedule, such as monthly.

In contrast, for online businesses such as Flickr, Yahoo!, and Google, ad-based revenues make up a large part of the "average lifetime value of a customer." With web analytics and digital tracking of PPC and page impressions, most online businesses can calculate the "average revenue per search query," and from that, the "average revenue per customer" per day, month, or year. For example, at the 2006 Web 2.0 Summit, Mary Meeker, top Internet analyst at Morgan Stanley, mentioned that Google's average revenue expectation was $13 per customer:

> If we look at advertising revenue per user [per year] for some of the top sites on the Internet, Google gets about $13; YouTube gets less than $1. We think that helps us to get a sense of what the monetization upside is for some of the other sites with Google as a benchmark at that level (*http://www.oreillynet.com/lpt/a/6848*).

In Flickr's case, in which the company was acquired largely for its loyal and active customer base of 2 million users as well as its Web 2.0 platform, a $40 million acquisition could mean that these 2 million users have a combined average ad-revenue, premium, and partner revenue stream of $20 per user over the next 3 to 5 years. Although a "multiple" like $20 per user might seem too simple, several of the analyst commentaries on Facebook's recent valuation used a similar user-based approach. After all, advertising and market access to 2 million users (in Flickr's case) or 50 million users (in Facebook's case) is extremely valuable, and thanks to pay-per-click, it is immediately monetizable as revenue from advertisers and sponsors.

Some informal discussions with Yahoo! executives indicate that they are also weighing the value of the attractive segment of the 1% to 10% most active contributors to the Flickr community. This would make a lot of sense—the lifetime value of an active and influential user should be higher, both in tangible collective user value and in contributions back into the user community. Such highly active users also trigger an increase in the number of customers through the improved value and quality of the overall system, the higher level of community engagement, and viral and referral marketing.

For example, in his blog titled "Creators, Synthesizers, and Consumers," (*http://www.elatable.com/blog/?p=5*), Bradley Horowitz, Yahoo! vice president of product strategy, mentions the following:

> In Yahoo! Groups, 1% of the user population starts the group, 10% participate actively and may actually author content, 100% of the user population benefits from the activities of the above groups.

> Even in Wikipedia, half of all edits are made by just 2.5% of the logged in users...social software sites don't require 100% active participation to generate great value.

For customer-facing businesses, this approach to valuation emphasizes the importance of customers and growth in the value of the company. (It could also include the ongoing nonfinancial contributions of customers, although that may be a challenge to quantify.)

In Flickr's case, this may be the only relatively simple way to gauge the company's value.

Looking Back: Netflix's Different Challenges

Netflix is a proud survivor of the dot-com boom and bust, and in the years since then, it has added more and more community features to its site. Like Flickr, Netflix:

- Appeared at a time when the nature of a communications medium was changing
- Distributes a huge quantity of visual information to its users
- Depends on an ever-evolving web interface for interacting with its customers
- Grew rapidly thanks to users reporting their experiences to their friends (quickly developing market share that couldn't easily be challenged)

Unlike Flickr, however, Netflix began in an era when it was still difficult for people to create shareable content, and delivering its services meant physically moving a DVD from its warehouse to the customer and back. The physical nature of the DVD and the cost of purchasing DVD content gave Netflix a set of problems whose solutions point the way toward many of the advantages of a pure-web approach.

The Costs of Growth

"Burn rate" was a popular term during the dot-com boom. Because economies of scale were a critical advantage of the Web, the general idea was to grow a company's market share rapidly. The cash flow curve that looks like a J-curve, shown in Figure 1-8, demonstrates what would happen as startup companies tried to buy new customers and market share with their investors' dollars.

The first part of the slope reflects the period when a company is spending more to build market share than it's making in revenue. The burn rate is initially steep, as the company spends money on marketing, hiring, and expanding infrastructure, but customers haven't yet rewarded that investment. As more customers come in, revenue should start to exceed expenditures, and the curve should

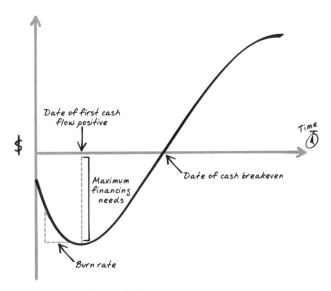

Figure 1-8. *A J-curve for cash flow*

fall less sharply, flatten, and then start climbing. When the curve climbs, cash flow is positive, and that will (hopefully) lead to eventual profit.

Netflix faced a very basic problem: acquiring new customers was tremendously expensive. Building the web infrastructure was expensive, of course, but the bigger, more difficult problem was the cost of what it was sending to customers: DVDs. DVDs were new technology in 1997 (and even in 2000), and each DVD cost a lot. Netflix was serving an audience of early adopters, successfully creating an initial frenzy by offering expensive movies at low cost—even free—for the initial offer. It's hard for a lending library to stay afloat when its customers want to be assured that they can always have the latest and greatest, even when there are thousands of customers.

The price of DVDs had a drastic effect on the costs of customer acquisition and the time it took to recoup those costs. By following a single customer (and ignoring marketing costs), we can see how how those costs add up. (For details, see the upcoming sidebar "The Profitability and Expected Value of a Netflix Customer.")

The Profitability and Expected Value of a Netflix Customer

The profitability of an individual subscriber is the average revenue (monthly subscription fees paid) minus the costs of acquiring and retaining that subscriber.

If Caroline starts subscribing to Netflix in January and immediately puts four DVD rentals on her "Movie List," she will receive the four DVD rentals in the mail at a cost of $80 to Netflix (each of the DVDs costs $20 to purchase from the movie studios). Netflix will also pay $8 for shipping, or $2 per round-trip postage, so the total new customer acquisition cost can be calculated as $88, and it is a cash outflow or upfront expense incurred by Netflix. Meanwhile, as Caroline is taking advantage of the free-month promotional offer, there is no revenue or cash inflow to Netflix in January. Although Caroline is an important new subscriber, she is unprofitable in the first month, and her first month of membership results in a net cash *outflow* of $88.

If Caroline is one of the 30% of new subscribers who drop out after the first month trial promotion, her profitability and her lifetime value after one month will be negative.

However, Chris, who started his subscription at the same time, decides to continue, paying $20 a month for six months. The cash flow for a subscriber who drops after six months equals five months times $6 net monthly cash flow ($20 minus $4 shipping, minus $10 incremental DVD costs), since Chris chooses several of the DVDs that are freed up by dropped subscribers and increasing inventory stock. Additionally, Netflix benefits from a one-time $80 avoided disc acquisition cost. The cash flow for a six-month subscriber like Chris is close to $30 + 80 = $110.

Meanwhile, if Peter started his Netflix service in January and stays longer than six months like 28% of the other subscribers starting in January, he will generate revenue and a net cash flow of $6 per month, or a yearly positive cash flow of $110 + 36 = $146 to Netflix.

Given these assumptions and the simplifications of no other costs, we can average the expected value of these three prototypical new subscribers—Caroline, a free-trial-month-only subscriber; Chris, a subscriber for six months; and Peter, a longer-term subscriber who after the first year becomes a loyal subscriber for five years in total.

—Continued—

We can easily calculate that the average expected value of a new subscriber is 30% chance of –$88 weighed against the 42% chance of $110 for the six-month subscriber and the 28% chance of $146 for the long-termer for a total expected value of $60 annual net gain or profit per individual Netflix subscriber.

So, how does this simplified individual subscriber profitability analysis and tracking of cash flow timing help us evaluate the viability of the Netflix's current business model and its chances for a successful IPO?

Step 1: is the cash flow situation good or bad? We can first see that over a year's time, there is an average profit per individual Netflix subscriber. But there is a lag between the cost of acquiring a new customer with a free-trial-month subscription at about $88 and a return, because the net cash flow is only $6 a month. This upfront problem is magnified in high-growth situations where, for the first few years, the installed base of loyal subscribers cannot fund the high cost of new customer acquisition, as shown earlier in Figure 1-8. We can make a calculation of the yearly aggregate cash flow of Netflix subscribers, assuming that there are 110,000 subscribers in 1999, 420,000 in 2000, 630,000 in 2001, 945,000 in 2002, 1.4 million in 2003, and 2.1 million in 2004 by estimating a 50% growth rate based on published DVD player sales in the period. Depending on assumptions for overhead, fixed costs, and product development expenses, Netflix would have cash outflows of $15 million to $20 million in 2000. This would make a successful IPO in the summer of 2000 unlikely, especially because of the collapse of the NASDAQ market in the spring. More seriously, it looks as though Netflix will run out of cash in 2000, trying to fund its high growth rate.

Step 2: how can we change the business model to dramatically improve the cash flow situation? Looking at the individual subscriber cash flow analysis makes the timing and size of the cash flows in and out more visible. The first month is a big cash drain—because there are no subscriber fees and because of the cost of the DVDs—so these are the key things to work on.

First, we can eliminate the free-month-trial promotion. This would generate an additional $20 per month per new subscriber for the first month, significantly reducing cash flow requirements for new subscribers. However, it might also significantly reduce the number of new subscribers and the growth rate—maybe by as much as 50%.

—Continued—

Second, we can reduce the most significant new customer acquisition cost—the cost of new-release DVDs—by negotiating with the movie studios. In the VHS rental world, large retail chains like Blockbuster had 60/40 revenue-sharing agreements with the studios that allowed Blockbuster to guarantee the availability of the new releases that customers wanted and to "maximize revenue on a title-by-tile basis for both the rental chain and the movie studios."

Third, we can change the number of DVDs sent to users per month. If, in the first month, three rather than four DVDs went out to the new subscribers, this would save $20 per new customer in cash outlay. Alternatively, we could charge different amounts for different levels of service—acknowledging and segmenting the subscriber base into usage, frequency, and number of DVDs rented per month. This would certainly make sense if the composition of users turned out to be a "long tail" as in the LinkedIn case described in Chapter 3, where 90% of users were stable but relatively infrequent basic users and 10% were premium and highly active users.

Because of the very high cost of the four (mostly new-release) DVDs sent out to each new subscriber, it takes four to six months of each subscriber's monthly fees to recoup the initial cash outflow. Shipping costs are relatively insignificant compared with the cost of acquiring the DVDs.

In theory, Netflix was worth a lot of money—it had a lot of customers happily paying for services. Using the total enterprise value formula described earlier in the "Calculating Company Value" section, Netflix was valued at about $120 million in 1999.

However, the relatively simple analysis of that Netflix business model yielded a cash flow curve that proved Netflix was unlikely to survive long enough to even realize this total enterprise value.

Escaping the Trap

Escaping the high costs of customer acquisition and maintenance required several different steps. The overall cost of DVDs— around $20 each—was a looming problem, and not just during the customer acquisition phase. Netflix was an independent company, not attached to any of the studios, so there wasn't any direct reason for studios to be helpful. The studios enjoyed the money they made from selling DVDs to Netflix, a major customer, but their business interests didn't match Netflix's interests.

According to *Rentrak News*,[6] a home-media retailing online newsletter, the movie studios were getting $65 for outright purchase of their VHS cassettes in the "heyday of the high-priced rental cassette," mainly from smaller rental chains, which preferred to be able to sell previously viewed titles within 30 days for new releases. The large chains like Blockbuster had an estimated 70% of their new titles on 60/40 revenue-sharing with the studios but had contractually strict selloff restrictions to avoid cannibalizing new-release direct sales.

Netflix now brings in about 60% of its new releases through revenue-sharing, according to Chief Content Officer Ted Sarandos: "Revenue-sharing is a way to maximize customer satisfaction in a margin-neutral way...."[7]

Surprisingly enough, in December of 2000, Netflix was the first Internet DVD dealer to have a revenue-sharing agreement with the major motion picture distributors Columbia TriStar and Warner Home Video. At that time, Netflix stocked 9,000 DVD titles and had a subscriber base of 250,000 members, who paid $19.95 a month for unlimited movie rentals. Reed Hastings, cofounder and then-CEO of Netflix, said:[8]

> We are extremely pleased that these major studios recognize Netflix as an important distribution channel for their content. With these revenue-sharing deals, we can continue to deliver on our promise to provide the best movie experience possible— giving our customers the titles they want, when they want them, and allowing them to enjoy the movies for as long as they like. The agreements also help us keep pace with our extraordinary growth, without compromising our quality of service.

---

6 Kurt Indvik, "Rev-Share Still Lives," Rentrak News online, Sept. 16, 2005, *http:// www.rentrakonline.ca/content/news/news_09-16-05.html*.

7 "NetFlix Signs Revenue-sharing Pacts with Warner, Columbia," *Ultimate AV* magazine online, Dec. 17, 2000, *http://ultimateavmag.com/news/10893/*.

8 Ibid.

Warner Home Video President Warren Lieberfarb[9] also pointed out the importance of the DVD as the format standard of the future and the realization that DVD rentals could open up a market much larger than the one for new releases:

> DVD is the entertainment format of the future, and Netflix is our fastest growing customer for DVD rentals. We look forward to working with Netflix to expose the DVD viewing audience to Warner's vast library of films.

Steve Lyons,[10] Columbia vice president of sales, also focused on the future of the DVD market and movie lovers:

> We entered into a business relationship with Netflix because they have developed outstanding relationships with DVD viewers, many of whom are knowledgeable about film and looking for new ways to enhance their movie viewing experience. We believe that Netflix is the way to introduce movie lovers to our films.

DVD technology was still in its infancy, requiring an investment in a (then) expensive DVD player. It took a while for the benefits of DVD technology over videotapes to become apparent to the public. Netflix had taken major advantage of the DVD's form to ship them through the mail, creating a business model that appealed to customers who were fed up with the problems related to video rental stores, such as late fees. DVDs were a disruptive force, and Netflix promised to make them much more disruptive, bringing them directly to customers at a lower price with greater convenience and quality.

Netflix would probably have been happier if the manufacturers of DVD players, which benefited tremendously from Netflix's enhancing the appeal of DVDs, had offered Netflix a subsidy in return for its help with DVD adoption. That, unsurprisingly,

---

[9] "Netflix announces agreements with major motion picture distributors," Netflix press release, Dec. 6, 2000, *http://www.netflix.com/MediaCenter?id=1024.*

[10] Ibid.

didn't happen. Instead, Netflix turned to its suppliers, looking for a way to lower costs.

Suppliers were also benefiting from Netflix's work because they sold Netflix a lot of expensive DVDs. However, Netflix's inventory, once acquired, wasn't doing much for them except suppressing sales of DVDs—people knew they could always "Netflix a movie," instead of buying their own copy. Netflix managed to change this equation, although it meant taking a long-term revenue hit.

The solution? A deal that aligned the interests of Netflix and its suppliers, allowing Netflix to buy DVDs for $1 each, but in return granting the suppliers 40% of the revenue those DVDs generated. The lower upfront costs eased Netflix's cash burn, and suppliers now had a greater interest in seeing Netflix succeed, but the potential revenue per customer in the long run declined.

That wasn't the only major step Netflix took in 2000, even as it withdrew its planned IPO. It also took a risk in its customer acquisition strategy, ending the first-month-free plan and reducing the number of DVDs a customer could rent at one time from four to three. This gave new customers less than first adopters got, but at that point, Netflix had a customer base that was happy enough with the services to continue using it and spread the word.

Much to Netflix's surprise, despite discontinuing the free-trial month, the company continued to experience extremely rapid growth. Revenue grew to $37 million during 2000, almost eight times its 1999 revenue. By March 2001, Netflix had 310,000 subscribers, a full 100% increase over the previous year. Due to fine-tuning its business model, Netflix reported positive cash flows at 500,000 subscribers in October 2001. It had a successful IPO on May 24, 2002 and raised $86 million, despite it being a lackluster period for IPOs.

Lessons Learned

Flickr and Netflix have carefully crafted web sites and substantial paying user bases. Flickr's path forward yielded different results for a number of reasons.

Customer Acquisition Costs, Inventory, and Growth Rate

The most obvious business difference between Flickr's digital photo-sharing community and Netflix's DVD movie-sharing club is Netflix's customer acquisition costs. These costs were directly tied to how much it cost to build and keep the media-lending library/inventory/database up-to-date. Flickr still has an easier time of it than Netflix, despite Netflix's major changes, as shown in Table 1-2.

Table 1-2. Comparing Netflix and Flickr

	NETFLIX BEFORE REVENUE SHARING	NETFLIX AFTER REVENUE SHARING	FLICKR
New customer acquisition cost	$100 (five DVDs at $20/each) DVDs + $5 shipping + platform	$3 DVDs + $3 shipping + platform	0+ Platform
Number of customers	300,000 after three years	600,000 after five years	2 million in two years

Flickr's digital photo database of 100 million-plus photos—85% of which are tagged—is completely user-generated. Netflix's DVD inventory comes from suppliers that expect to be compensated. So, *collective user value* has an immediate and recognizable impact on the cost structure and cash flow requirements in growing a customer-focused business.

Cash Flow Curves and Time to Profitability

Flickr followed the Web 2.0 curve in Figure 1-9 rather than Netflix's Web 1.0 curve or a more typical physical-world curve.

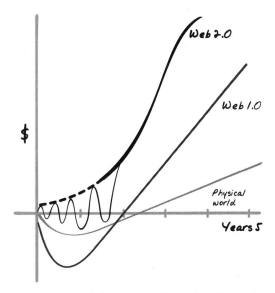

Figure 1-9. *Comparing cash flow in the physical world, Web 1.0, and Web 2.0*

The physical-world curve shows a more traditional path to profitability and is spared the Web's huge investment aimed at locking in users, but it doesn't make the same kind of return, either. The Web 1.0 curve shows the higher expenses of seeking a huge audience, but also the greater return on possible investment that lured investors in. As Gil Forer, global director of Ernst & Young's venture capital advisory group, said in a March 2007 press release:

> From the investor perspective, the low capital requirements, potential high return, and the faster time from development to revenue are the primary drivers of the increase in venture capital investment in the Web 2.0 segment. In addition, success stories such as YouTube have had a positive impact both on entrepreneurs and investors.

See *http://www.ey.com/global/content.nsf/International/Media_-_Press_Release_-_VentureOne_New_Web* for more.

The Web 2.0 curve is different (and attractive) for a number of reasons:

Customer acquisition costs start small

Building a community is not the same as attracting as many users as possible. The initial investment is small (although it may be a lot per user), and then the community itself helps attract users.

Product costs are reduced

The lack of a physical inventory (or, in some cases, on-demand creation of such inventory) also reduces upfront costs.

Development costs have shifted

The huge initial investment in hardware and software needed to build a large-scale web site has declined, as free software and low-cost—but easily extended—hardware setups have reduced the initial bite.

Iterations change the shape of the curve

The smaller-scale, community-based model lends itself to an iterative development approach. Companies can start basic and get a revenue stream going before making major investments.

Exponential effects play a much greater role

When a community achieves critical mass, value is created that isn't possible for a site that is in one way or another only a catalog. As Flickr grew, its usefulness increased dramatically, drawing in more people and expanding it further.

As always, J-curves can come to a sudden halt, as there is no magic formula for success. Web 2.0's community-based approach, however, can help lower costs at the outset when budgets are tight and increase rewards when (and if) success blossoms.

Company Financial Valuation

The total enterprise value calculation offers a customer-centered approach to valuing a company, but it is only one of many different tools analysts and managers use to determine company value.

As noted earlier, Flickr's final separate valuation was the $40 million that Yahoo! paid for it. It's not entirely clear how that value was determined, but working backward from the total enterprise calculation suggests that each customer is worth about $20. Because Flickr's primary assets are its customers and its brand (which ties the company to the customers), it seems likely that the valuation was based on customers.

By contrast, Netflix went to the public market, and its IPO brought in $86 million. The total enterprise value calculation suggests that 600,000 customers with a lifetime value of $20 should have been worth about $120 million. However, the market didn't see it that way, perhaps counting Netflix's ever-growing inventory of DVDs to be a cost as well as the key benefit to its customers.

Entrepreneur/Founders' Net Worth at Exit

Company valuations also influence a financial calculation—net worth at exit—that is very important to the entrepreneur/founders of a startup company like Netflix or Flickr.

Netflix, like many companies founded during the dot-com era, was funded by venture capitalists. But Flickr, like many of the companies founded with Web 2.0 technologies, had such low capital, inventory, marketing, and development costs that the two cofounders never needed to take venture capital funds to grow their startup into a profitable and sustainable company. This allowed them to retain a large proportion of their equity ownership, which ended up being worth around $40 million to Yahoo!.

When Netflix received its $86 million from the IPO, the venture capitalists that had waited five years for Netflix to break even and become profitable needed to receive an internal rate of return (IRR) of about 50% for their patience with a continued risky investment.

That leaves the likely net worth of the original founders at IPO, five years after launch, with a lowered percentage ownership due to multiple funding rounds and cash flow issues.

Questions to Ask

Flickr and Netflix may seem far from your own plans, whether they include an existing business or a startup. The following questions will help you evaluate the lessons of this chapter and possibly apply them to your own projects.

Strategic Questions

Consider how your business and industry currently work...

To what degree have you opened up to collective user value—multiplying the ways that users inside and outside of your project, team, or organizational unit can easily leverage, aggregate, and spark collective work, knowledge, and systems?

If you took the perspective of a CEO and strategic leader...

How and when do you see Web 2.0-enabled collective user value disrupting the current practices, business model, competitive advantages, and economics of your business and industry? What's the risk of being a leader or laggard? When should this become a boardroom agenda item?

If you took the perspective of a CIO and program manager...

How could you better benchmark, analyze, compare, and quantify the impact of shifts in collective user value and community in key functional areas, such as marketing and sales, product and services development, customer support, inventory management, logistics and operations, recruitment and training, partner and supplier relations and procurement? How can quantifying new customer acquisition costs, cash flow curves, per-user analytics, and per-click metrics provide a new basis for enterprise and financial valuation?

If you are a project team member...

Are you ready to brainstorm together with your group members on how the collective user value practices described for Flickr could be applied effectively in your business—whether consumer-focused or industrial, product or service-oriented, offline or online, local or global, small or large? What event could become a pilot project?

Tactical Questions

- Are your web site, storefront, web presence, development ecosystem, and user experience aligned with and open to collective user value best practices?

- Are you (or is your management) comfortable with letting users have their own independent voices on your site?

- Do you allow users to participate on your site? Can they share their own questions and ideas there?

- How do you attract users to participate on your site? What brings them there initially, and what encourages them to come back?

- What features of your site help users make connections with each other? Can users form groups with other users?

- How sense-rich is the participation you support? Can users present sound, video, or even just formatted text?

- Do you provide mechanisms (tagging, for example) to help users create their own navigation through your site?

- Do you support user annotation of your site?

- How could your site learn from user behavior and adapt itself to users? Which categories of user behavior have the most potential in your situation?

- How do you encourage users to bring other people to your site?

- How do you encourage users to share information in public, where it can generate positive network effects? In other words, is your site "public by default"?

- Can you create—or tighten—feedback loops between user requests and your company's ability to fulfill them?

- Can users keep up with your site through syndication—RSS or similar approaches?

- Do you provide programming interface (API) access to developers who want to combine, or mash up, the contents of your site with complementary materials from elsewhere?

- What licensing do you use for your site contents? And what licensing can users specify for their own contributions? (For example, All Rights Reserved versus Creative Commons with some rights reserved.)

- Do users feel they can control their information once they've entrusted your site with it? Can they extract it later?

- How do you support your active community members?

- Is there an opportunity to charge for the services your site provides? If so, can you structure those charges so that the people benefiting most directly from your site are the ones paying, while those contributing pay less or nothing?

CHAPTER TWO

Networks Multiply Effects

FOR MOST OF US IN THE REAL (OFFLINE) WORLD, TRAFFIC IS A BAD THING. More cars on the highway at rush hour create negative network effects. Each driver reduces the quality of the experience by congesting and overloading the highway network past its limit. But in the online world, traffic is a powerfully good thing.

Positive network effects created the Web 2.0 network platforms and contributed to the online hypergrowth of networks such as Google, Yahoo!, eBay, Skype, Wikipedia, Craigslist, Flickr, and others. These enterprises have strategically combined different kinds of network effects—including direct, indirect, cross-network, and demand-side—to multiply the overall positive impact of network value creation. Positive network effects explain, for example, why it could make brilliant but counterintuitive economic sense for GoTo—an early search engine innovator—to pay 5 cents to acquire a new search user just to get advertisers to pay 1 cent or more for that search user's pay-per-click keyword advertising.

Latecomer Google demonstrated a complete set of two-sided network effect multipliers that enabled it to be the first to reach critical mass and sustainable profitability in the paid keyword search race, even before first-movers GoTo and Excite. Ad-revenue-based online competitors, like Google, are disrupting the rules of the game for their offline rivals in the technology and media industries by providing free services to *search engine users* (the consumer-focused side of the Google platform), subsidized by *advertisers* (the second side or group linked to the Google platform by the AdWords self-service advertising network).

U.S. advertising expenditures were about $100 billion in 2007, nearly half of the global total. Just for comparison, U.S. venture capital investment in all stages (from early to late) during the first quarter of 2007 was a relatively modest $7 billion and was probably less than $30 billion for the year. U.S. marketers will continue to shift their spending into online advertising for a projected total of $19.5 billion in 2008, with $8.3 billion being spent on paid search ads, which are typically PPC, cost-per-action (CPA), and online sponsorships. Growth is coming from "new money": 44% of the companies in search advertising started in the past two years and are buying more keywords, leading to higher prices and overall increases in budgets and spending.

Google is the big winner in online advertising, dominating in the U.S. and internationally. It not only generated the most global online revenue in 2006, but it also grew at nearly two times the rate of its peers. Despite competition from other U.S. online advertising networks—such as Yahoo!, Marchex, AOL, Monster, Gannett, the *New York Times* online, and Knight-Ridder—Google grew its net advertising revenue by 63% year to year.

Google's amazing success makes it easy to forget that it faced at least two critical make-or-break junctures in its race to dominate the "winner-takes-most" paid search marketplace. Two natural experiments in Google's past were especially critical:

- Despite being a latecomer, Google used a powerful combination of network effects strategies to defeat its strongest competitors.

- AOL helped tip the paid search market to make Google's average U.S. search revenue per query more than triple that of its competitors. Positive network effects explain why the value of AOL's 7–9% market share points were worth as much as $4 billion to Google, although analysts argued at the time that $1 billion was too much to protect Google's traffic from falling into Microsoft's hands.

Web-Enabled Online Network Effects

Positive network effects increase the value of a good or service as more people use or adopt it. The simplest network effects are direct: increases in usage lead to direct increases in the value of the system. Telephone service is a great example of this. The more people available to call, the more valuable the system becomes.

Web-enabled online networks have generated several new types of positive network effects. They combine the powerful economic characteristics of digital economics—high upfront costs but negligible incremental costs—with the opportunities of exponential network growth in users and usage, as well as willingness to pay. When increases in usage create more value across all users, a rise in returns is generated that alters the nature of the competition substantially. Achieving critical mass offers the potential for exponential growth, as we saw with Flickr in the previous chapter.

In Web 2.0, managing combinations of online network effects is key to competitive success for the following reasons:

- *Upfront capital costs have dropped* so that there are lower barriers to entry and frictionless scalability in online networks compared with physical networks. As a result, customer acquisition costs are reduced, and free basic services (rather than only promotional or trial usage) are relatively low-cost and sustainable in the long term.

- *Online networks have strong demand-side scale economies* where users bring other users. Social and/or late users can increase the overall global value of the network for all members and create a bandwagon or "tippy" effect, whereby the market tips in favor of one company or another. This is rarely seen in physical networks—which tend to be dominated by economies of scale in production—where higher volume leads to lower unit costs and commoditization, rather than higher or premium prices and increased market attractiveness.

- *Online networks form faster, more frequently, and more interactively* than before. Active *one-percenters* and *uploaders* can rapidly trigger a critical mass of online adoption and formation of communities. Many-to-many network effects become more commonplace.

- *Online networks and services can expand rapidly and often virally* across borders, geographies, market segments, media types, and channels.

- *Barriers to entry are low, but barriers to success are high* because of timing sensitivity and customer volatility, as expressed in winner-take-most competitive races, tippy markets, path dependency, standards, and compatibility battles.

There are different kinds of network effects:

Direct network effects

The value of a good or service increases as more people use it. Each new customer boosts the value of the network and often increases the willingness of all participants to pay for network services. The fax machine is a classic example of direct network effects because the first buyer of a fax machine finds it useless with no one to fax, but as his network of users expands, so does the value of having a machine.

Indirect network effects

More usage of the product spawns the production of increasingly valuable complementary goods, resulting in added value to the original product or service. For example, although some direct network effects are associated with Windows and file compatibility, the indirect network effects that arise from the increased quality and availability of complementary applications software are more significant.

Cross-network effects (sometimes referred to as two-sided network effects)

A rise in usage by one group of users can increase the value of a complementary product or service to another distinct group of users. Hardware and software platforms, reader/writer software pairs, marketplaces, and matching services display this kind of network effect.

Social network effects (sometimes referred to as local network effects)

Instant messaging shows local network effects. A user is influenced directly by the decisions of a typically small subset of other consumers; for instance, those she is connected to via an underlying social or business network. The extent and density of clustering in the network, as well as information access, becomes strategic in technology adoption and pricing choices.

N-Sided Markets

Most markets connect only two groups: buyers and sellers. Buyers are the source of revenue; sellers provide goods or services in return. Economists call markets that connect two or more different groups of customers/users to sellers/partners *n-sided markets*, with the *n* referring to the number of different groups (see Table 2-1, which was modified from tables and examples in Marco Iansiti and Roy Levien's book *The Keystone Advantage* (Harvard Business School Press) and *HBR* article "Strategies for Two-Sided markets" (Eisenmann et al.), see end notes N-sided markets and ecosystems.).

American Express, eBay, Kaiser Permanente, Nintendo, and Microsoft are all examples of companies that orchestrate or provide a platform for n-sided markets.

Visa is often cited as an n-sided market because its credit cards connect communities of retailers, banks, and consumers. In the case of credit cards, it's easy to see that n-sided markets unite interdependent communities. The whole ecosystem would fall apart if there weren't enough of each group present to provide a critical mass. So, although some markets can operate with a small number of customers—maybe by pricing a premium amount for each additional user or customer—Visa has zero value to retailers without a critical mass of cardholders, and vice versa. We can see a cross-network effect: the more retailers that participate worldwide, the more beneficial the card is to its users. Thus, it is important to Visa to be "Everywhere you want to be"; American Express positions itself similarly with "Don't leave home without it."

Table 2-1. *N-sided markets in a variety of sectors*

Industry	Platform	Side 1	Side 2	Free or minimal	Sources of revenue
Search	Search engine	Searchers	Advertisers	Side 1: searchers	Google earns 97% of its revenue from keyword searches, about $8 billion per quarter.
Payment services	Credit card	Card-holders	Merchants	Side 1: cardholders	American Express earns more than 80% of its revenue from merchants in the form of transaction fees.
Media	Newspapers	Readers	Advertisers	Side 1: readers	80% of newspaper revenue comes from advertisers.
Online recruiting	Web	Job seekers	Recruiters, hiring companies	Side 1: job seekers	100% of Craigslist revenue comes from employers (and in New York, real estate classifieds). More than 90% of Monster.com's revenue comes from recruiters.
Video games	PCs, game consoles	Game players	Game developers	Neither: both sides pay	Xbox and PlayStation producers get revenue from hardware and licensing to third-party developers. EA and others sell games directly to end users. Shanda provides a pay-to-play system in China.
Open source software	Linux	Users	Application developers	Side 1: users	IBM, Sun, HP provide hardware platforms and get indirect revenue from hardware and services.

Table 2-1. N-sided markets in a variety of sectors (continued)

INDUSTRY	PLATFORM	SIDE 1	SIDE 2	FREE OR MINIMAL	SOURCES OF REVENUE
Web 2.0 software	Linux, Apache, MySQL, PHP, Perl, etc.	Users	Application developers	Side 1: users	Ad-supported, software as a service (SaaS), pays per usage or user.
DVD	DVD players	Users	Movie studios	Side 1: users (free Netflix promotions)	Netflix online DVD rental and free promotion is partly subsidized by movie studios.
Online auctions	Web	Buyers	Sellers	Buyers	Sellers pay an 8% transaction fee to eBay.

What is the value of a free customer? N-sided markets provide a compelling answer to that question. eBay wouldn't have a profitable transaction business, charging its sellers 8%, if there were no online buyers searching its auction listings. IBM, HP, Sun, Facebook, Amazon, Apple, and even synthetic worlds such as World of Warcraft and Second Life would not attract networks of application developers, partners, affiliates, value-added resellers, and related or complementary product/service providers (and indirect network effects) if they didn't have an actively growing installed base and critical mass of users.

Exponential Growth

Bob Metcalfe, the inventor of Ethernet, concluded early on that the value of a network increases as does the square of the number of users. Each new user n can connect to $n-1$ existing users, who also benefit from new users. This rule, often called *Metcalfe's Law*, helps explain the bandwagon effect: why growth and profitability accelerate as a system obtains more users.

Metcalfe's Law does a good job of explaining why people found the Internet more valuable as it expanded, but it's also a simplification that assumes users aren't making a contribution beyond their availability on the network. When users make a contribution (even though this may be a side effect of their activities, unnoticed by the user), networks can experience even faster value growth.

Reed's Law, created by David Reed, another network scientist, proposes that Metcalfe's n^2 isn't quite enough—the effects may be more like 2^n. Why? Because the benefits accrue on the basis of the combinations among the users and the total many-to-many possibilities, not just the one-to-one possibilities of Metcalfe's network (*http://en.wikipedia.org/wiki/Reed's_law*).

In the examples examined in this chapter, the existence of millions of advertisers willing to pay Google top dollar per click daily for keywords is possible only because there are already billions of online queries and searchers worldwide.

Google's Combination of Network Effects

Google had a great foundation to build on: the PageRank algorithm that used links among sites to determine their likely relevance in a search. Google succeeded because it was able to build on network effects PageRank created in one area, then spread the results of that work to other areas where more network effects could multiply its resources still further. Consider the following:

Direct search engine network effects

Each new search query from users dynamically updates the PageRanking and user relevance of the search engine. Google also increased traffic and usage through affiliate deals with AOL, AskJeeves, and others, using a different revenue split with affiliates than was normal at the time.

Direct advertiser network effects

Performance-based pay-per-click made it easy for customers (and Google) to monitor advertising. Google made AdWords cheap and easy to use for small- and medium-size businesses that were new to online advertising, giving them a do-it-yourself system for creating and monitoring ads. Google's $5 to enroll and 5 cents paid per click enticed a lot of new people and got them talking.

Advertiser–searcher cross-network effects

Both small and large advertisers wanted the search engine with the most search queries and users.

Demand-side network effects: the advertiser's willingness to pay

AdRanking dynamically priced keywords and created pricing auctions for advertisers. Pay-per-click delivered return-on-investment metrics and customer behavior information, and revealed the cost-effectiveness of online versus offline advertising for direct marketing and branding. Advertisers started putting more marketing and ad dollars into Google's coffers.

All four of these effects reinforced each other. Before we talk about the first three—the better-known direct, indirect, and cross-network effects—let's backtrack and fill in some background on the last network effect.

Demand-Side Network Effects and Critical Mass

Businesses tend to be most familiar with increasing returns created by supply-side-driven scale economies. On the supply side of Figure 2-1, the cost curve shows that as a manufacturing company increases its output, its marginal and average unit costs decline to a point. On the supply side, the curve tracks average cost per unit as it varies with output production or scale. As average unit costs decline, the difference between revenue and costs increases, creating growing returns and increasing profitability over time until the cost curve stops its decline.

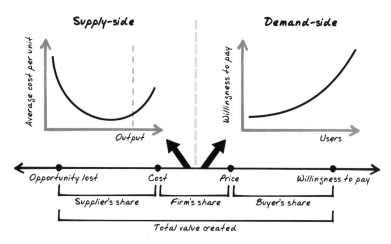

Figure 2-1. *Differences between economies driven by supply and economies driven by demand[1]*

[1] Based on Exhibit of "Mauboussin on Strategy: Exploring Network Economies," October 11, 2004, *Legg Mason Investment Report*, modified for Web 2.0 increasing returns.

By contrast, networks are characterized by demand-side scale economies. The demand side of Figure 2-1 has a vertical y-axis of willingness to pay and a horizontal x-axis of number of users. Once a network has passed the *critical mass* point on the S-curve of growth, it enters an exponential growth stage, driven by positive network effects. After the critical mass point, *willingness to pay* increases because the value to the users grows sharply (as described in the earlier "Exponential Growth" sidebar with Metcalfe's Law). As value increases, revenue and the average price that users are willing to pay tend to go up.

We can look at the relative size of the supplier's, firm's, and buyer's share of the total value created by a network like Google and relate that to the value creation diagram at the bottom of Figure 2-1.

Supplier's share

> In many network systems, the average cost per unit cost curve starts out with a high upfront cost followed by a low incremental cost. Common examples of this include software, books, and music. Writing the first copy is time-consuming and costly. Once that code or digital product is finished, however, the cost of replicating and distributing it is very small or close to nothing.
>
> When the suppliers are users, or if a significant part of the value can be contributed or donated effortlessly by volunteers, the supplier's share of the total value created can be large, while costs remain low. Although creating an expert-edited entry for the *Encyclopedia Britannica* is costly, the users who volunteer to share and publish their knowledge on Wikipedia do so for free, donating their share of the total value created. Once information is entered, the cost of replicating and distributing, and editing or improving, that knowledge is also very low.
>
> Similarly, Google's PageRank algorithms use a popularity-driven ranking of relevant search listings in response to keyword search queries. This continuously improves search result relevancy by aggregating the valuable information that is supplied or generated by the clicks of all its users. Just by searching on Google, users help generate value by improving the relevancy of frequent keyword searches.

Firm's share

> Google's share of the total value created is the difference between the average price advertisers are willing to pay per keyword search query and the cost of acquiring and maintaining a leadership position in search engines with an installed base of search users making billions of queries.

Affiliate's share

> Google revenue shares its advertising dollars with partners or affiliates that bring traffic and help spur positive network effects.

Buyer's share

> Advertisers pay-per-click on a performance basis. The keyword price approaches their willingness to pay because priority positioning is based on both the auction price of the keyword and the ad ranking or click popularity. This allows for perfect price discrimination.

Getting Advertisers to Pay for Keywords: GoTo

Bill Gross, the founder of Idealab and GoTo (later renamed Overture), built GoTo on the fundamental insight that search engines could offer searches for free and be profitable if they could charge the advertiser a *price for keywords* used in the search. In his book, *The Search* (Portfolio), John Battelle quoted Gross:

> All of our false starts made me realize that the true value of search lies in the search term.... I realized that when someone types "Princess Diana" into a search engine, they want, in effect to go into a Princess Diana store—where all the possible information and goods about Princess Diana are laid out for them to see.... (The Search, 106–07)

Gross took an enormous risk to prove his keyword system. He built a pay-per-click performance-based advertising model into GoTo. An advertiser paid for a visitor only when the visitor clicked through an ad and onto the advertiser's site. Instead of demanding upfront money from advertisers, GoTo required advertisers to pay only when their ads were clicked on.

To further convince a critical mass of advertisers that this pay-per-click keyword advertising system was risk-free, he priced his search engine at 1 cent per click at a time when everyone else was charging 7 to 10 cents per click for banner ads. In fact, *The Search* recounts that Gross was buying traffic and search query users at 5 to 10 cents in at least one case and selling advertising access to these users at 1 cent per click. How could this possibly make sense?

It made sense only if you believed that it was essential to reach critical mass and then harvest positive network effects in search users and usage. It made sense if the cost to drive a search was declining rapidly at the same time that price and willingness to pay on the part of advertisers were increasing, driving both revenue and increasing returns.

Gross explained his reasoning:

> Eventually, with volume, I was able to drive traffic acquisition costs down to six and sometimes four cents. Then people would exit paying a penny, or possibly two, as some might click on more than one link. But people were also bookmarking the site and using it again, which drove down my average cost to acquire a searcher/search. With volume and loyalty, my cost to drive a search was declining each month and my earnings for each search were increasing. (The Search, 110)

For consumers, GoTo provided relevant search results for free. For advertisers, GoTo provided traffic to their sites at pennies a click. Advertisers that were using online advertising for the first time were amazed at the ROI, motivating them to shift their advertising expenditure from offline to online media.

Advertisers started to compete for scarce and valuable keywords, driving the price up for keywords such as "auto" and "camera." Gross had already developed models explaining how buying traffic and generating positive network effects would turn profitable as advertisers bid up various keywords from one cent to as high as two dollars. Gross recalled:

> In about six months, the average price paid by an advertiser rose past the average price GoTo paid to acquire a searcher...we were way ahead of schedule...I knew bid prices would increase to their true value over time and...in the range of 25 cents per click to $2.50 per click and even higher on some terms. (The Search, 110)

Additionally, GoTo had made some major traffic acquisition deals with Microsoft, Netscape, and AOL—providing search services on these web sites in exchange for a fee or a split in revenue, said to be 50/50.

Google's Entry

So, how did Google win the race by 2003? GoTo was a first-mover and innovator in many of the powerful network effects and paid search strategies that Google later adopted.

Direct search engine network effect

- PageRanking organic search optimization
- Paid search
- Affiliate traffic partners

Direct advertiser network effect

- Performance pay-per-click
- AdWords—self-serve and easy to use for small advertisers

Advertiser-searcher cross-network effect

Advertiser willingness to pay for demand-side network effect

- Dynamically priced keywords and auctions on keyword pricing for advertisers
- AdRanking also used to determine positioning
- Pay-per-click delivered ROI metrics and customer behavior information and revealed the cost-effectiveness of online versus offline advertising for direct marketing and branding; advertisers started spending more marketing and ad dollars

The three important ingredients Google added to the mix were:

- PageRanking optimization of organic search
- AdWords' self-service model, which allowed advertisers to buy text ads online with a credit card and separated advertising from organic search results
- AdRanking used to assess an ad's popularity and click-through rate, as well as its auction and pay-per-click

PageRanking optimization of organic search

Google's PageRank algorithm calculated a site's relevance by counting the number of links into a particular site, reinforced by calculating the number of links into each of the linking sites.

The more popular sites rose to the top of its annotation list, and less popular sites fell toward the bottom. PageRank's results were not only more relevant—*and less advertiser-driven*—than competing search engines, which ranked mostly on the basis of keywords, they also benefited directly from the increasing scale of the Web. PageRank analyzed links and link popularity; as the Web expanded, the engine improved.

The direct positive network effects came from both the number of users linking to Google's search engine and the wisdom of the crowd: popularity information generated from each new search query fed back into the system.

By mid-2002, Google had the highest loyalty of any online brand— its users were rabidly loyal, and the press was in love with it.

AdWords: A self-service way of reaching the long tail of search query

Google had to beat a lot of competitors. Joe Kraus, founder of the early search engine Excite and the wiki startup JotSpot (later acquired by Google), wrote about what Google did that Excite didn't. Kraus examined the power law distribution of query searches, now known much more widely as a *long tail* after Chris Anderson's best-selling book, *The Long Tail: Why the Future of Business Is Selling Less of More* (Hyperion).

Kraus explains (*http://bnoopy.typepad.com/bnoopy/2005/03/the_long_tail_o.html*) that when Excite analyzed its keyword search queries, it discovered that only 3% of the keywords actually received a substantial number of hits each day, leaving 97% of the keywords to a query rate of less than 1,000 hits per day. As shown in Figure 2-2, "Britney Spears" might be a keyword that received 10,000 hits on a given day, but "mesothelioma," a rare cancer, might receive considerably fewer than 1,000. Despite Excite's rapid growth and search technology, Kraus and his management team could not figure out how to get revenue from the long tail of the search query marketplace—and that's what killed Excite.

How did Google figure out how to effectively monetize the long tail of the search query marketplace through paid keyword searches? By observing its closest competitor at the time: Overture.

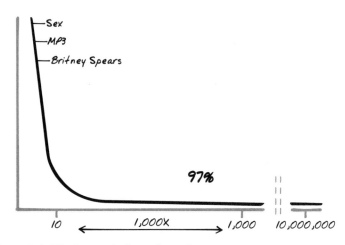

Figure 2-2. *The long tail of search results*

Although Google was late to the paid search listing space, it was just in time to capitalize on the shift in the market and in the popular press toward pay-per-click textual advertising as a way to subsidize billions of inquiries and free search. Although Overture filed for patent infringement and settled before Google's 2004 IPO, Google is now the company most search users associate with the keyword PPC paid listing business model. Overture was later purchased by Yahoo! and is a key component of its paid search system.

As John Battelle quipped in *The Search*, Google reached "a billion dollars, one [advertising] nickel at a time." Those nickels came from millions of small and mid-size companies that were new to advertising. In October 2000, Google introduced a new service called AdWords, an automated self-service model that allowed advertisers to buy text ads online with a credit card. The announcement read, "Have a credit card and 5 minutes? Get your ad on Google today." The online self-service market opened up for millions of small and mid-size companies that had never advertised online before.

At Google's first shareholders meeting, CEO Eric Schmidt elaborated:

Google's mission to serve The Long Tail—advertisers from the largest companies—Wal-Mart—in the world, all the way down to the smallest companies in the world, the single individual.... So we went in both directions, we brought out a whole suite of tools for very large advertisers...to drive lots of revenues because, of course, in our model the advertising drives predictability, it drives conversions, and so forth.

And what about the individual contributor, the small business, the company where Joe or Bob is the CEO, the CIO, the CFO, and the worker, and the support person? A one-person company, two-person company, a three-person company? We built a whole bunch of small, self-service tools which allowed them to almost automatically use this service.

So [we went] in both directions. By going to the bottom with self-service, we were able to reach advertisers who fell below the threshold of traditional advertising. And by going all the way to the top, we were able to capture very large and historically underserved businesses as well as a whole new area that never had access to these kinds of online services...maybe the last entry is a person in India with a basket selling something they made—but if there's an Internet connection and they have a small business, we help them do business outside their own village, reaching a large market, get more suppliers, better price competition, and so on....

AdRank to determine advertisement positioning

With the growth of AdWords, Google's 2001 revenue was on pace to hit nearly $85 million. But Overture was doing better because its auction-based, pay-per-click advertising network had tens of thousands of clients. In February 2002, Google launched a new version of AdWords that included auctions and pay-per-click, as well as a new metric called AdRank. AdRank was based on an ad's popularity and clickthrough rate.

As David Vise commented in Harvard Business School's case *Google Advertising*:

> Overture's model was strictly capitalistic—pay more and you are number one. Google has more socialistic tendencies. They like to give their users a vote.

The press loved it because they interpreted it as not allowing advertisers to buy their way to the top but requiring they get there through popularity. Google benefited financially because it placed businesses with the most clickthroughs at the top spot, giving it a percentage of every click and more money.

As with PageRank, the direct positive network effect came from the number of advertisers linking to Google's advertising platform, as well as the "wisdom of the crowd" popularity that clickthrough information dynamically generated from each new search query. AdRank and the high ROI of online paid search for advertisers created positive network multipliers, driving more and more advertisers from offline to online advertising.

AdRank also rewarded the most effective and relevant ads—the ones with the highest clickthroughs—with higher placement. This helped trigger a shift toward keyword relevance rather than attention-getting visuals.

Compounding network effects

The three important ingredients Google added to the mix were PageRank optimization, the AdWords self-service model, and AdRank. Each of these multiplied direct positive network effects by increasing the value of the Google system with every new search query or clickthrough, not just by the sheer numbers of users or advertisers. The secret sauce of Google's direct positive network effects was the aggregation of the wisdom of the crowd as expressed by popularity and frequency of usage of linkages, sites, and advertising clickthroughs. Google could then monetize or capture the value of this information through dynamic pricing. Table 2-2 shows some of the most profitable keywords, according to a 2006 study by Xedant.

Table 2-2. Profitable advertising centers for making money from search terms

Keyword	Cost per click	Clicks per day	Cost per day
Insurance	$17.41	49,893	$868,645.81
Hotels	$3.52	200,636	$706,238.75
Film	$2.88	183,044	$527,166.75
Home	$3.89	102,282	$397,878.91
Car	$5.09	52,069	$265,033.75
Schools	$4.13	60,913	$251,570.69
Acting	$2.28	106,337	$242,448.36
Credit	$8.67	25,705	$222,862.34
Cheap	$2.71	82,139	$222,598.05
Digital	$1.70	130,607	$222,031.91
Hotel	$2.38	84,776	$201,768.06
Film schools	$5.64	35,501	$200,228.45
Software	$3.23	61,259	$197,868.19
New	$2.17	90,415	$196,200.55
Auto insurance	$29.48	6,453	$190,234.44
Rental	$5.97	31,635	$188,863.94
Free	$1.06	172,680	$183,041.33
Travel	$5.02	35,084	$176,124.19

Blogging for dollars

Google's AdSense system was also a perfect match for blogging. Blogs are web sites, often either personal or focused on specific topics, that have regular postings and maintain a history (the "log") of old postings. Thousands of people were setting up and contributing to blogs, and the combination of Google's low initial cost with context-based advertising helped AdSense flourish in the blogging world. In the *Google Advertising* case, it was put as follows:

> AdSense was the flip side to AdWords. Instead of giving advertisers a mechanism via which they could buy space for their ads, AdSense gave content providers a mechanism via which they could add advertising space to their websites.

Blogs helped Google place ads on sites where users were especially likely to click on them—sites with specific focus or simply lots of personality. Google's revenue-split approach gave many blogs their first source of regular revenue, and blogging became possible as a business, not just as a hobby.

The Google advertising platform uses an estimated 80/20 revenue split, sharing value capture and revenue distribution with its ecosystem partners. Figure 2-3 is a simpified version of a block diagram originally posted by a blogger (Vaughn's One-Page summaries) who was trying to map the interdependencies of Google AdWords, AdSense, and the payout to a blogger. For the full version, see *http://www.vaughns-1-pagers.com/internet/adwords-adsense-diagram.gif*.

As Mary Meeker noted in her 2006 "State of the Internet" presentation (*http://www.oreillynet.com/lpt/a/6848*), these cycles bring a lot of cash to Internet business, and much of what comes to Google goes back out to its partners:

> Google and Yahoo! account for about 60 percent of U.S. online advertising revenue, per IB data. In turn, they share 30 percent of that with their partners and affiliates. That's a lot of money shared with a lot of other players.

Google started with a base of users doing searches, built an advertising engine on that base, and then managed to connect that advertising engine back into the Web by sharing advertising

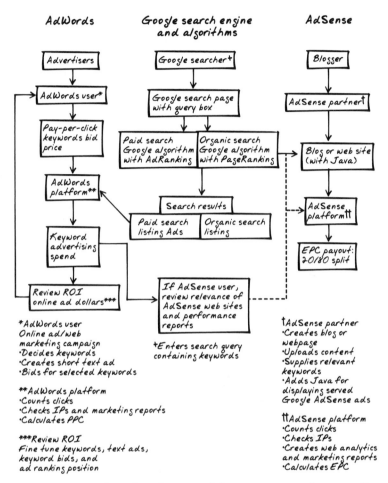

Figure 2-3. *How AdWords, AdSense, and their customers and partners fit together*

revenue with bloggers and other businesses. The positive feedback cycle was working well.

The Ups and Downs of Positive Feedback

Positive feedback can easily be confused with rapid growth because with positive network effects, success seems to feed on itself—the strong get stronger and the weak get weaker. Positive feedback amplifies *virtuous cycles*—the strong getting stronger.

Just as quickly, however, positive feedback can amplify the shift in the other direction, a *vicious cycle* where the weak get weaker. Figure 2-4 is a conceptual illustration of this.

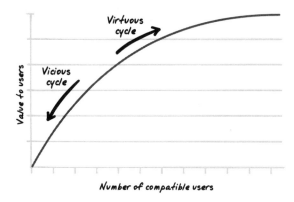

Figure 2-4. *Virtuous and vicious cycles created by network effects*

When two or more companies are in a competitive race for market share where there is strong positive feedback due to network effects, only one company emerges as the winner. (Economists call this market tippy because it can tip in favor of one company or the other.) Strong positive feedback can lead to a winner-take-all market dominated by a single firm or technology.

To show how a winner-take-all market evolves, Carl Shapiro and Hal R. Varian developed the diagram shown in Figure 2-5 and in their book *Information Rules: A Strategic Guide to the Network Economy* (Harvard Business School Press). A race may be very close, with one company or technology starting with an initial lead and more than half the market, and then experiencing a virtuous cycle and growing to nearly 100%. However, the company or technology that lags in this critical period with a little less than half the market will experience a vicious cycle that drives a decline to less than 10%. The positive feedback that starts the virtuous or vicious cycle is amplified by the perception and bandwagon desire of the users to select the company or technology that looks like it is going to win and have the most users. No one wants to be stuck with an incompatible (or worse, orphaned) technology that no one else uses or services.

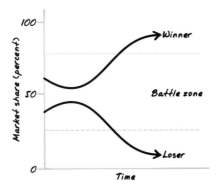

Figure 2-5. Competitive race with positive feedback

A classic example of this kind of tippy market is the videotape recorder market in the 1980s, when the VHS standard (backed by and licensed to a global group of companies led by JVC and Matsushita) competed against the Beta standard (backed by Sony). Notice in Figure 2-6 that the key crossover point between the VHS technology standard and Beta actually occurred in 1978 at the 50% market share point.

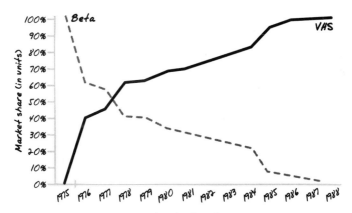

Figure 2-6. How the VHS/Beta battle played out[1]

[1] Based on Table 1 from "Strategic Maneuvering and Mass-Market Dynamics: The Triumph of VHS over Beta," by Michael A. Cusumano, Yiorgos Mylonadis, and Richard S. Rosenbloom, in *Business History Review*, Spring 1992.

The AOL/Google Story

In December 2005, Google paid $1 billion for a 5% equity stake in Time Warner's AOL unit and provided a $300 million credit for ads on Google promoting Time Warner products. In this deal, Google cemented a 5-year paid search and revenue-sharing deal with AOL, services that accounted for about a 7% to 9% share of the U.S. paid search market. It also shut the door on Microsoft's proposal for a joint venture with AOL in paid search.

According to the Harvard Business School case study *Google, Inc.*, there was some controversy among analysts about whether Google had paid too much to protect its traffic. At first glance, Google overpaid by $300 million for AOL's equity and could have expected to earn about $200 million in net ad revenue (an estimated $500 million during the five-year period from 2006–2010), which was offset by the $300 million ad credit. It appeared that Google paid about $100 million too much.

However, as the previous section demonstrated, in competitive markets with strong positive network effects, the crucial battle zone is between 40% and 60% market share. At this point, one company or technology harnesses the virtual cycle and market expectations to become the winner, and the other falls into a vicious cycle of collapse and loses.

As shown in Figure 2-7, in December 2005, Google's share of search traffic was just around 50%. Losing the AOL deal would mean a decline of overall paid search share to 43%, just under the 50% point. Given that Yahoo! was at the 37% market share level, Google would not be a clear or dominant leader at 41% to 43%. Winning the AOL deal meant a dominant leadership position for Google with 57% to 59% of market share. AOL could be seen as the swing vote in harnessing the virtual cycle and market expectations.

So, was Google's extra $100 million only a strategic investment in securing Google's 59% market share for the next 5 years?

A back-of-the-envelope calculation shows why 7% to 9% market share in a tippy market with strong positive effects can be worth $4.45 billion, not just $100 million.

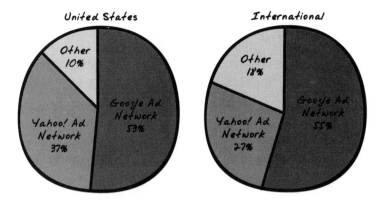

Figure 2-7. In 2005, Google dominated advertisers in both the U.S. and international markets—but not by that much

The key is to realize that the revenue per search (RPS) of advertising varies dramatically with market share. Advertisers are willing to pay more to advertise with the online search engine that has the dominant share of search users and overall number of search queries. By protecting its 7% to 9% of AOL's share of traffic, Google protected all of its 50% of paid search traffic from a precipitous decline in RPS. According to equity analysts, the RPS gap between Google and its followers, including Yahoo!, was very large. RBC Capital Markets estimated that Google's RPS exceeded Yahoo!'s by at least 40%.

Looking at simplified numbers may make this easier to see. If the entire industry made $12 billion in total online ad revenue and there were 400 billion inquiries, the industry-wide RPS for 2005 would be 3 cents. Google's ad revenue was $8 billion, and its queries totaled 200 billion. This would imply an RPS of 4 cents for Google and 2 cents for all others.

So, if Google's share is around 50% at the end of 2005, losing AOL would mean a decline of overall paid search share to 43%. This would have caused the advertiser base to contract in response, as well as the average RPS. If Google fell to a 2 cent RPS as a result of negative network effects and falling out of its dominant leadership position, it would not only lose 28 billion queries at .04 (7% share), but also 172 billion queries at .02 in revenue (its 43% of the total query market but only monetized at 2 cents per query rather than 4 cents), creating a revenue loss of more than half—$4.56 billion of its $8 billion.

An extra $100 million for AOL's traffic is a tiny price to pay for avoiding a possible loss of $4.56 billion in a tippy market in which the leader is just at the 50% point.

Lessons Learned

The two natural experiments in Google's past turned out to be tipping points early in its evolution and tippy markets a few years later:

- Google, as a latecomer, was able to match or copy several paid search network strategies innovated by Bill Gross of GoTo/Overture. However, its distinctive positive network multipliers—as featured in PageRanking, AdRank, and AdWords—were critical deciding factors.

- AOL helped tip the paid search market to make Google's average U.S. search revenue per query more than three times that of its competitors. Positive network effects explain why AOL's 7–9% market share points were worth as much as $4 billion to Google, even though analysts argued at the time that $1 billion was too much to protect Google's traffic from falling into Microsoft's hands.

Google's experience may seem unique, as its explosive growth and status as an icon have led to tremendous capitalization. However, although Google has seized the search engine market, there is still plenty of room for others to follow a similar path in other markets—and even use Google's tools. Figure 2-8 shows a critical sequence of events on the path to success.

Following these curves—and not sliding back on them, or suddenly stopping—requires several events to occur in the right combination:

Starting up the adoption curve

> If no one ever hears about your product, it's going to be very hard for it to succeed. To create buzz, you must combine ease of use, attractive results, and an initial user base. Early adoption is critical, and the climb up the S-curve is rarely easy.

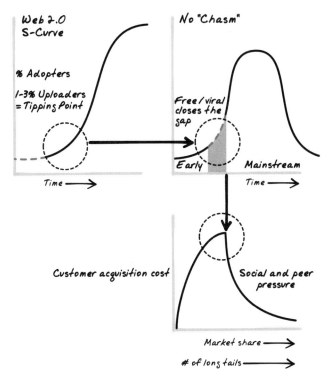

Figure 2-8. *A Web 2.0 path to growth*[1]

[1] Based on Exhibit 10 of "Mauboussin on Strategy: Exploring Network Economies", an October 11, 2004 Legg-Mason investment report, but modified for Web 2.0.

Avoiding the chasm

Too many products reach a certain market of early adopters and then halt, unable to reach a broader mainstream audience. Product cost is a classic adoption barrier, one that's fairly easy to avoid in a web environment. Reputation is also critical; anything that alienates adopters may send them to your competitors. Try to ensure that in addition to providing users with direct benefits, you also make it easy for them to stay with your service.

Taking advantage of the long tail

As more users join a service, it becomes easier to justify serving specific audiences. Broad critical mass makes it easier to create specialized critical mass, and people are much more likely to stay (and contribute or pay) when services provide rare features they can't find elsewhere. It's now much easier to monetize the long tail through online advertising.

Google may be unique in combining so many different aspects of network effects across such a broad audience, but there is still plenty of room to use similar strategies for more targeted projects.

Questions to Ask

Your company may not be Google, and even if you work at Google, you're probably not planning to reinvent what's been done. However, these questions will help you apply the lessons of its experience to your own projects.

Strategic Questions

Think about positive network effects...

Taking place in your business, ecosystem, and industry. To what extent do you actively consider and work with positive network effects as a fundamental process for accelerating and multiplying your business value? Are you effective at monetizing network effects? Why or why not?

If you considered positive network effects as a fundamental strategy...

What specific implications would it have for how you run your business and compete effectively?

What are some immediate and practical ways...

You can imagine to raise the awareness of those in your business, organization, and ecosystem about the power of monetizing and multiplying network effects?

As a project team member...

Are you ready to systematically analyze with your group members the full range of network effects described for Google that could be applied effectively in your business— whether consumer-focused or industrial, product- or service-oriented, offline or online, local or global, small or large? What event could become a pilot project?

Tactical Questions

- As users visit your site, do you learn from them, or just present information to them?

- Can you make users happy by helping them find information you don't control?

- Are you prepared to serve large numbers of users if they arrive?

- Can you reach critical mass for your business by buying other businesses or providing them with services?

- How much does it cost you to acquire a new customer? Are there ways to reduce that cost?

- Do users trust your site, your services, and your business?

- Do you serve enough people to see distinct niches forming among your user base?

- Can you provide tools that help users address their own needs and wants? Does your site have do-it-yourself features?

- Would auctions offer you the chance to maximize income for the services you provide?

- How can the different facets of your business or site reinforce each other?

- If you are in a competitive race, how do your users perceive your offerings versus competitors' offerings?

- If you are starting in an empty space, how will you bring users to a new field?

- If you're challenging existing giants, how can you differentiate your services from theirs? Are there ways to capitalize on "new" so that you don't stay small for long?

- To accelerate adoption, how low can you go? What can you give away to draw people in, and how can you monetize on those people's presence to pay for and profit on that giving?

CHAPTER THREE

People Build Connections

IN OCTOBER 2007, SILICON VALLEY WAS BUZZING. Microsoft's $240 million advertising deal and investment in Facebook, for a 1.6% equity share, valued the 3-year-old company at a total enterprise valuation of $15 billion (compared to Google's public stock valuation of $181 billion at a stock price of $600 a share). Some observers immediately dismissed the number as a throwback to the dot-com bubble, the "irrational exuberance" of naïve and enthusiastic stock purchasers in the late 1990s. But the "smart money" venture capitalists and private-equity firms took notice.

After all, Microsoft and its investment bankers were sophisticated mergers-and-acquisitions dealmakers. There were whispers of a closed round of bidding where Google's outright offer of $11 billion had been the "floor" for anteing up, with all of the large multinationals and media firms expressing interest. From the point of view of Facebook and Microsoft, the final deal was a win-win. Facebook's privately held stock was ratcheted up as if it were already publicly valued by the $240 million transaction, and Microsoft's stock gained as well upon the announcement.

Financial deal making aside, what kind of financial analysis might tell us whether Facebook was worth $15 billion? Let's turn to the generalized framework of the customer-based financial valuation model we explained in Chapter 1, in valuing Netflix as the sum total of the lifetime value in subscription fees of its installed customer base (a methodology originally developed for cable and cell phone subscription companies).

A Web 2.0 online social network like Facebook has three immediate and powerful advantages over those previous customer-
based enterprises:

- Facebook has proven itself to be a much more powerful
  customer-acquisition engine, using its viral social marketing
  and distribution online to attract 47 million customers in less
  than 3 years.

- These 47 million free users are highly interactive and engaged
  with Facebook.

- Facebook is a social network advertising platform. The value
  of this installed base of 47 million free users is immediately
  monetized through target advertising revenues—cash flows in
  much faster and more predictably than it would from monthly
  subscription fees. More importantly, the cross-network value
  to the advertiser is *already* multiplied by these users' uploaded
  collective user value—the huge database/inventory storehouse
  of digitized personal and social information, photos, bios,
  interests, music, content, applications, preferences, and lists of
  friends they have volunteered to upload openly to Facebook.

Just as in the Flickr case, Facebook users had a mostly individual
or social motivation for developing and sharing a digitized personal and contact database. However, their openness benefits and
contributes to the positive network effects and value of the system
both as a one-stop social communication/directory site and also as
a treasure trove for algorithmic, targeted advertising and social-
influence marketing. If Google's average revenue per user is $15 in
pay-per-click ad-revenue monetization, Facebook hopes to do
even better by leveraging Microsoft's technology resources and the
advertising/IM platforms developed with MSN.

Google may know my keyword search queries, Amazon may have
my wish list, and Flickr may know which photos I tag as interesting or cute—but Facebook knows my face, the photos of my
friends, my personally created profile, the evolution of my digital
persona, and my interactive social milieu.

Facebook could skyrocket because the emergence and rapid
growth of online social networks have made it possible for people
to communicate and work together in ways that simply weren't
possible before. People with common goals and interests—even

highly specialized and unusual pursuits—can find each other more easily and build groups. One person can help vast numbers of people without ever knowing who she has helped. These recent developments build on the possibilities that online social networks have opened and lead to new business opportunities.

Social Roles: Online and Offline

In *The Tipping Point: How Little Things Can Make a Big Difference* (Back Bay Books), Malcolm Gladwell tells the story of Paul Revere and William Dawes. Every American schoolkid knows the basics of the story. In April 1775, in Boston, a young stable boy overheard a British army officer tell another that there would be "hell to pay tomorrow." The stable boy's news tip was passed to the local silversmith Paul Revere, who mounted his horse and began his famous midnight ride from Boston to Lexington, crying, "The British are coming! The British are coming!" He spread the news like a virus and mobilized a critical mass of neighbors, farmers, and merchants who jumped out of bed and armed themselves.

But not many people remember William Dawes. Dawes rode just as far, on a different route, knocking on just as many doors. Why is Paul Revere remembered while William Dawes is not? As Gladwell tells it, because Revere had a gregarious and social personality that could bring people together. Dawes had only ordinary social abilities. Gladwell suggests that certain kinds of people matter to "tipping" word-of-mouth epidemics; we're all familiar with them in our everyday offline social world (see Figure 3-1):

Connectors

> The "social glue" who know and want to introduce you to everyone "you should know" whether for matchmaking or career mentoring

Mavens

> "Information brokers" who can't wait to tell you about the best deals and give you advice on where to stay and what to buy

Salesmen

> "Evangelists" who get you to act and convince you to buy

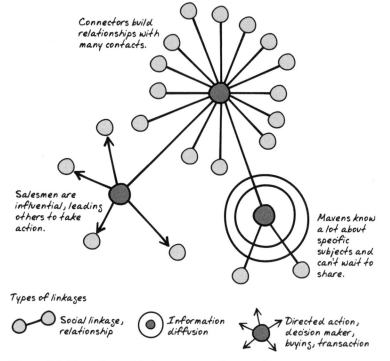

Figure 3-1. Key roles and linkages in social networks

Paul Revere was a potent combination of connector, maven, and salesman, with late-breaking news to broadcast, thanks to the news tip from the stable boy—who was a natural maven.

You probably know some connectors, mavens, and salesmen, especially if you participate in business networking groups or community organizations. The combinations of people playing these different roles in social networks are critically important for convincing a broad audience to use a company's services.

Some of the most popular services on the Web today are online social networks built to help people find each other, share their stories, and connect. Their business lessons apply to a broad group of situations, whether or not you plan to run a social network site yourself. Flickr, for example, is most commonly thought of as a photo-sharing site, not a social networking site, but the social aspect is critical to its success. Even more simply, Amazon relies on rankings from readers to give its reviewers a sense of enhanced status and recognition.

How Online Changes Social Networking

In some ways, online networking is much like offline networking—the social skills you know from the offline world are still helpful. However, connecting by web sites and email makes it more like a network of people who are all in the same room, ready to make introductions without the small talk. It's not a replacement for face-to-face conversation, but it's certainly a supplement that changes the rules.

Two things change the "tipping" of word-of-mouth epidemics in the online world:

• The availability of personal content uploaded online

• The speed of connecting online to someone who you don't know but want to be linked to or get a message to

Online is a small world. With just a few clicks, users can reach people they want to know. Increasingly, people get their first impressions from online rather than offline encounters.

The Shift from Snailmail to Hotmail

In the late 1960s, the sociologist Stanley Milgram investigated what came to be known as the "small-world phenomenon." He conducted an experiment to find connections linking people in the United States who did not know each other. He gave a letter to someone in Nebraska, with instructions that the letter had to reach a particular person in Massachusetts. The first person was told only basic information about the "target," such as his address and occupation, and was told to give or send the letter to someone she knew *on a first-name basis*, and that person was given the same direction, to deliver the letter to the target as efficiently as possible. Anyone who received the letter would follow the same instructions until the target was reached. Through repeated trials, Milgram found that it took five or six "steps," on average, to get a letter from Nebraska to Massachusetts. This formed the basis for the well-known concept of "six drgrees of separation" (shown in Figure 3-2).

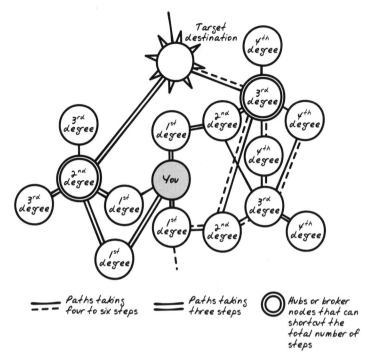

Figure 3-2. *Degrees of separation*

In his book *Six Degrees* (W. W. Norton & Company), Duncan Watts points out that certain paths were considerably shorter because the Milgram package reached a "hub" or "broker" node that shortcut the average six steps. Figure 3-2 illustrates this by putting an additional circle on the hubs or broker nodes and showing the different paths on the right and left side.

In the online world, using LinkedIn or a similar network, members can easily browse lists and profiles of past business contacts who now live in Boston or who are stockbrokers in Massachusetts, and see on a map how many steps it would take to get an email introduction forwarded to the stockbroker online through first-degree contacts (see Figure 3-2).For example, LinkedIn will tell you how many steps there are between you and your destination mailbox (as shown in Figure 3-2).

Online social and professional networks use the connections found in the offline world and magnify them proportionally. In the LinkedIn system, the intermediary roles of the connectors, mavens, and salesmen remain basically the same but are enhanced by orders of magnitude. Easy and speedy digital connectivity shifts the focus in online social networking from creating, mapping, and expanding your network toward finding new ways to exploit, capture value in, and monetize your own network (see social network mappings in Figures 3-3, 3-4, and 3-5).

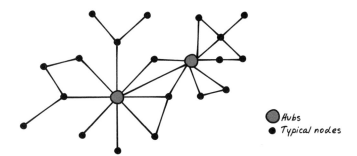

Figure 3-3. Social network hubs are keys to connection

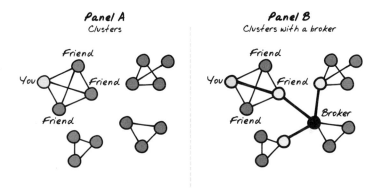

Figure 3-4. Ties connecting separate groups may be weaker

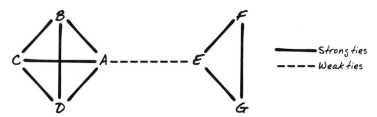

Figure 3-5. How brokers connect separate social units

According to an *MIT Tech Review* article,[1] Marcus Colombano, a media and technology marketing consultant in San Francisco, read about a company he thought should be his client. He popped its name into LinkedIn and found he was connected to four people with contacts at that company. He wrote up a proposal and sent it to a friend who had a contact who knew the CEO. Four hours later, he got an email from the CEO requesting a meeting (see Figure 3-6).

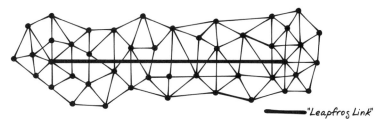

"Leapfrog Link"

Figure 3-6. *Connections across a large network can have tremendous value and speed*

Do these speedy introductions lead to revenue for the startups that create and run these online networking platforms? The surprising answer is yes. Perhaps even more surprising, the case of LinkedIn, examined more closely later in this chapter, gives us a pretty good idea of what online connectors, mavens, and salesmen are willing to pay for access to these visibly more efficient search and linkage networks, as well as an idea of when the network's best move is to offer some services for free. Of course, this presents new choices for the online social and professional networking companies that provide these services and platforms. Should advertisers or sponsors pay the freight or "freemium" users who are willing to pay for a "leapfrog link"?

---

[1] Michael Fitzgerald, "Internetworking: new social networking startups aim to mine digital connections to help people find jobs and close deals," *MIT Technology Review*, April 2004, *http://www.technologyreview.com/Infotech/ 13526/page1/?a=f.*

Connectors, Mavens, and Salesmen at Broadband Speed

The Web and related technologies help online connectors, salesmen, and mavens reach an exponentially larger audience, more frequently, more easily, and almost instantaneously. In comparison:

- Offline connectors develop relationships over time in face-to-face meetings with many other individuals. Online connectors benefit from using the Web, IM, email, audio, and video to connect directly to more people, more frequently, and more interactively.

- Offline mavens have in-depth knowledge about a particular subject and are eager to share it. Online mavens have an instantaneous means of broadcasting and publishing the knowledge they want to share and become information providers and brokers through referrals, reviews, forums, and communities that supplement emails, syndication (RSS) feeds, blogs, and wikis.

- Offline salesmen influence people to take action; online salesmen do the same thing but are supported by many different interactive formats and media.

Social networks moved online steadily, but businesses took different approaches and found themselves with different groups of people doing different kinds of things. Business networkers needed one set of features, whereas social networkers needed another. Varying preferences led people to cluster on different sites, to move from site to site, and even use multiple sites at the same time.

How Many Customers and How Quickly?

Facebook, YouTube, Skype, MySpace, and Flickr show that a Web 2.0 company's business and financial valuation depends on the number of users and how quickly those users accept, adopt, and bring their positive network effects to a new online service. In the social networks and advertising platforms, these users can be monetized immediately, through advertising and n-sided market sponsorship. Clickstreams, average revenue per user (ARPU), individual customer profitability, and advertising ROI can be tracked with web analytics daily and even hourly.

Rogers Adoption Curve

In the study of high-tech marketing and management of innovation, the Rogers Adoption Curve is often used to explain the rate of adoption of a new technology or product.

In 1962, Everett M. Rogers, in his book *Diffusion of Innovations*, gauged how populations adopt new products and technologies. He later suggested that five factors explain why some new products succeed with high growth rates and rapid customer adoption and others fail:

Relative advantage

> How much better the new product is compared with the old one. Angioplasty is 10 times more effective than open-heart surgical bypasses, it is less invasive, and it allows faster recovery.

Compatibility

> If a new product fits with current values and usage, it broadens the initial audience. Major changes are more risky and appeal to a relatively smaller group of early adaptors, independent thinkers, and innovators.

Complexity

> Ease of use and understanding of features make adoption faster and easier.

Trialability

> Products can sell themselves if customers experiment with them and get hooked by the personal experience. Free trials, demos, and test drives reduce the risk.

Observability

> How visible product usage and impact are to others. Social influence plays a role in adoption of the very visible iPod and the hybrid Prius automobile. Preventative medicine and tax-preparation software usage is less visible and requires a more targeted effort to market virally.

The power of Web 2.0 technologies coupled with a freemium n-sided business model shows up in all five of these factors for Facebook, compounding its advantages and triggering its hypergrowth rate of adoption.

Relative advantage

Facebook offers the perception of increased or new benefits—especially in greater reach. If a large number of campuses are connected to the Facebook directory and applications, users can keep up with high-school friends who went elsewhere for college and renew acquaintances with long lost connections.

Compatibility

Facebook's web application was easier and more instantaneous than the printed college facebook. This was very comfortable for a digital youth generation that is used to being always online, instant messaging constantly, being connected wirelessly with their friends through various devices and media.

Complexity

Facebook was easy to use, with information pushed to users through RSS feeds.

Trialability

Users could try Facebook for free, paid for by n-sided cross-network effects.

Observability

Observability is built into the company name—users could easily identify who was on and using the Facebook "wall" by name, frequent messages, and uploaded photos. Facebook viral applications raised this observability to a whole new level of referral, subtle peer/friend pressure, and social influence. Not only were friends inviting friends to "join the party" and play an application with them—they got constant numerical updates and reminders of how many of their circle of friends were participating. Why not click and try it out for yourself? How bad could it be if 80% of your close friends were doing it? Talk about a bandwagon effect.

The Rogers Adoption Curve provides a useful framework to evaluate where on the adoption curve your product or service is getting roadblocked. For example, Geoff Moore's book *Crossing the Chasm* (HarperBusiness) identifies a marketing "chasm" between the early innovators and adopters and the mainstream. As mentioned in Chapter 1, Web 2.0 companies like Flickr have attempted to close that chasm by using a freemium strategy and social network effects.

However, there are no variables or factors in Rogers framework that directly take "social influence" and the peer-to-peer pressure of online social networks into account. It's difficult to quantify the impact of viral marketing, costless distribution, or viral distribution on adoption or growth rate. Nor are there quantifiable and standardized growth and diffusion patterns so that different kinds of products, services, channels, and marketing strategies can be measured and compared. The Rogers Adoption Curve and model rely on some fundamental assumptions about new technology adopters and markets:

• The available population and market of adopters for all new technologies, products, and services follow a normal distribution or bell curve characterized by 2.5% innovators.

• The key attributes for market projection are individual-user-centered. Factors to consider are the behavior and risk profile of the individual user toward new technology, interest in new things, risk aversion, etc.

• Even in the more detailed product-related model, user behavior is independent.

The Bass Diffusion Curve

The Bass Diffusion Curve is an important update to the Rogers model because it provides a radically different framework of customer/user adoption rates based on social influence. Social influence is arguably the key factor completely missing from the Rogers Adoption Curve. It also uses an exponential form, mathematically speaking, which makes the modeling assumption that the process of diffusion is viral, as in an epidemic. The general shape of the Bass Curve reflects a type of propagation through a population with a modified power law distribution. (And again, for quantitative projections of how many customers will adopt a new product and how quickly, the Bass Curve has been regularly empirically tested and validated.)

Frank Bass introduced this model in 1969 in a famous paper titled "A New Product Growth Model for Consumer Durables," published in the *Management Science* journal. The key concepts are intuitive and simple: some users start the process by adopting a new product independently of the actions of others; others are influenced to adopt the innovation when they see others using it, being socially influenced by those who have already adopted the product.

The simple version of the Bass model has only three major parameters—m, p, and q:

- m is the estimated total number of eventual adopters.

- p is the variable describing the rate of growth of first-time adopters who act independently.

- q is the variable describing the rate of growth of first-time adopters who are influenced by social effects and interpersonal influence.

The level of social influence can be expressed as the ratio of q/p. If the ratio is low, fewer social "followers" or "imitators" are influenced by the early independent adopters. If the ratio is medium or high, a substantially larger proportion of the potential first-time adopters in the market are strongly influenced by the initial group of independent adopters.

A few consumer durable goods examples make the curve intuitively easy to understand. The Bass Curve has been used to gauge the adoption of washing machines, TVs, leaf blowers, and cell phones.

- The p in washing machines and TVs is relatively high, but the q is relatively low, because although these consumer items may be highly useful, they are not easily observable or conspicuous status items, the way cars might be.

- Leaf blowers have a surprisingly high q/p ratio, and adoption grew much faster than expected—potentially because they are highly observable in their weekend usage and in their effect on neighborhood sidewalks and walkways, while not being very costly to purchase or try.

- Cell phones had a higher q and p than wired phones.

These kinds of examples provide analogies in making marketing predictions for newer technologies. So, for example, an analyst might estimate the diffusion pattern of satellite radio to be similar in shape to that for satellite TV but faster because of ease of replacement and lower cost.

But what about online viral marketing and distribution?

The size of the Oakland Hills, California, firestorm in 1991 that burned more than 2,000 homes had more to do with the hot dry season and the gusty Santa Ana winds that spread the fire than with the actual spark that started it. Structural and coincidental factors were at work. In a similar way, fads and social influence "cascades" are triggered by influencers or sparks, but they require the right conditions to spread with explosive speed.

Highly influential people—celebrities like Oprah Winfrey—can make a book an overnight bestseller. But thousands of computer simulations reveal that global cascades are more likely to be triggered by accidental and unintentional influencers within a receptive social network structure. A cascade needs just enough of a critical mass of easily influenced people to propagate a chain reaction, one degree of separation at a time.

Sometimes, personal characteristics make a difference. Rogers' risk profiling and psycho-graphic profiling of early adopters, mainstream users, and laggards—combined with Moore's explanation of "crossing the chasm"—does a good job of explaining many high-tech marketing successes and failures. However, online web social networks make it easy for a relatively small number of users—like you and me—to trigger network effects.

Do we know how to "seed" and shape these new product adoption cascades or epidemics?

Not yet, but current research findings seem to indicate that the raw number of early users and their first-degree "friend" or online "buddy" linkages, along with their social interactivity or frequency of contact, someday may be more critical in this "online cascade" viral distribution model than highly paid influentials such as celebrities or brokers.

LinkedIn and Facebook are great Web 2.0 examples of the newer models of applied online social networks. LinkedIn offers a fascinating online business application of small-world networks and social network analysis mapping brought online. In contrast,

Facebook provides a natural example of large-scale diffusion and node-to-node cascading behavior in social networks.

LinkedIn: The Rolodex Moves Online

For a lot of people, LinkedIn defines business networking. Its contact management enables people to connect to each other easily, offering a self-updating contact list that helps them find the connections they need. It even looks a bit like a classic address book, as shown in Figure 3-7.

Figure 3-7. LinkedIn's connections list for a small set of connections

Even this simple address book, however, leads into the possibilities that electronic contact management offers. Note the icons in the right column, just to the left of the ad. The address book tells users how many contacts their contacts have, letting them see at a glance how well-connected their contacts are. Clicking on that icon displays the other person's contacts, making it easy for users to dive into a network of people they might be interested in knowing.

Searches also let users find more people they might want to contact and tells them how many degrees of separation stand between their personal contacts and them, as shown in Figure 3-8.

Figure 3-8. Search results with relationship information

The relationship column shows how many degrees of separation stand between the searcher and the contact. Clicking on a name brings up a profile, with a "Get introduced through a connection" option. Mutual friends can then help establish a more direct LinkedIn connection.

LinkedIn put members' existing networks of business relationships and business contact information onto the Web. By putting members' rolodexes (the rotating file devices used to store business contact information such as business cards) online, these networks became more easily searchable, and the networks of people who knew each other could be easily connected and linked. The signup or joining process had a strong viral online word-of-mouth effect—anyone could become a member, but 90% of members joined in response to an email invitation from an existing member.

Most businesspeople have received scores of email invitations to join LinkedIn or Plaxo, and now Facebook. The email invitation allowed you to click through to a membership page. Then you could upload a simple profile with name, region, and industry, or a longer bio with photo, education, career, and other professional affiliations. As soon as the profile was loaded, new members were linked to the member who invited them and could then extend their networks by inviting others to join, asking existing members to connect to them, or accepting invitations to connect from existing members. Connections had to be agreed to by both parties, and members were free to disconnect from any unwanted contact.

LinkedIn illustrates some challenges that first- and second-generation online social networking sites faced:

- Growing quickly
- Creating trust and maintaining privacy within an open or professional network
- Monetizing social networks—deciding how to price services and who should receive free services

According to a Harvard Business School case study on LinkedIn (Mikolaj Jan Piskorski), Stanford grads Reid Hoffman and Konstantin Guericke started discussing online professional communities in 1997. The founders invited their contacts, who invited others and yet others onto the beta site. By April 2004, the network had 550,000 members. LinkedIn was funded by Sequoia Capital ($4.7 million), Greylock ($10 million), and well-known angel investors such as Marc Andreessen (cofounder of Netscape) and Peter Thiel (cofounder of PayPal).

Rapid Growth

In 2004, there were 12,000 requests for introductions per month; 85% of requests approved by all the intermediaries were accepted by the target recipient. By mid-2005, requests for introductions had reached 25,000, and acceptance rates had increased slightly to 87%. As the membership base grew, so did search activity. Members executed 2 million searches in April 2004. By mid-2005, that number had more than doubled to 5 million.

LinkedIn's ability to track the electronic activities and linkages of its membership gives us new insights into online social networks.

The Harvard Business School case study revealed an unexpected usage pattern:

Online relationship managers

Ninety percent of LinkedIn users are first-degree contact managers and treat LinkedIn like an improved rolodex or Microsoft Oulook inbox. They maintain their own lists of close contacts, adding new contacts as they find them in the offline world through input, conferences, new jobs, and meetings. The main features that LinkedIn provides are automatic updates and easy organization.

Online connectors

Online networkers, like their real-world counterparts, are actively seeking new contacts. Five percent of LinkedIn users are online connectors or brokers.

Networkers, unlike relationship managers, often send invitations to people they never actually meet in the offline world. The strength of the bond is less important for networkers than the general quality of the network—they typically aim for large groups of contacts that they can navigate to find just the right person.

Privacy is also less of an issue for networkers—many of them display their email addresses to allow other people to contact them easily. There's also something of a competitive streak among this group—TopLinked.com lists the top 50 networkers on LinkedIn, with the most-networked user having 36,480 contacts in October 2007.

Online salesmen, connectors

The last 5% of users are focused searchers, people seeking contacts that address specific needs. Contactors are often recruiters, analysts, business-development consultants, or salespeople. Like networkers, they find that the value of LinkedIn grows as the number of users climbs, giving them a broad range of people to search for and reach out to.

Contactors typically combine searches with referrals, finding people who fit the profile they need and then tracking them down through their own contact list. Their focus on finding key people makes them especially appreciate—and sometimes find—the "leapfrog link" shown earlier in Figure 3-6.

Trust and Degrees of Separation

"A friend of yours is a friend of mine." The common saying echoes the feeling that most of us have: two degrees of separation can be trusted. After all, you know your friend directly, and he wouldn't introduce you to someone he didn't trust or think highly of online or offline. "A friend of a friend of a friend," however, is three degrees of separation, and already we feel a little less comfortable because we are further from a direct link. On the other hand, LinkedIn realized that allowing the possibility of four degrees of separation between a requestor and a recipient exponentially increased the reach of the system. For example, mathematically, if each contact had 20 ties, a requestor could access 137,180 unique contacts with 4 degress of separation:

20 contacts × (20 contacts − 0 friends in common − 1)³ [4 degrees of separation−1]

So, although it might be awkward for the "friend of a friend of a friend" to pass along an introduction when he does not know the originator of the message or the recipient, anyone along the path could decline the request anonymously. In mid-2005, LinkedIn announced that monthly requests were 25,000 and acceptance rates were at 87%. Part of the reason for the higher acceptance rate was the added endorsement feature. Members could collect endorsements or testimonials from their contacts, describing their qualifications and performance specific to a particular position or project. In the Harvard Business School case, LinkedIn noted that members were 3 times more likely to select an endorsed member from a search list, and requests initiated by endorsed members were 25% more likely to be accepted by both intermediate connectors in the path and the final target destination.

Monetizing Social Networks

By carefully mapping and separating LinkedIn users into three distinct groups—relationship managers, connectors, and focused searchers—we see that Guericke and Hoffman were able to create a virtual two-sided network system. LinkedIn offers free services to the 90% installed base of relationship managers, while networkers and contactors are willing to pay a per-contact fee, as well as a monthly subscription fees for highly desired premium contact and networking services.

We see a pricing strategy similiar to the other freemium cases where one side of the market sponsors or pays for the other, for example, Visa credit cards, eBay, and Google.

Note the importance of the relationship managers. In a classic business model, they might be seen as troubling parasites—90% of customers are using valuable services for free? (They see ads, but nothing makes them click on them, of course.) In LinkedIn's model, relationship managers may be getting something for free, but they're also giving LinkedIn the key information it can sell to other people. The cost of supporting those free users, even when it's 90% of the base, is still less than the income potential from the 10% of paying customers.

LinkedIn makes much of its money by selling members the ability to contact anyone in the network for a fee, through three programs of highly focused feature changes:

- LinkedIn kept its free referrals through intermediaries but reduced the degrees of separation from four to three. (Four-degree introductions were often uncomfortable anyway.) This reduced the free services and increased the value of LinkedIn's paid services.

- The new InMail system gave members a way to contact other members directly for a subscription fee. LinkedIn also provided a reputation system so that contactors could demonstrate that their messages were actually appreciated and focused to the right people and not merely paid-for spam.

- The new OpenLinkNetwork helped networkers find each other without having to use the formal introduction process. The subscription-based service simplified the kinds of tasks that networkers like to do without changing the rules for relationship managers.

Figure 3-9 shows the features LinkedIn offered in July 2007, along with their price points.

Compare Account Types

	Personal Free	Business $19.95 per month or $199.50 per year (2 months free) ➡ Upgrade	Business *plus* $50 per month or $500 per year (2 months free) ➡ Upgrade	Pro $200 per month or $2000 per year (2 months free) ➡ Upgrade
Receive Introductions	✓	✓	✓	✓
Send Introductions	✓ 5 at a time[1]	✓ 15 at a time[1]	✓ 25 at a time[1]	✓ 40 at a time[1]
Receive InMails	✓	✓	✓	✓
Send InMails		✓ 3 per month	✓ 10 per month	✓ 50 per month
Receive OpenLink Messages		✓	✓	✓
Reach over 11 million users		✓	✓	✓
Unlimited reference searches		✓	✓	✓
More LinkedIn Network results		✓ 100	✓ 150	✓ 200
Expanded LinkedIn Network profile views		✓	✓	✓
OpenLink Network membership		✓	✓	✓
Upcoming feature sneak peeks		✓	✓	✓
Priority customer service		✓ 1 business day	✓ 1 business day	✓ 1 business day

Learn more about Business and Pro account benefits.
Please **contact us** to learn about more account offerings.

[1] Maximum number of pending Introductions

Figure 3-9. LinkedIn's many offerings, all built on the same basic set of personal data

LinkedIn epitomizes the Web 2.0 model of free access to users who help build critical mass, while charging those who seek to use that mass for their own larger purposes. LinkedIn has stayed slim, focusing tightly on a core mission of business connectivity and leaving richer but much more resource-intensive forms of social networking to other companies.

Facebook: Introduce Yourself Online

It started out as a pretty simple application—an upgraded version of the classic print photobooks some universities hand out to new students—and has grown into a much richer set of tools. Figure 3-10 shows a typical profile, and Figure 3-11 shows the interface for editing that profile. Users can present a lot of information without having to master a complex interface.

Figure 3-10. A Facebook profile

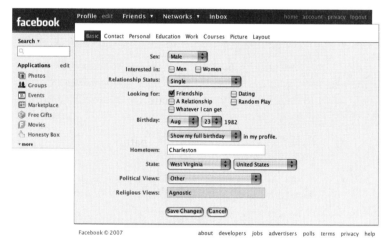

Figure 3-11. Editing that Facebook profile

Facebook (like most social networks) also lets users communicate within their network, as shown in Figure 3-12.

Figure 3-12. Communicating within Facebook

Facebook's Initial Growth

The hypergrowth of the Facebook user base continued as it developed, from 5 million online users in late October 2005 to more than 7.5 million in mid-April 2006.

Facebook enjoyed an exponential growth pattern much like the S-curve discussed in Chapter 1. It benefited from direct network usage effects: the more a user's friends use Facebook, the more valuable it is to the user. Additionally, peer pressure and social influence fuel the "contagion" and word-of-mouth effect. If your friends are not using Facebook, why should you?

College students didn't want to have to wait to see their friends show up and start using Facebook. So, speed of adoption is important to get to critical mass quickly.

Speed is also important in the race to reach a high enough market share to tip the market and lock out competitors. Facebook reached critical mass and tipped the market before other competitors entered the same space. The Korean social network site Cyworld seized a similar early-mover advantage in its national market. When first-movers in strong network-effects markets reach a dominant market share, they become hard to displace.

The usage patterns were impressive for the frequency as well as retention. Facebook's Mark Zuckerberg explained:[2]

> On a normal day, about two-thirds of our total user base comes back to the site. A lot of sites measure monthly retention, and if you have 25%, you are doing really well. I don't know any other site that measures their retention in daily retention. Facebook is a clearly different type of application.

Facebook had competition. MySpace had become the fifth most popular web site by number of page views. It had already grown as a music destination to include more than 350,000 bands and artists. Its growth rate was phenomenal as well; in October 2004, it had 3.4 million users, and one year later it had 24.3 million unique visitors—an increase of 600%. On July 18, 2005, the multinational media conglomerate News Corporation announced that it would acquire MySpace's parent company Intermix Media for about $580 million in cash. As of August 2006, MySpace had broken through the 100 million account mark.

Although MySpace and Facebook are targeted toward social rather than professional networks, Facebook focuses on relational clusters and existing groups and circles of friends; MySpace is targeted at helping users find new friends—discovering social affinity groups related to music, bands, and artists. Facebook helps college students keep up with high-school buddies in other colleges, as well as peers from sports, music, extracurricular, and volunteer activities. MySpace supports much more customization of profiles than Facebook, which has stuck with a simpler look.

---

[2] The quotes from Mark Zuckerberg are from the Stanford Business School case on Facebook (*http://harvardbusinessonline.hbsp.harvard.edu/b01/en/common/item_detail.jhtml?id=E220*). Quotations were taken from his interview with venture capitalist Jim Breyer at the Oct. 26, 2005 Stanford Technology Ventures Program or from an interview with Professor Willam Barnett, case author, April 2006.

This is consistent with Zuckerberg's creation of Facebook as a directory utility for people to keep tabs on the people in their lives and as a way to express themselves. One-third of Facebook users list their cell phone numbers, and a large number check their Facebook pages a couple of times a day. Of course, college students are concerned about how their online Facebook profile and photos appear to others. They're also interested in identifying others on campus who have similar interests and in looking for potential dates.

By January 2006, Facebook had become so vital to the university lifestyle that eMarketer reported that incoming students were creating their Facebook profiles long before they even set foot on campus. By contrast, MySpace has a lower frequency of usage, and its users are doing different things on it—uploading music and playlists, and exploring new music and artists. College students might categorize MySpace with sites such as Last.fm, a popular site for finding new music.

Because the utilities and motivations for college students who join Facebook are different than for those who join MySpace, it's not yet clear whether the two can coexist in equilibrium or will spark a competitive race—in the college market and overseas.

Viral Growth at Facebook

Mark Zuckerberg recalled that:

> At Harvard, a few of my friends saw me developing Facebook and they sent it out to a couple of their friends and within two weeks, two-thirds of Harvard was using it. Then, we started getting emails from people at other schools asking, "How do we get Facebook? Could you license us the code so we could run a version of Facebook for our school?" But when I started it, there was no concept of having Facebook across schools.

In early March 2004, Facebook launched at Yale, Columbia, and Stanford:

> We started with the schools which we thought the people at Harvard were most likely to have a lot of friends. We decided that those were Yale, Columbia, and Stanford. It was not really scientific; it was just intuition and probably wrong.

At Stanford, half or two-thirds of the school joined Facebook in the first week or two. At Yale, there was a similar story. Columbia's community, on the other hand, was a little more penetrated by an existing application and Facebook didn't pick up right away. A little later, when we launched at Dartmouth, half the school signed up in one night.

By June 2004, Facebook was serving 30 colleges and had about 150,000 registered users. Zuckerberg and his two roommates, Dustin Moskovitz and Chris Hughes, spent the rest of the 2004 school year trying to respond to the demand from colleges across the nation:

> Early on, we weren't intending this to be a company. We had no cash to run it. We actually operated it for the first three months for $85 a month—the cost of renting one server.

They were able to build their system with minimal customer acquisition costs. The popularity of Facebook made it something users signed into automatically:

> We have natural growth built into our system in that over 3 million people leave high school and enroll in college every year. Last year, we had between 700,000 to 800,000 seniors graduate and are now alums on the site. About 45% of that group still returns to Facebook each day.

In September 2005, when Facebook opened its platform to high-school students, college students were asked to send invites to their high-school friends, who could then invite others:

> The high school network reached a million users way faster than the college network did. The college network took almost 11 months to reach a million, and the high school took only six or seven months.

In 2004, Facebook was a free service and accessible to anyone with an ".edu" email account, limiting its use mostly to college students. Members of the network were encouraged to create a personal profile, including contact information, interests, and current course schedule.

> It's essentially an online directory for students where they can go and look up other people and find relevant information about them...I guess it's mostly a utility for people to figure out just

what's going on in their friends' lives, people they care about...
Friendster, MySpace, and Facebook are all different things, but
you can apply the [term] social networking to them because they
have this model of having friends sending invitations [to
friends].

Unlike MySpace or Friendster, Facebook made its members'
schools their primary networks and offered only limited access
beyond that, making it a network of peers, rather than a random
assortment of people. In the past few years, Facebook has opened
itself to anyone who wants to join.

Facebook was fairly open by default: everyone at a member's school
could see his profile, but members could control their settings so
that only their friends could view their profiles on the web site.

Viral Applications

In May 2007, Facebook launched a set of application programming interfaces and services that allow outside developers to add
their own ideas to the Facebook user experience. Marc Andreessen,
a founder of Netscape, posted a detailed and enthusiastic analysis
of the Facebook applications platform:[3]

> The Facebook Platform is a dramatic leap forward for the
> Internet industry.... Facebook is providing a highly viral distri-
> bution engine for applications that plug into its platform.

> As a user, you get notified when your friends start using an
> application: you can then start using that same application with
> one click. At which point, all of your friends become aware that
> you have started using that application, and the cycle continues.
> The result is that a successful application on Facebook can grow
> to a million users or more within a couple of weeks of creation.

> Finally, Facebook is promising economic freedom—third-party
> applications can run ads and sell goods and services to their
> hearts' content....

> Facebook is providing the ease and user attraction of MySpace-
> style embedding, coupled with the kind of integration you see
> with Firefox extensions, plus the added rocket fuel of automated

---

3 Marc Andreessen's blog, June 12, 2007, *http://blog.pmarca.com/2007/06/
analyzing_the_f.html*.

viral distribution to a huge number of potential users, and the prospect of keeping 100% of any revenue your application can generate.

Facebook's API offers its users a wide choice of new services, as shown in Figure 3-13. Users don't have to wait for Facebook to provide new functionality for them—anyone can develop applications, and good applications will get shared across user networks quickly.

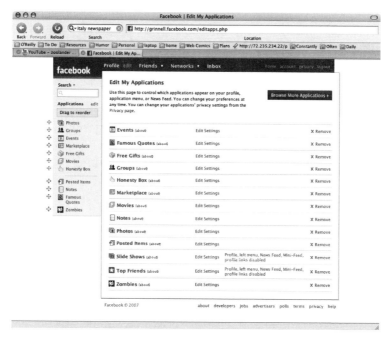

Figure 3-13. Facebook's application editor

Perhaps more startlingly, the Facebook API also gives developers a place to see their ideas zoom across a huge number of people. The amazing effectiveness of this viral distribution is best told in the words of the iLike blog, shortly after its launch as one of Facebook's first third-party applications:[4]

> In our first 20 hours of opening doors we had 50,000 users sign up, and it is only accelerating. (10,000 users joined in the first 12 hours. 10,000 more users in the next 3 hours. 30,000 more users in the next 5 hours)....

---

[4] *http://blog.ilike.com/ilike_team_blog/2007/05/ilike_as_a_serv.html*

Facebook's rapid user-base chewed up our 2 servers almost instantly...we doubled...we doubled it again. And again. And again. O crap—we ran out of servers....

Tomorrow we are picking up over 100 servers from different companies to have them installed just to handle the weekend's traffic....

Today was a critical day in iLike's history. The Facebook Platform enabled us to build a service that in a single day matched and beat the impressive traffic we built on iLike. com in over 6 months. iLike is now growing at more than twice the pace it was yesterday, and accelerating. Fasten your seatbelts everybody, here we come! :-)

Facebook's API approach is somewhat different from that of, for example, Google Maps. Rather than support new functionality outside of Facebook, it adds new functionality inside users' familiar Facebook environment. Working this way, Facebook can share its success with a much broader ecosystem of potential partners who can leverage the huge social network inside of Facebook. Facebook itself, rather than the broader Web, acts as the platform here.

During the writing of this book, Facebook changed its application-sharing tools to make the viral marketing feel less to users like a massive influx of spam. Developers still have many ways to promote their products among Facebook's tightly networked users. For one perspective on how this changes the adoption rate and business model, visit *http://500hats.typepad.com/500blogs/2007/07/marketing-faceb.html*.

The Limits of Viral: Facebook Beacon

Beacon is Facebook's targeted social advertising system. From the press announcement and launch on November 6, 2007, 44 high-traffic web sites—from eBay to Fandango to Travelocity—were enthusiastic supporters of a new way to socially distribute information and connect businesses with relevant users and their trusted network of friends on Facebook.

For example, the chief marketing officer at Travelocity used the following example:

> Travel is naturally a social activity that travelers enjoy discussing with the people they know...Using Beacon, Travelocity users can now easily choose to spread the news of their latest vacation plans on Facebook as a complement to their activities on the Travelocity web site.

The Beacon announcement was taken as a major step toward justifying the $15 billion valuation by Microsoft's investment and proof of a business model for "monetizing" the reported 50 million Facebook users.

It didn't work out, though, because users objected, and loudly. How did a platform hyped as the "most important marketing breakthrough in the past 100 years" become a major controversy about privacy and, in the eyes of several observers, "a disaster" that could bring Facebook down? After all, Facebook's News Feed feature, introduced in 2006, was arguably even a bigger "privacy trainwreck," and yet it's a feature that many users now enjoy and consider positive and useful.

The most succinct explanation I heard online came from Andy Carvin, National Public Radio's senior product manager for online communities and former coordinator of the Digital Divide Network, an online community:

> One of the reasons Facebook is popular is that it makes it so easy for users to follow their friends' activities.... For people who want their lives to be an open book, it's a great tool. It seems that Facebook took that idea one step too far by making users' purchasing decisions equally transparent, then not making it an opt-in service.

In other words, Charlene Li, a prominent Forrester Internet analyst, could purchase a cocktail table at Overstock.com and discover that all her "friends" had received a message via news feeds about her purchase. Or some number of the 55,000 protesters who signed the petition from MoveOn.org to demand that Facebook change the Beacon system had their holiday gift purchases broadcast to all of their friends, including the intended recipients.

Coca-Cola, one of the early advertisers, stated that it had chosen to withdraw its participation in Beacon, stating that it had had the impression that Beacon would be an explicit opt-in program.

Facebook's CEO Mark Zuckerberg apologized publicly on December 5 and made Beacon an "opt-in" system rather than a default. But trust was further eroded by independent tests that seemed to indicate that Facebook was continuing to collect information on click and purchase activities for data mining, whether or not its users opted-in. Legal experts and advocacy groups continue to look closely at the advertising program, and complaints have been filed with the Federal Trade Commission.

But the larger question had been raised in too many minds and blogs: does social advertising and marketing mean the end of privacy?

> The more you reveal about yourself online, including your daily habits, your friends, your shopping habits, etc.—the more that data can be used to create value for the social networking company and their partners.... A lack of privacy becomes a fundamental part of their business models.

Lessons Learned

The online social networking experience teaches three critical lessons:

- The importance of social networks and network effects for building your business to scale
- The value that users can generate by sharing even basic information with a larger group
- The incredible acceleration provided by bringing this kind of task to the Web

While all of these clearly apply to the explicit social networking applications examined in this chapter, they also apply to other projects that may not be thought of as explicit social networks.

Climbing Social Networks

Social networks have always been a key part of sales and marketing. When you're trying to sell a product, you want to find key influencers. The acceleration that social networks provide in a Web 2.0 market has two major effects in this regard:

- Social networks (even informal clusters) can make or break a product by spreading positive news of its existence to other potential users or by recommending a competitor.

- The potential of online social networks to help people meet others they want to meet can entice ever-growing numbers of people to join an existing network.

LinkedIn provides clear paths for its customers to invite other customers to join its system. Members who invite their friends receive clear and direct benefits, and joining the network costs nothing (except time) for the invitee. This makes it very easy for people to give or get a positive impression of LinkedIn, accelerating its growth tremendously. Facebook's viral marketing benefited from similar effects, amplified by its appeal to contained groups of people. Figure 3-14 shows how growth curves may vary by the nature of the kinds of people who spearhead the use of the system and their social influence.

> Some people have taken this message to mean that marketing will have the greatest effect if it's targeted to key influencers. It's a good idea as a general rule, but always remember that influencers are already used to being targeted and the pool of influencers is constantly changing. Achieving critical mass requires not only reaching influencers but also making it easy for everyone to feel welcome at the party.

Similarly, both LinkedIn and Facebook grew more and more rapidly as the value of their networks climbed. "Are my friends using it?" is a critical question for possible customers, and it's vastly easier to convince them to join as the number of their friends involved increases.

Value Generation in Social Networks

The value of a social network lies in its members. Social network software and sites are tools for connecting and finding the mem-

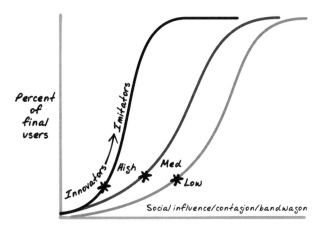

Figure 3-14. *Social influence drives growth*

bers, but in a strong sense, the health of the business isn't the software, it's the customers (see Figure 3-15).

Social networks don't have to be like Flickr or Wikipedia, where users spend lots of time creating material to share with others. Basic social network software focuses on capturing what users already have—acquaintances—and creating a forum that can be shared and expanded. Directories are still powerful tools, and enhancing those directories to support new kinds of contact between users draws in more people on the basis of the same relatively small amount of information.

Some social networks give their users considerably more freedom to add information. LinkedIn sticks to the basics; Facebook lets users add more information in a fairly structured environment; MySpace lets users do all kinds of things to present themselves. The kind of information users are likely to add to an explicitly social network application may be different from what they post to Flickr or Wikipedia, but it can still draw new customers, often even more motivated customers.

Acceleration

Social networking is a hallmark of Web 2.0. Users are willing to share a certain amount of themselves, and that sharing creates new opportunities. It's a situation where users who like the site will probably want to invite their friends to join, creating an army

Online social networks...

95% *First-degree clusters*   **5%** *Hubs/ connectors*   *Small-world network Leapfrog Link*

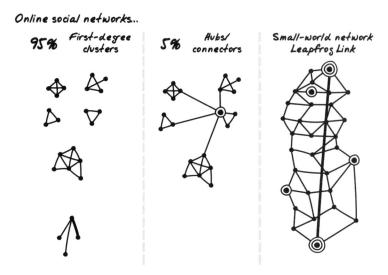

Figure 3-15. *Emerging and useful patterns in social networks*

of potential marketers and evangelists. It's a situation where anyone looking for a targeted group of people may be interested in paying for access to all of those people who just showed up, making it possible to sustain growth.

As noted back in Chapter 2, looking at the virtuous and vicious cycles in Figure 2-5, the acceleration can also run backward. Keeping a vast number of users requires gaining their trust and providing them with what they've come to expect. The same networks that promote growth can destroy market share and build up competitors if they give users reasons to depart.

Social networking creates an optimal arena for positive network effects to appear, and it also offers opportunities that can be integrated into projects that aren't necessarily "social networking" projects. Any time a site has registered users—or even identifiable users—there may be an opportunity to offer them a place to call their own and share it with others. Building a community of people who use the same product and who can interact with each other, for instance, is a lot more likely to generate user interest than sites where customers interact only with a company. It's less controllable, of course!

Questions to Ask

Your business probably isn't Facebook, LinkedIn, or even something that looks much like them. However, social networks are becoming a more and more common aspect of web sites of all kinds, giving participants opportunities to connect and share, and to invite others to do the same. With that in mind, consider your own projects in the light of the questions below.

Strategic Questions

- Think about your own business, professional, and social networks. With whom do you keep in touch and how often? What is it about your linkages, know-who, and "social capital" that contributes to the effectiveness and value of your network in situations ranging from mentoring and career planning to summer internships for a friend of a friend of a former boss. What is your online persona?

- Consider an upcoming product or service launch for your business. Based on the key elements of online social networks that were explored using Facebook and LinkedIn, what might you pay more attention to in your planning now? What might you do to help identify the 1–3% active uploaders in your current community and support them as customer evangelists? How could you put into place platforms and services that invite viral marketing as well as viral distribution?

- How might you have reacted as an key advertiser on Facebook during the MoveOn protest? What are your individual and company principles regarding user privacy?

- What are some immediate and practical ways you can imagine to raise the awareness of those in your business, organization, and ecosystem about the power of social networks and communities in triggering social influence and adoption?

- As a project team member, are you ready to systematically map and analyze with your group members the social networks of customers and partners critical to your business?

Tactical Questions

- How might your users relate to each other? (Or, how do they presently relate to each other?)
- If you have an existing place for users to communicate, would you benefit from enriching it with profiles and contacts?
- Do you provide mechanisms for your users to communicate among themselves?
- Do you provide tools for users to invite others to join your site?
- How much information are your users really willing to share about themselves?
- What balance of openness and privacy is appropriate in your business's context? What mechanisms do you have to maintain that balance?
- What value might user information create for you in this context? Advertising value? User happiness value? A new business of people who want to contact your users?
- Do you know how tightly knit your current users are? Are they tightly clustered, loosely clustered, or purely individuals who haven't yet formed connections?
- Have you identified key individuals in your user base who have developed the trust of others and can make things happen on your site?
- Would your site benefit from a full-blown social networking component, with contact lists, degrees of separation, and more, or might simply adding a profile page for users provide more immediate benefits?

- How does the current nature of your user base influence your potential for expansion? Are there specific subjects you should explore or projects you should undertake to maximize network effects building on who your current users know?

- What are the ratios of different kinds of users on your site? How many are contributors, how many are readers, and how many are active in community-building or networking? How can you monetize some groups without alienating others?

CHAPTER FOUR

Companies Capitalize Competences

WEB 2.0 TRANSFORMS THE ECONOMICS OF KNOWLEDGE-BASED BUSI-NESSES EVERYWHERE. Companies of all sizes are being forced to rethink their strategies for competing in a hyper-connected, web-savvy world. These fundamental shifts in how work gets done are zooming across organizations, business and social networks, and an increasingly "flat world." Executives, managers, and policymakers no longer have the luxury of a "wait and see" attitude, given the speed and volatility with which local and seemingly small events triggered by a few individuals and groups—users, partners, employees, and knowledge workers—can result in ripples throughout the world.

The speed and exponential nature of change in the business world is why 60% of the CEOs surveyed by PricewaterhouseCoopers consider networks and the networked world the most important factor in their strategies, much more than innovation or technology. Many of the "strategic inflection points" or "tipping points" disrupting their businesses and challenging their competitive leadership are cultural, social, and global, as well as user-generated. Some of the more unexpected items on the boardroom agenda include the knowledge economy, local and open innovation, global warming, social responsibility, and "creative capitalism."

The terms "dynamic" and "dynamic capabilities" take on a whole different meaning and time frame in the Web 2.0 world. I was part of a team that first asked the research question, "How do companies manage successfully in turbulent environments?" in the 1990s, when the U.S. was losing its technology lead in semiconductor chips to the Japanese. We published our "Dynamic Capabilities" article in the *Strategic Management Journal* (*SMJ*) not long after the Netscape IPO but before the dot-com boom. We heralded the shift of strategic management toward the knowledge economy and external "capabilities" using intangible assets such as knowledge and know-how. We encouraged CEOs and top corporate strategists to move away from the industrial economics and structural approach of viewing strategy as primarily tied to industry-level forces and bargaining power. We put these ideas into practice at top European and Japanese multinationals, while following the guideposts of earlier thinkers.

It's time for an update. Although this *SMJ* article has become one of the most cited in the strategy field, Web 2.0 changes the relevant research question to:

> *"How do industry leaders create value in a very fast-changing global networked knowledge environment?"*

Now the mainstream industry leaders, International 100s, and Fortune 500s that are having the hardest time adjusting their hierarchical organizations, outdated business models, and strictly in-house capabilities to the new strategy challenges of the digital and knowledge economy. The goals have changed from being a steward and "managing successfully" the gains, products, services, and legacy of the past to "creating value." The companies detailed in this chapter have found innovative ways to capitalize on that created value, either with direct revenue streams or, more often, using indirect revenue streams. For the first time, the level and pace of knowledge-based productivity are being driven by a diverse group of users like you and me, not just digital natives, credentialed scientists, or salaried employees.

The speed at which relevant knowledge is produced, accessed, distributed, and validated is constantly accelerating. This shifts the costs, revenues, and cumulative benefits from closely held research-and-development and internal function areas to a broad network of suppliers, partners, advertisers, affiliates, communities, and individual users. Eric von Hippel called this trend the "democratization of innovation" to emphasize the shift from hierarchically managed research and development (R&D) toward lead users and learning-by-doing. Web 2.0 makes it just as easy for physicians across nationwide hospital chains to "Flickrize" CAT, MRI, and NMR scans as for photo hobbyists to share their work.

"Dynamic capabilities" now means evolving your slower-moving organization into a fast-moving team focused on the innovative combination and orchestration of a multicompany ecosystem of global partners, users, and customers. To survive and compete, companies must quickly leverage and capitalize on the range of internal and external capabilities, know-how, know-who, and networks needed to solve problems faster, better, and cheaper.

Satyam Computer Services in India has thrived in this fast-changing global networked environment, growing from a $350,000 company in the 1990s to a multibillion-dollar company. At the 2008 World Economic Forum, B. Ramalinga Raju, the company's founder and chairman, suggested that "the trouble with our times is that the future is not what it used to be." In a world where manufacturing industry rules no longer apply, "all of our various businesses are incidental—the issue is to create value in a world that is changing...we are more akin to an ant colony—each with a mind of its own...but carrying out a group strategy...."[1]

According to Forrester, companies are adopting Web 2.0 technology for business productivity (74%), competitive pressure (64%), specific problem solution (53%), partner recommendation (53%), employee request (45%), and bundled service (25%).

But what are these companies actually doing? We'll look at why Web 2.0 matters to the following companies' financial results and way of doing business:

---

[1] From the summary of the "Developing Strategy in a Networked World" session at *http://www.weforum.org/en/knowledge/KN_SESS_SUMM_22310?url=/en/knowledge/KN_SESS_SUMM_22310.*

IBM

   Local to global network effects

Salesforce.com

   Software as a service

Amazon

   Competence syndication

But first, a brief background on dynamic capabilities and online syndication.

External and Internal Forces

The industry analysis, or "five forces," approach to strategy developed by Michael Porter looks at the external conditions facing the firm—the forces that are determining the profitability of the industry, such as new entrants or overly powerful suppliers. In contrast, the resource-based approach to strategy (exemplified by the work of Edith Penrose) looks primarily at the company-level internal and organizational factors, such as combining tangible and intangible assets—people, systems, skills, processes, and capabilities—as key determinants of strategic performance.

The original dynamic capabilities framework,[2] written before the advent of the Web, was quite prescient. It suggested that both firm-level and industry-level factors are critical. Companies must dynamically adjust to turbulent outside forces by combining inside and outside capabilities, assets, and resources.

Developing Dynamic Capabilities: Before the Web

If these dynamic capabilities are so important to a company's strategic performance and profitability, how do you acquire them? We know from economists that it's hard enough to create, value, transfer, and replicate individual knowledge, especially if it is in a "tacit" form of know-how and personal experience in someone's brain or muscle memory, rather than in an "explicit" or "codified" form, such as a mathematical formula or blueprint. That is

---

2   David Teece, Gary Pisano, and Amy Shuen. "Dynamic Capabilities and Strategic Management." *Strategic Management Journal* 18, no. 7 (1997): 509–533.

why it is difficult to explain how to ride a bike to someone without that person actually doing it. Unfortunately, accumulated individual learning-by-doing limits the rate of diffusion and the scope of proliferation of capabilities or skills.

Michael Polanyi called this *personal knowledge;* see his book *Personal Knowledge: Towards a Post-Critical Philosophy* (University of Chicago Press). He developed much of the terminology we still use today for explaining the difficulties of international technology transfer and the *stickiness* or *lumpiness* of knowledge. "Knowledge goods" behave differently in markets and transactions than other digital and physical goods of economic value. Communities accelerate knowledge and competence transfer and replicability by sharing experiences and increasing peer-to-peer social interaction and communication. They also provide the feedback that is necessary for cumulative and aggregated learning.

Because individual competences and experience are embedded in the brains and memories of individual people, companies can "buy" brains and talent and "acquire" experience and competences in that way. But how can they keep this intellectual capital from walking out the door and across the street to a competitor?

Companies have developed ways of turning individual competences into group or organization-level capabilities, for example, Sony's core competence in miniaturization, or Apple's capabilities in cool design. These capabilities combine and orchestrate talented people inside and outside the company with resources and tangible assets, such as network infrastructure, IT systems, equipment, inventory, laboratory, and manufacturing facilities. This leads to the development and leverage of valuable intangible assets, including market capitalization, network effects, brand, reputation, buzz, business models, relationships, ecosystems, goodwill, and momentum.

However, the pace of organizational learning is still tied to the company's prior experience in its domain of interest, often referred to as *absorptive capacity,* as well as its level of organizational inertia due to "not-invented-here" (NIH) syndrome, which slows information and knowledge transfer because of structural rigidities, bureaucracies, and functional silos.

Web 2.0 technologies provide an unexpected and new answer to the age-old challenge of how big companies in slow-moving but highly competitive industries get dynamic capabilities without turning the clock back.

From Online Syndication to Competence Syndication

Anyone who subscribes to a local newspaper because they like *Dilbert* or *Doonesbury* has seen syndication in action. Scott Adams and Gary Trudeau, the creators of those strips, are originators, or original content creators. A syndicator collects and packages original content, specializing in comic strips, and sells them to print publications. Thousands of local newspapers deliver the cartoon to avid readers, along with late-breaking news articles, photographs, and classified ads. They choose which cartoons go into their paper from the selection offered by the syndicator.

Syndication is common in the entertainment world for TV programs, cartoons, and articles, but it's unusual elsewhere. That is because syndication is actually the sale of the same good, sometimes remixed and repackaged, to many different customers, who then integrate it with other offerings and redistribute it. This is hard to do with physical goods such as cars or watches that can be sold to only one customer at a time.

In contrast, digital goods—being electronic bits, not physical atoms—can be copied at no cost; furthermore, the information or content contained within these digital bits can be reused by an infinite number of people. Thanks to the instant access and easy distribution mechanisms of the Web, syndication has become a more radical disrupting force than the redistribution of repackaged digital content.

Online syndication accelerates the rapid transfer of digitized know-how and competences. RSS is a technology standard that allows any online publisher to broadcast information onto the Internet in *feeds*. Users can link to the information in these feeds in a number of ways, clicking buttons or links (often orange) in the page or the web browser, or through other tools.

If users have a personalized home page, such as MyYahoo! or Google Gmail, they are probably already RSS users. MyYahoo!

and Google Gmail provide a web-based news aggregator that alerts users to new content from their favorite sites as soon as it hits the Web, and aggregates all their favorite sources of information so they can peruse them on one page.

Online syndication or RSS (along with link lists) is the highly viral distribution engine for the blogosphere. With one initiating click of the RSS button, users get notified by headlines when their favorite blog authors write something new on their topics of interest. If users comment or hyperlink in their next blog entry, the positive feedback loop starts—leading to the observation, and sometimes the criticism, that the blogosphere is an amplifier, an echo chamber for a few loud voices.

Syndication has grown rapidly from a means for a few technically literate bloggers to share their postings into something that people do without even thinking. Most blogging software generates feeds by default and makes them available to potential readers. Thousands of sites now collect those feeds and filter or aggregate them to present them to readers who have particular interests. Readers explore them through many different viewers in many different formats, and some of the readers are computers (from search engine crawlers to complex aggregators), not just human customers.

Blogging has emerged as a powerful force, but its use of syndication isn't all that different from the syndication of news articles, photos, comic strips, and TV shows. Syndicating organizational competence takes syndication to a whole new level.

Because organizational competences, know-how, and processes can be embodied and packaged in digital form, these valuable services can also be syndicated and sold to many different buyers and companies. One company can syndicate a shopping-cart ordering and payment system to many online retailers. Another company can syndicate a logistics platform. Another might syndicate fraud-detection and credit-scoring algorithms, and yet another could syndicate human resource processes, recruiting, and training. In the first generation of the Web, the distribution of these digital services and applications was more complicated and expensive, with high upfront costs. As businesses have learned to take better advantage of the Web, those costs have declined.

Software as a Service (SaaS)

Software as a service (SaaS), a web-enabled software application distribution model, has created explosive growth in the syndication of business services and processes. In SaaS, a *creator* is often a business software application developer, an independent software vendor (ISV), or a software value added reseller (VAR), rather than a consumer or media-oriented blogger, YouTuber, or citizen journalist/cartoonist. The creator develops a web-native software application and hosts and operates (either independently or through a third party) the application for use by its customers over the Internet. The *syndicator* or *distributor* is often an SaaS platform provider like Salesforce.com or IBM's On Demand and Utility computing services.

Customers pay for using the software application *only when they need it* (service-on-demand) rather than actually buying the software as a product or license. This reduces upfront costs and is especially attractive to small- and medium-size businesses. It has the same benefits as commercially licensed, internally operated software with its accompanying IT support staff, but avoids the complexity and high initial cost of buying or building a custom application.

SaaS revenue streams are attractive to the creator or developer as well. Because these applications are priced on a per-user basis, they encourage positive direct network effects and increasing returns rather than an an upfront perpetual license supplemented by ongoing maintenance and support fees over time.

By applying economies of scale to the operation of applications, and distributing applications directly to web browsers online, a service provider can offer better, cheaper, and more reliable applications to a wider population, as well as being able to reach a more targeted global market. A company that makes software for human resource management at boutique hotels might once have had a hard time finding enough of a market to sell its applications, but a hosted application can instantly reach the entire market, making specialization within a vertical market not only possible but preferable to a "shrink-wrapped" product.

Part of the consumer-driven Web 2.0 and "Google effect" is a level of comfort and trust with new external applications that are web-based and ubiquitous, from searching, calendaring, keeping spreadsheets, and sending emails to expense reporting and applicant screening. As shown in Figure 4-1, SaaS fills a gap in the existing software market, giving customers a more formal opportunity than hacking but a lower barrier than is needed to build software or sustain a market for shrink-wrapped applications.

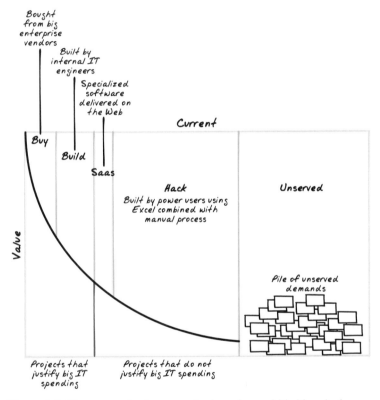

Figure 4-1. *The range of software tasks, by value and likelihood of happening in typical models*

Many businesses view Salesforce.com as emblematic of SaaS. Founded in 1999 by former Oracle executive Marc Benioff, the company helped drive the rapid shift from on-premise Siebel, PeopleSoft, and Oracle enterprise-level software for sales force automation (SFA) and customer relationship management (CRM) to on-demand, web-browser-based, hosted software services.

Salesforce.com's AppExchange product allows external or third-party developers to create add-on applications for email marketing tools, sales analysis, and finance; and to sell and distribute their applications through the AppExchange web site. Close to 600 applications are now available in the AppExchange ecosystem.

This changes the nature of competition among software developers. Instead of hoarding valuable, proprietary, and internal competences and processes, established and successful companies can compete over how quickly they can package these services into applications to distribute them to clients, provide platforms for related applications, and support ecosystem development to multiply the number of direct or indirect revenue streams. The balance is shifting toward agility in recreating, dynamically integrating, and acting as a platform and host to rapidly distributing the best available syndicated components, systems, and services.

This kind of web syndication faces unique rewards as well as competitive risks. On the bright side, browser-based competence syndication:

- Opens up many opportunities for customer and traffic acquisition
- Offers growth and flexibility
- Enables businesses to choose where they wish to concentrate their efforts
- Piggybacks on a myriad of other businesses and application creators for the software, web services, and related components and specialized systems it needs

The syndicated world of the Web has different rules from those of the offline business world, where assets tend to be fixed and roles and relationships stable. To thrive in this environment of competence syndication networks, companies have to change many of their old assumptions and strategic approaches. They need to connect and interact with other companies and customers, open their ecosystems, and maximize their connections to other companies and users. Companies also have to be agile in managing these positions and connections because they are evolving and dynamically changing.

Finding Competence Across the World: IBM

Opening up and orchestrating inside and outside comptences was the major transformation that Lou Gerstner, former CEO of IBM, set into motion at the major Fortune 500 company. IBM shifted from controlling a dominant share in one major pie of IBM-centric computing to becoming a sliver in thousands of little pies— fields in which IBM participated but did not necessarily dominate, many of which provided no direct revenue stream to the company. That may sound like a dangerous and risky strategy, but there was more downside in being only in major pies.

Integrating Linux and Apache

When Linus Torvalds posted his first version of Linux on an obscure software bulletin board in 1991, he could not have foreseen a multibillion dollar ecosystem that allows large corporate champions of open source, like IBM, to challenge Microsoft's operating system in major emerging software marketplaces, such as China, India, Russia, and Brazil. The old model of companies competing on the basis of their own homegrown proprietary solutions faced a free alternative built by a loose network of programmers who seemed more motivated by community, robust software, and bug-fixes than by profit-making or industry leadership.

IBM showed that "the elephant could dance," transforming itself into a champion for open systems and embracing a new kind of collaborative innovation and learning culture, becoming a trusted member of a very decentralized developer community of thousands. IBM, with the zeal of the recently converted, estimates that by including open source programming, contributing to the community, and adapting the open source philosophy, they have saved nearly $1 billion per year compared with what it would have cost to develop a Linux-like operating system on their own.[3]

Collaborations can produce more robust, user-defined, fault-tolerant products in less time and for less money than the conventional closed approach. (And anyone can contribute to open source: large companies, governments, individuals, and pretty much any group that is willing to accept the basic philosophy.)

---

[3] From Don Tapscott and Anthony D. Williams. *Wikinomics*. Portfolio Hardcover, 2006.

IBM is showing off its dynamic capabilities, demonstrating how an industry leader can strategically transform the uses, combinations, and interactions of assets and resources from inside and outside the company. IBM used to be recognized for its success using its capabilities—resources, systems, people, and organization—to dominate large corporate markets with proprietary and highly integrated hardware and software enterprise systems. In this case, however, IBM showed a remarkable capability to deeply transform its strategy, people, organization, and systems through its involvement in the open source communities of Apache and Linux.

Mentoring

IBM is invested in supporting the emerging vast and vibrant ecosystem of startup companies and developers that are driving the next wave of development in open source business applications and services, especially in emerging markets, such as China and India. Explicit partnering agreements are part of the approach, but a broader set of initiatives is designed to build the number of developers in these countries. Developers don't have to work for IBM directly to contribute to the projects IBM would like to see succeed.

In 2004, IBM announced a new initiative called *virtual mentoring* not only to help the new generation of application developers but to raise its new products, services, and innovations to certification standards (to ensure compatibility), and to actively comarket these new products and services globally. About 400 emerging-market developers join IBM's developer networks daily.

This next generation of location-specific Linux developers and software innovators may well redefine the IT market. Already everything from enterprise applications to enterprise resource planning (ERP) to content management and business intelligence to retail and e-commerce payment services and inventory management—basically anything you need to run a small or enterprise-level business—is available as a low-cost, open source, online distributed, pay-as-you-go web service.

The full array of new ventures and applications is astonishing (around 10,000 and growing). Although these new applications help IBM around the world, they also address the needs of billions of users in the emerging markets of Brazil, Russia, India, and China (often referred to as the BRIC countries).

The open source community supports the heavy lifting by helping produce and debug the software, while IBM provides the certification and cross-national marketing, access, and support. The money that these developers and small companies spend can go directly into developing regionally localized features and services. This is a big change from the proprietary enterprise model, where more than 70% of the costs go into development, sales, and marketing. Competence syndication occurs when regional developers create Linux-based, value-added, local applications for their home countries that are ideal for proliferating and distributing with equal or higher value in many other locations.

Ecosystems and competence syndication

IBM's strategy reflects more interest in developing ecosystems than in syndicating its own competence as such. Ecosystems are about technology platforms and competence syndication is about distribution. It's like comparing hub-and-spoke airplane companies like United and American with regional upstarts like Southwest.

IBM, like many other enterprise software vendors, talks about the number of partners in its ecosystem as though many vendors signing up for a partner program were a sure indicator of success. To its credit, IBM is one of the few companies that has realized that the application developer landscape has shifted dramatically. First, 14 million new Linux developers will emerge in China and India in the next 5 years.[4] Second, the most significant cost and barrier to success that these developers will face is sales and marketing, not the cost of hardware, servers, or storage.

Giving Away the Store: Amazon

Amazon's strategy can be best understood within the framework of competence syndication. Although Amazon started as an online book retailer, founder and CEO Jeff Bezos soon realized that

---

4 Amy Shuen, corporate venture research on IBM presented to the Fall Meeting of NVCA Corporate Venture Group, Sept. 2005.

Amazon's early advantages could not be guaranteed to sustain its scale, as thousands of competitors were always just a click away.

First steps: letting other sellers into the store

In 2001, Amazon opened zShops, providing virtual shelf space to online competitors. They could sell their goods through the same system Amazon used, paying a listing fee plus commissions on sales. At little cost, Amazon became a distributor of easily found online storefronts and products, and it was able, like Google's AdWords, to reach a long tail with small- and medium-size businesses—some of which had never even advertised online before.

Both Wall Street and some of Bezos' own management thought it was risky to push into these uncertain markets while the core online book business still had yet to make a profit. As Bezos said:[5]

> It was the kind of thing that became controversial internally. It made people nervous. But the reality is that if you give customers what they want—price, selection, and fast delivery— you're going to get more sales.

Giving competitors a piece of the action primed the pump for Amazon's own business success. Sales grew by 34% in 2003, climbing to more than $5 billion. And at the end of 2003, after nearly a decade of operating at a loss, Amazon posted its first profit.

It helped that Bezos never considered Amazon to be merely a distributor and that he creatively repositioned it to play many different syndication roles. Early on, Amazon launched an aggressive affiliate program to take its site where customers were clicking. Amazon Associates provides a way of syndicating its online store to affiliates' web sites. Affiliates provide specialized content and organize product listings for a specific audience or community. Thousands of nonemployees act as a virtual sales force that gets paid only on a success-fee basis when a sale is realized.

These techniques follow a key Web 2.0 practice: give something away for free, but always do it in such a way that it ends up expanding your business. Positive network effects can make this

---

[5] Susanna Hamner and Tom McNichol, "Ripping up the rules of management," *Business 2.0*, May 21, 2007, *http://money.cnn.com/galleries/2007/biz2/0705/ gallery.contrarians.biz2/2.html*.

strategy work. Bezos was one of the first people to stop thinking of the world of retailing as bricks and mortar, and to see it as a way of turning competitors into customers. In the Web's syndicated world, core capabilities are no longer secrets to protect, but instead are just the thing to sell to your competitors as web services, which could potentially become your most popular product.

Amazon is using syndication to turn distinctive capabilities, such as ordering systems and online shelf space, into an easy-to-use shopping cart system that can be sold to stores and content sites throughout the Web. Potential competitors become customers and users, actively participating in Amazon's ecosystem.

Next steps: sharing back-office competences

After leasing its cash-register services, Amazon moved from the storefront to the back office, spending millions on web services that take advantage of its experience running an enormous site with millions of users.

The first component of this strategy is storage capacity. As shown in Figure 4-2, Amazon's Simple Storage Service (S3) charges 15 cents per gigabyte per month to store data on the company's servers, plus costs for data transfer. S3 is designed to do very little, but to do it on a vast scale at low cost.

S3 may seem extremely distant from Amazon's core retail business; however, it extends talents that Amazon has already demonstrated to a whole new audience. Web 2.0 startups, for example, are using S3 to save money while they develop an audience for their projects.

More recently, Amazon has been renting out computing power for 10 cents per hour through the Elastic Compute Cloud, EC2. (For more information on EC2, see *http://www.amazon.com/gp/ browse.html?node=201590011*; there's much more involved than in S3!) Bezos asked a simple question when deciding to pursue these kinds of projects:

> If we needed this kind of technology internally, then chances are a bunch of companies could also benefit.

Figure 4-2. *Amazon's S3 fundamentals*

Amazon's vision isn't limited to its web expertise but extends to its tightly integrated warehouse and logistics services. Having given away online shelf space to competitors, Amazon is now providing them with physical room in its warehouses. Fulfillment by Amazon lets smaller companies leave their inventory management to Amazon. When a customer places an order, Amazon ships it out.

Helping others share competences

Some sections of this book were transcribed from lectures and presentations. Amazon's support for a service called CastingWords is another example of a low-tech, high-labor-cost, fragmented industry—transcription services—that has benefited from networked and global dynamic capabilities. I uploaded an audio WAV file of my iPod-recorded lecture to *http://www. CastingWords.com*. One or two days later, I received a high-quality transcription in Word format at the unbeatable rate of less than a dollar per minute of recording. Inspired by the story of the Mechanical Turk, the chess-playing "computer" that had a real person inside the box, Amazon's service routed my WAV file online to a pool of transcribers—somewhere worldwide—who were immediately ready to provide services and who were paid online through some agreed-upon revenue share by PayPal.

Encouraging Competence Mashups: Google

Musically, *mashups* combine two or more songs to create a new song or dance track.[6] Over the last few years, the mashup concept has spread to the Web, encompassing much more than just popular songs. Developers can now mix, match, reuse, and morph web content, data, and services. These "high-tech versions of Tinkertoys" are changing the way companies and users look at information. Mashups are starting to fulfill some of the promises of web services, software, and data services that can be tapped on demand. "They're taking little bits and pieces from a number of companies and sticking them together in a clever way.... You'll start to see the real power of web services," noted Amazon's Bezos.[7]

HousingMaps.com (*http://www.housingmaps.com*), shown in Figure 4-3, was a mashup created by Paul Rademacher. While looking for a place to live, he was frustrated with having to pore through Silicon Valley rentals on Craigslist and then separately look for the locations on Google's map service. So he decided to combine the two sites and create a truly useful web service. The listings on his mashup creation are transformed into interactive pushpins on maps of different regions that provide rental details when the pushpins are clicked. Similarly, on Chicagocrime.org (*http://www.chicagocrime.org/*), shown in Figure 4-4, Adrian Holovaty combined a Chicago Police Department crime web site and Google Maps to show recent crimes close to any address.

Mashups evolved because commercial applications, services, and data (see the earlier "Software as a Service (SaaS)" section) were distributed via the web browser, and application programming interfaces (APIs) were opened to offer developers easier access to data and services. Vint Cerf of Google commented:[8]

---

6 See *http://www.mashuptown.com*.

7 Robert Hof, "Mix, Match, and Mutate," *BusinessWeek*, July 25, 2005, *http://www.businessweek.com/magazine/content/05_30/b3944108_mz063.htm*.

8 Juan Carlos Perez, "Q&A: Vint Cerf on Google's Challenges Aspirations," *Computerworld*, Nov. 25, 2005, *http://www.computerworld.com/developmenttopics/development/story/0,10801,106535,00.html*.

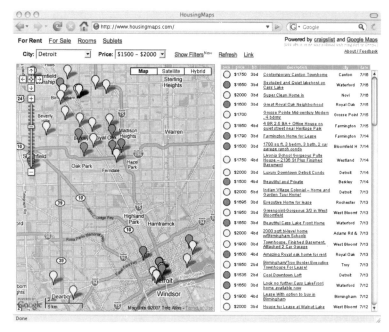

Figure 4-3. Rental properties from Craigslist combined with maps from Google to create HousingMaps.com

> We know we don't have a corner on creativity. There are creative people all around the world, hundreds of millions of them, and they are going to think of things to do with our basic platform that we didn't think of. So the mashup stuff is a wonderful way of allowing people to find new ways of applying the basic infrastructures we're propagating. This will turn out to be a major source of ideas for applying Google-based technology to a variety of applications.

John Musser's ProgrammableWeb site (*http://programmableweb. com/*) forecasts 1,000 mashups a year, based on a daily creation rate count. Why is the Web 2.0 mashup ecosystem growing? One factor is the combinatorial effect: there is simply an amazing amount of readily available, democratized content, and collective interaction. The other factor is the appearance of positive network effects. Smart aggregation, recombination, and hyperdistribution make the online world and its user services exponentially better than the simple sum of its parts.

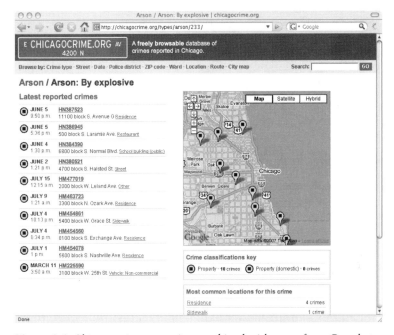

Figure 4-4. Chicago crime reporting combined with maps from Google to create Chicagocrime.org

Mashups are inherently cool, but they present challenges as well as opportunities. A laboratory of mashups will find all kinds of new opportunities in existing data, but the results of those mashups don't always look like what the data providers had planned. Advertising may vanish, for example. Providing data to mashups may also incur costs, from simple processing and bandwidth to data licensing costs. Because of these issues, many companies require registration for their APIs, and terms of service agreements often let experiments and nonprofit projects use data at lower (or no) costs than businesses that want to incorporate data into their own work.

Lessons Learned

The Web has created new opportunities for businesses to sell software and services, including features and content that used to be kept tightly proprietary. Businesses can look around at what they do well, and find ways to sell it over the Web, or newcomers can create possibilities that didn't exist before—often from parts they've gleaned from other companies. The old content syndication models have led to new service syndication models. Often, making this work demands a shift in perspective on the business itself. Jeff Bezos looked at Amazon as a set of capabilities with a regular audience of customers rather than as a bookseller, and thus found new ways to sell those capabilities. Lou Gerstner and his successors at IBM focused on making IBM a key provider of computing talent and have made huge investments in creating ecosystems that allow talent to flourish, producing harvestable goods.

Even in new projects, creating value often means letting some of that value flow elsewhere. The creative energy of mashups appears in large part because the companies providing the services being mashed up no longer insist on total control over their products. That flexibility allows a different dynamic than the usual system of "create, patent, and license" that has dominated intellectual property for the last few decades.

That flexibility may apply both inside and outside of companies. Facebook's API, explored in the previous chapter, is an open invitation for developers to come work inside of Facebook. Salesforce. com thrives because a wide variety of companies are willing to replace their own systems with Salesforce.com, bringing these new tools inside their businesses.

Finally, these kinds of collaborative approaches create new questions about privacy and user data. It may be easy to move data from one place to another, shifting it to the place that has the most competence to handle it, but users may not always be happy about where their data lands.

Questions to Ask

Expanding dynamic capabilities by sharing competences means examining how many different aspects of your company operate, from traditionally outward-facing aspects to tasks that are traditionally handled in-house.

Strategic Questions

Consider how your business and industry currently works...

To what degree have you opened up to dynamic capabilities—multiplying the ways that users inside and outside of your project, team, or organizational unit can easily leverage, aggregate, and spark collective work, knowledge, and systems?

If you took the perspective of a CEO and strategic leader...

How and when do you see Web 2.0-enabled dynamic capabilities disrupting the current practices, business model, competitive advantages, and economics of your business and industry? What's the risk of being a leader or laggard? When should this become a boardroom agenda item?

If you took the perspective of a CIO and program manager...

How could you better benchmark, analyze, compare, and quantify the impact of shifts in dynamic capabilities in key functional areas such as marketing and sales, product and services development, customer support, inventory management, logistics and operations, recruitment and training, partner and supplier relations, and procurement? How can this provide a new basis for enterprise and financial valuation?

If you are a project team member...

Are you ready to brainstorm with your group members on how the dynamic capabilities practices described for multinationals, such as Cisco, IBM, and Amazon, could be applied effectively in your business—whether consumer-focused or industrial, product- or service-oriented, offline or online, local or global, small or large?

Tactical Questions

- What kinds of online data, besides the basic web site, does your business provide?

- Do you (or your management team) feel comfortable letting outsiders work with your data? Put their data into your processes?

- Does your business currently syndicate content it generates? Press releases? Articles? Reporting?
- Are third-party services aggregating your data?
- How do you monitor the use of content you syndicate?
- Are you aware of specific markets that might want to work with the data you syndicate?
- Are your software products available as APIs and web services?
- Do you have clear and accessible policies and systems for letting outside developers connect to your services or data?
- How do you charge for the use of your APIs?
- How do you encourage developers to use your APIs?
- What kinds of benefits do you derive from your APIs?
- Are there aspects of your business that are so far ahead of the competition that you could sell them as services?
- On which communities does your business and technical infrastructure depend?
- Can you risk investing in communities without a clear direct payback?
- Are there areas of your business where you could benefit by letting someone else provide the services instead?
- Do your internal cost structures fit better with upfront software purchases or with software as a service?
- How much data sharing are your users willing to accept?

New Recombines with Old

WEB 2.0 MAY APPEAR TO BE SOMETHING NEW, DIFFERENT, AND INCOM-
PATIBLE with business platforms that came before. Although much
of the point of this book has been to show that Web 2.0 *is* different, that difference doesn't mean that the old world halts and a
new world begins.

Web 2.0 strategies can be a component of other business models.
One common option is to build communities on the basis of
existing products and brands. Another is to build relationships
between up-and-coming firms with new technologies and older
companies with experience in a field and a strong user base. Along
the way, businesses can explore new relationships with their customers and with each other.

Styles of Innovation

Even before economist Joseph Schumpeter described innovation as
the "creative winds of destruction" back in 1942, businesses have
feared the dark side of innovation. New technologies disrupt the
old order and destroy the comfortable relationships, profitable
markets, and leadership positions that current companies—called
industry incumbents—have successfully carved out for themselves
through years of investment and infrastructure. Clayton Christensen's bestseller, *The Innovator's Dilemma* (HarperBusiness),

reminded even high-tech winners that innovation comes in disruptive waves from emerging technology niches and ignored market segments, making today's heroes next year's zeros.

Using the disk drive as an example, Christensen defines *disruptive innovation* as a "sleeper" technology that poses an unanticipated threat to industry incumbents, as the new entrants initially satisfy only the requirements of a niche or an emerging low-performance, low-end market. Thus, established firms—even those that are quite capable of the new technology—are led to complacency and inertia by their own mainstream and premium customers, until it's too late.

Of course, that is not quite the story in digital and online networked technologies or in disruptive business models that change the way businesses make money and cover costs in an increasingly connected online, mobile "flat world."

- Amazon.com certainly did not start with low performance when it immediately attacked the mainstream mass market for books and quickly moved to a range of retail products and affiliate storefronts.

- Digital cameras started out more expensive than film cameras of similar performance but held out the promise to all recreational photographers of lower lifetime usage costs because film and development could be replaced by digital images, distribution, sharing, and storage.

- Skype and peer-to-peer (p2p) architecture for Voice over Internet Protocol (VoIP) offered free basic or low-end service, but they targeted and reached a global mainstream and business market through viral marketing and distribution (allowing users themselves to be the routing hub for their international calling rolodex).

For the purposes of this chapter, we will start with a simplified 2×2 innovation typology, shown in Figure 5-1, that positions disruptive innovation (or, as it used to be called, "revolutionary innovation") along the axes of old-new markets and old-new technologies.

Clearly, new technologies that capture old or existing mainstream markets are disruptive—a bit like revolutionaries who turn the entire population against the old order. But for the mainstream market to move wholesale to a new way of doing things, a large

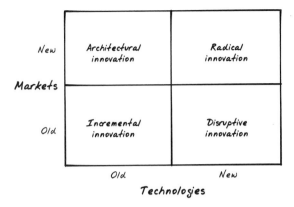

Figure 5-1. Categorizing different kinds of innovations

population must believe that it's worth switching—and that the basis of competition and of how people are measuring and comparing value has changed.

It's easy to place incremental innovation and radical innovation in this matrix. *Incremental innovation* is old technology in old markets; *radical innovation* is new technology in new or emerging markets. Finally, we have *architectural innovation,* old technologies in new markets, recombining and repackaging existing technologies within redesigned system and product architectures to reach new market segments and niches. Scholars have used these terms for decades to categorize the kinds of technological innovations that cause shifts in the competitive landscape and the relative profitability and market share of incumbent firms compared with new entrants.

Of course, whether one views these innovations as "world-saving" or "creative destruction" depends on where she sits. Specifically, if any of these kinds of innovation or technologies is *competence-enhancing* and increases the value of the organizational and intellectual assets a company already has in-house, she is likely to be a cheerleader. However, if one of these technologies is *competence-destroying* and destroys the value of the organizational and intellectual assets a company possesses, she is likely to be a defender and will do her best to eliminate, strong-arm, or legally wipe out these threats. This is the typical zero-sum, win-loss battle between the incumbents, who have a lot at stake, and the new entrants, who have everything to gain.

However, Web 2.0 and its particular brand of collaborative, digital, and online networked/interactive user-led innovation doesn't fit neatly into this conventional 2×2 competitive innovation matrix. That isn't surprising, as these innovation categories were coined to describe technological breakthrough innovations in the physical world of disk drives, semiconductors, steel mini-mills, photolithography equipment, and manufacturing processes. In the following sections, we'll discuss some newer categories of online digital networked collaborative innovation that are breeding disruptive business models in high- and low-tech industries.

Competitive or Collaborative Innovation?

A few industries—media, telecom, and banking, among others—seem to stay above the competitive fray. Initially, these industries were well protected from the turbulence of emerging technologies, pure-play competitive startups, and global new entrants. Governmental regulations, high barriers to entry through committed investments in irreplaceable and costly infrastructure, complex contracting structures, and relationships combined with strong and enforceable property rights had, to this point, insulated them against the changing landscape.

Yet in erecting walls against all possible disruptors and competitors, while assuming away the option to become network partners and ecosystem allies, the companies in these protected and highly regulated industries may have been mistaking the good Dr. Jekyll for the evil Mr. Hyde.

In the early 1980s, during the advent of videocassette recorders, the movie studios fought major legal battles to try and stop home recording and video rentals. So, at first, studios priced their movies so that rental stores could afford to buy only a few copies, disappointing many customers who wanted new and popular releases. Of course, with the high video prices and artificial scarcity of video rentals, "cannibalism," or eating into live-at-the-theater big-screen profits, was reduced. It took 15 years to see that the actual outcome of the new videocassette recorder technology was to enormously expand the entire market. In 1980, industry revenues from both big screen and video were $2.4 billion, by 1995, the market was $12.3 billion, with home video rentals bringing in $7 billion.

Figure 5-2 shows the multiple revenue streams and network effects that are now possible for movie studios with online and digital distribution. The challenge for the movie studios has changed from creating blockbuster movies and distributing them through a limited physical channel of distribution—the movie theater— toward more effective monetization and value capture of the expanded digital distribution market in cable pay-per-view, DVDs and rentals, network TV, video games, music soundtracks, and other potential syndication, licensing, and remixing opportunities.

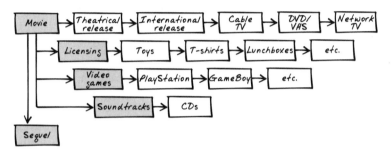

Figure 5-2. *Value chains deriving from a movie*

Another example comes from e-commerce. It would be easy to see offline independent and chain bookstores as strict competitors of online booksellers like Amazon. However, just like the video story, sales in one domain seem to produce a "lift" in the other, and vice versa. The key to Netflix, Flickr, Amazon, and other online companies is that the sales of offline physical products can get online "buzz." These online sales, referrals, rankings, and reviews enjoy a wider and more targeted word-of-mouth marketing, creating a chain reaction or critical mass of adoption and social influence.

Even when industry leaders recognize a potential network partner or ecosystem player, they will sometimes turn down the opportunity in order to protect their own cash cows or maintain control of their "walled garden." In the financial world, this could be one of the explanations for why, of all the major retail banking centers in the world, only Japan had a different magnetic strip on its credit cards that made the cards usable only at Japanese ATMs. It certainly seems to have been why Citibank, the first bank to introduce and invest in the ATM infrastructure back in 1977, waited until 1991 to allow its ATM cards to work on other banks' ATM networks. A simple analysis of indirect network effects would have shown that everyone's ATM cards are more valuable when they work on all machines.

At least some of the explanation of Europe's surprisingly strong recent economic health comes from both the European Union and the euro with its integration and positive network effects compared with the once-independent currencies and fragmented markets of the European nations.

PayPal's person-to-person online payment system, piggybacking on the hypergrowth and the success of eBay's online auction transactions, was viewed as a startup competitor rather than a potential ally by the major banks that wanted to protect their finely tuned and highly profitable SWIFT cross-border and inter-bank system for wire transfer of funds. (Several of them tried to develop their own person-to-person online payment systems.) PayPal's system never reached a critical mass of networked online users because it lacked the visibility and daily volume of n-sided market transactions of an online partner like eBay. Not surprisingly, eBay acquired PayPal in 2002, listening to its customers who preferred it over eBay's homegrown system.

The key is that allies and ecosystems can join forces in expanding and opening up markets to create a win-win situation. Competitors and a competitive perspective on innovation tend to divide markets and leave a lot of potential expanded network-effects value and opportunities on the table.

Styles of Collaborative Innovation

In the new-style online collaborative innovation, the entire perspective of innovation changes. We move away from a situation in which new and old companies *compete* in an industry for competitive advantage in capturing new and old markets using different kinds of innovative technologies. Instead, we have big and small companies whose users *collaborate,* often across industry boundaries, in innovative ways. So, the fundamental axes of the *collaborative innovation matrix* are different from those of the *competitive innovation matrix*.

The styles of collaborative innovation are distinguished by whether the collaborative interaction is between

- Crowds of users, called *user-led* or *democratized innovation*.
- Dissimilar companies, called *recombinant innovation*.
- Crowds collaborating to solve problems for companies, called *crowdsourcing*.
- Companies that provide new platforms on which innovation communities and ecosystems can form, including *open source*, *ecosystem*, and *platform innovation*. This yields a number of different paths for innovation, as shown in Figure 5-3.

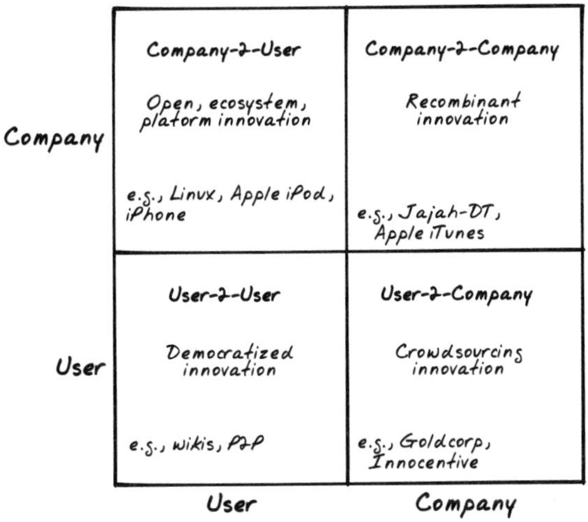

	Company-2-User	Company-2-Company
Company	Open, ecosystem, platform innovation e.g., Linux, Apple iPod, iPhone	Recombinant innovation e.g., Jajah-DT, Apple iTunes
	User-2-User	User-2-Company
User	Democratized innovation e.g., wikis, P2P	Crowdsourcing innovation e.g., Goldcorp, Innocentive
	User	**Company**

Figure 5-3. Types of online collaborative innovation

Democratized Innovation

Eric von Hippel's book *Democratizing Innovation* (The MIT Press) observes that lead users often develop and modify products for themselves and freely reveal what they have done so that others can adopt the developed solutions. He calls the trend toward these primarily user-centered innovation systems the "democratization of innovation."

As open source software projects show, horizontal or peer-to-peer innovation communities, consisting entirely of users, can function as self-organizing and regulating entities without manufacturer or corporate involvement. So, the keys to *democratized innovation* in the online collaborative world are the wide distribution, ease and low cost of tools for innovation, combined with the tools for interaction and communication. Peer interaction and recognition between users catalyze innovation, personal expression, and creativity. The Linux open source community is a good example, says Chris Hanson in *Democratizing Innovation*:

> Creation is unbelievably addictive. And programming, at least for skilled programmers, is highly creative.... Community standards encourage deep understanding.... For many, a free software project is the only context in which they can write a program that expresses their own vision, rather than implementing someone else's design or hacking together something that the marketing department insists on.... Unlike architecture, the expressive component of a program is inaccessible to non-programmers. A close analogy is to appreciate the artistic expression of a novel when you don't know the language in which it is written...this means that creative programmers want to associate with one another: only their peers are able to truly appreciate their art...it's also important that people want to share the beauty of what they have found....

Web 2.0 technologies such as RSS, wikis, podcasting, and social networks increase the intensity, frequency, and ease of online collaboration and community-building.

Crowdsourcing Innovation

Crowdsourcing or *crowdcatching* is a problem-solving and idea-generating process in which a company throws out a well-specified problem to a selected crowd or group of people for solution. Some well-known crowdcasts are in the form of competitions—prizes are used as an incentive, and the "winning" solutions are chosen by a set of judges. It provides a focal point for the "wisdom of the crowd" to emerge from unexpected and interdisciplinary sources and individuals.

Let's start with a simple framework used by economists for analyzing knowledge as an economic good and apply it to the recent
case of Goldcorp, a company in the "old-economy" mining
industry. Rob McEwen had become the CEO of Goldcorp, a low-
yield Canadian gold-mining operation, when the gold market was
depressed, operating costs were high, and the miners were on
strike. "Mining is one of humanity's oldest industrial pursuits.
This is *old* old economy. But a mineral discovery is like a technological discovery. There's the same rapid creation of wealth as
rising expectations improve profitability. If we could find gold
faster, we could really improve the value of the company."

McEwen realized that if he could speed up the "knowledge production" process—to find new ideas about where to dig for high-
grade ore on his property faster—he could turn around his failing
company. Most companies use three conventional forms of
knowledge production:

- R&D knowledge production in company and academic labs
  focused on basic research or applied research

- Learning-by-doing, involving lead users and communities of
  practice

- Integrative or coordinative knowledge including standards
  and platforms

McEwen needed results fast. He recalls that his "eureka" moment
came as a result of a seminar at MIT in 1999, where he first heard
about the impact of the Linux operating system and the open
source revolution. Here was an unconventional and revolutionary
approach to speeding up the "knowledge production" process
without costly long investment cycles or big, risky bets. "I said,
'Open source code! That's what I want.'" After all, if Linux could
attract world-class programmers to help make better software,
maybe Goldcorp could attract world-class geologists to help find
gold. McEwen issued the Goldcorp Challenge in March 2000—
Goldcorp revealed all of its geological data regarding their Red
Lake gold mine online, asking geologists to tell them where to find
6 million ounces of gold. The prize money totaled $575,000; the
top award was $105,000.

More than 1,400 virtual "prospectors" joined the Goldcorp gold rush and downloaded company data. Like alchemists, many of the final contest winners turned Goldcorp's raw information and data into actionable knowledge about where to dig for gold. McEwen says that the contest was a major success: "We have drilled four of the winners' top five targets and have hit on all four." Additionally, the discoveries have been high-grade and high-yielding ore deposits. "But what's really important is that from a remote site, the winners were able to analyze a database and generate targets without ever visiting the property. It's clear that this is part of the future." Making the data available for download on the Web, allowed scientists, engineers, and geologists from 50 countries to participate, and the panel of 5 judges could evaluate and compare the creative approaches and targets of an astonishingly diverse set of submissions.

The numbers speak for themselves. In 1996, the Goldcorp Red Lake mine was producing at an annual rate of 53,000 ounces at a cost of $360 an ounce. After the contest and some modernizing in 2001, the mine was producing 504,000 ounces, about 10 times more, at a cost of $59 an ounce. With gold prices at $307 an ounce, that's like $248 in profit per ounce rather than a $53 loss per ounce.

The mining industry as a whole has benefited. As Michael Polanyi pointed out in his book *Personal Knowledge: Towards a Post-Critical Philosophy*, personal knowledge or "tacit" knowledge such as riding a bike, scoring soccer goals, or intuiting where to dig in 55,000 acres of Red Lake property is usually hard to transfer or reproduce. But any of us can make the effort to deliberately share and transfer this kind of knowledge and skills to others by "codifying" it in a formula, script, program, model, expert system, demonstration, or recording.

The problem comes when the inventor or idea originator wants to get paid. Once knowledge is produced and codified, as in a mathematical formula or digital code on the Web or video, it becomes fluid (an economic good that is difficult for the creator to control privately), "infinitely expansible" (like the Energizer bunny, it doesn't get depleted by usage), and cumulative—leading to a combinatorial explosion of social and public goods. This benefits many individuals and companies through knowledge "spillover," but it may or may not result in profit or payment to the sponsoring company or to the generators of the idea and the knowledge. Thus the term "externality" applies when an economic good produces positive or negative effects (value or noise) that cannot be captured or "internalized."

An online contest can turn out to be an unexpected solution to the externality problem. According to Ronald Coase in his article "The Problem of Social Cost," in the *Journal of Law and Economics*, and explained in Dominique Foray's *The Economics of Knowledge* (The MIT Press), the size of the externality can be reduced by expanding the area in which knowledge is voluntarily shared. So, the collective production of knowledge in technology consortiums, multicompany research centers, and R&D agreements can be used to "internalize externalities." Before the Web, coordination and organization costs made a very large number of knowledge-sharing partners infeasible.

The Goldcorp contest was well organized to allow the company to immediately judge the value and quality of the submitted ideas and mining targets and then pay the contest winners a fixed amount for their contribution. In economic terms, this provided a fixed incentive for the contest participants as well as a way for Goldcorp to internalize or monetize the virtual gold rush through actual mining operations.

In the Goldcorp Challenge, the top contest winner was a partnership of two Australian groups (Fractal Graphics and Taylor Wall & Associates) that developed a powerful 3-D graphical model of the mine. Winning the prize gave publicity to the firms' competence in 3-D models of mines, and according to Nick Archibald at Fractal Graphics, the industry now has a new way of doing exploration. "This has been a big change for mining. This has been like a beacon in a sea of darkness."

In short, Goldcorp struck gold on the Web by:

- Accelerating relevant "knowledge production" (on where to dig for gold) by world-class experts at a relatively low fixed cost (total prize money was $575,000).

- Incentivizing "collective production of knowledge" by making its company-proprietary (but raw) data sets available to download for the contest, while maintaining sole rights to mine and exploit the knowledge generated about target sites.

• Capturing knowledge spillover and cumulative learning across a range of disciplines by reviewing, judging, and evaluating the diversity of approaches and then testing the target sites.

• Monetizing the winning models immediately by exploring the mining targets and paying, publicizing, and promoting the contest winners.

The web sites of the Innovation Challenge, World Bank Development Marketplace, X PRIZE Foundation, Goldcorp Challenge, Bayer Material Science Prize, Netflix Prize, Ansari X PRIZE, Innocentive, and Red Hat Challenge illustrate the range of companies, industries, and technologies experimenting with crowdsourcing innovation.

It doesn't even require a well-publicized contest. The blog Billions With Zero Knowledge (*http://www.billionswithzeroknowledge. com/*) uses the T-shirt company Threadless as an example of creative design-intensive community production that seems to be much more powerful and innovative than just "crowd-sourced manufacturing."

Open Source, Ecosystem, and Platform Innovation

Companies have adapted to user-centered innovation in different ways. Several authors have described how companies have innovated by providing platforms from which externally generated innovations can result, and where users—as well as ecosystems of affiliates, third-party developers, and service providers—can form innovative communities.

After reviewing some definitions and examples, we'll discuss a more recent and wildly popular platform innovation: Apple's iPod and the ecosystems that have developed around it. Although the iPod does not use a Web 2.0 business model, it illustrates how companies can capture and multiply network value from ecosystems and passionate, loyal users.

Steve Weber's *The Success of Open Source* (Harvard University Press) explores how open source catalyzes innovation and enlarges the scope and scale of knowledge domains because "property in open source is configured fundamentally around the right to distribute, not the right to exclude." He echoes Larry Lessig's well-known argument that a "commons" functions as a "feedstock for economic innovation and creative activity." But he adds a more nuanced innovation benefit: the importance of DIY participation in creative activity by individual users, simply for the sake and value of the individual or community creative act—even if this participation is not immediately measurable as an increase in knowledge stocks or directly related to a breakthrough innovation.

Marco Iansiti and Roy Levien's *The Keystone Advantage* (Harvard Business School Press) argues that the very best companies are "keystones" or orchestrators of their ecosystem or "value network"—their large and distributed network of partner companies and customers. They use the examples of Wal-Mart, Microsoft, and Li & Fung to show how keystone companies provide "platforms" that other firms and users can leverage to spur innovation.

Geoff Moore, the best-selling author of *Crossing the Chasm* and recently *Dealing with Darwin: How Great Companies Innovate at Every Phase of Their Evolution* (Portfolio Hardcover), coined the term *platform innovation*. In his blog (*http://geoffmoore.blogs. com/*), he refers to Intel's shift from microprocessor products to all-purpose mobile computing and communications platforms and devices as a good example of platform innovation. The key is to leverage a potentially ubiquitous product or device into a market-making, online distribution platform and channel.

The biggest challenge to companies innovating in this area is to convert from an engrained culture of competition to the collaborative culture necessary for creating trusting relationships and developing myriads of new partners and ecosystems. It's not easy for a company like Intel—whose chairman and former CEO Andy Grove wrote a book titled *Only the Paranoid Survive* (Currency) and rose to power as a take-no-prisoners competitor—to turn around and preach "Give to get."

Online Recombinant Innovation

The recombinant DNA techniques discovered in 1973 founded genetic engineering and sparked a biotechnology revolution.

Recombinant DNA emerges from new combinations of DNA molecules that are not found together naturally and are derived from different biological sources. In an analogous way, innovation that shows recombination or new combinations of different companies' technologies, processes, systems, and business models can be termed *recombinant innovation* to differentiate it from innovation that comes from only one company and source.

Bridging, Not Disrupting

Rather than rebelling against or completely disrupting the old business order and replacing the infrastructure that took decades of development and investment, the new click-and-mortar, online-offline network partnerships are recombinant business model innovations. They focus on building new networks and business models based on collective user value and hypergrowth social network opportunities.

Integrating Ecosystems: Apple's iPod

Apple's iPod is not precisely a web application. At its heart, it combines iPod hardware for playing music (and pictures and video), iTunes software for managing that content (shown in Figure 5-4), and an iTunes store that runs over the Web (shown in Figure 5-5). The iPod exemplifies the integration of new technology with existing systems, and its continuing growth into new areas (such as the web-capable iPhone) demonstrates how different technological ecosystems can coexist. Physical hardware can both benefit from network effects and create surrounding businesses based on those effects.

However, the iPod combines much more than just components made and controlled by Apple. The first four ecosystems we'll discuss are illustrative examples of *platform innovation*, and they demonstrate how Apple has captured value from its ecosystems and expanded and widely distributed this value to its partners. You'll see the overall increased returns from collaborative innovation.

In this example, a lead company—here, Apple—conceives, designs, and orchestrates the external innovation and creativity of many other outside participants, users, suppliers, creators, affiliates, partners, and complementors to support an innovative product, service,

Figure 5-4. *iTunes software with a user's music library*

Figure 5-5. *Apple's music store running inside of iTunes*

or system. The final (and fifth) ecosystem—the iTunes and major record label partnerships—is used as a contrasting example of *recombinant innovation* and will be discussed later.

Platform Innovation Ecosystem #1: Production

To create the iPod, Apple first assembled a production eco-system—a group of companies all over the world that contributed to circuit design, chipsets, the hard drive, screens, the plastic shell, and other technologies, as well as assembly of the final device.

Although many people still think of the manufacturing process as the key place to capture added value, the iPod demonstrates that Apple—the creator, brand name, and orchestrator—has actually figured out how to capture the lion's share of the value: 30%. The rest of the value is spread across a myriad of different contributions within the network of component providers and assemblers, none of them larger than 15%. Researchers, sponsored by the Sloan Foundation, developed an analytical framework for quantitatively calculating who captures the value from a successful global outsourced innovation like Apple's iPod.

Their study (*http://pcic.merage.uci.edu/papers/2007/AppleiPod.pdf*) traced the 451 parts that go into the iPod. Attributing cost and value-capture to different companies and their home countries is relatively complex, as the iPod and its components—like many other products—are made in several countries by dozens of companies, with each stage of production contributing a different amount to the final value.

It turns out that $163 of the iPod's $299 retail value is captured by American companies and workers, with $75 to distribution and retail, $80 to Apple, and $8 to various domestic component makers. Japan contributes about $26 of value added, Korea less than $1, and the final assembly in China adds somewhat less than $4 a unit. (The study's purpose was to demonstrate that trade statistics can be misleading, as the U.S.–China trade deficit increases by $150—the factory cost—for every 30 GB video iPod unit, although the actual value added by assembly in China is a few dollars at most.)

Suppliers throughout the manufacturing chain benefit from sales of the product and may thrive as a result, but the main value of the iPod goes to its creator, Apple. As Hal Varian commented in the *New York Times*:[1]

> The real value of the iPod doesn't lie in its parts or even in putting those parts together. The bulk of the iPod's value is in the conception and design of the iPod. That is why Apple gets $80 for each of these video iPods it sells, which is by far the largest piece of value added in the entire supply chain.

---

[1] Hal R. Varian, "An iPod Has Global Value. Ask the (Many) Countries That Make It," *New York Times*, June 28, 2007, *http://people.ischool.berkeley.edu/~hal/people/hal/NYTimes/2007-06-28.html*.

Those clever folks at Apple figured out how to combine 451 mostly generic parts into a valuable product. They may not make the iPod, but they created it. In the end, that's what really matters.

Platform Innovation Ecosystem #2: Creative and Media

The iPod is also part of an ecosystem and contributes to the indirect network effects of Apple's other key product: Macintosh computers. Even though iPods, and the iTunes software that supports them, were originally compatible with Macs only, the cachet of the iPod has continued to help sell Macs even after the iPod developed Windows support.

Beyond the iPod and iTunes, Apple's creative and media ecosystem includes software such as iMovie, iDVD, Aperture, Final Cut, GarageBand, and QuickTime (a key technology for the video iPods). These are all Apple products, but many other companies also provide software and hardware for this space, notably Adobe and Quark.

Platform Innovation Ecosystem #3: Accessories

As any visit to the local electronics (or even office supply) store will show, the iPod has inspired a blizzard of accessories. Bose, Monster Cable, Griffin Technologies, Belkin, and a wide variety of technology and audio companies provide iPod-specific devices, from chargers to speakers. Similarly, iPod fashion has brought designers, such as Kate Spade, into the market for iPod cases, along with an army of lesser-known contributors. Also, automobile companies and car audio system makers are adding iPod connectors, simplifying the task of connecting iPods to car stereo systems.

iPod accessories are a $1 billion business. In 2005, Apple sold 32 million iPods, or one every second. And for every $3 spent on an iPod, at least $1 is spent on an accessory, estimates NPD Group analyst Steve Baker. That means customers make three or four additional purchases per iPod.

Accessory makers are happy to sell their products, of course, but this ecosystem also supports retailers, which get a higher profit margin on the accessories than on the iPod (50% rather than 25%). It also reinforces the value of the iPod itself because the 2,000 different add-ons made exclusively for the iPod motivate customers to personalize their iPods. This sends a strong signal that the iPod is "way cooler" than other players offered by Creative and Toshiba, for which there are fewer accessories. The number of accessories is doubling each year, and that's not including the docking stations that are available in a growing number of cars.

Most industry participants were surprised by the strength and growth of the accessory market. Although earlier products such as Disney's Mickey Mouse or Mattel's Barbie supported their own huge market for accessories, those were made by the company that created the original product or by its licensors. Apple has taken a very different path, encouraging a free-for-all; it accepts that its own share of the accessories market is small, knowing that the iPod market is growing.

Platform Innovation Ecosystem #4: User-Provided Metadata

Even before the iTunes music store opened, users who ripped their CDs to digital files in iTunes got more than just the contents of the CD. Most CDs contain only the music data, not information like song titles. Entering titles for a large library of music can be an enormous task, and users shouldn't have to do it for every album.

This problem had been solved earlier by Gracenote, which is best known for its CDDB (CD database) technology. Every album has slightly different track lengths, and the set of lengths on a particular album is almost always unique. So, by combining that identification information with song titles entered by users only when they encountered a previously unknown CD, Gracenote made it much easier for users to digitize their library of CDs.

Rather than reinventing the wheel, Apple simply connected iTunes to CDDB, incorporating the same key feature that made CDDB work in the first place: user input. Whenever a user put in a CD that hadn't previously been cataloged, iTunes would ask that user if he wanted to share the catalog.

Apple has no exclusive rights to CDDB, but it benefits from its existence nonetheless. Users get a much simpler process for moving their library to digital format, and contributing to CDDB requires only a decision, not any extra work.

Recombinant Innovation

The music industry is perhaps the most difficult ecosystem the iPod has to deal with—and the most frequently discussed. The music industry has dealt with the Web and the Internet broadly as a threat rather than an opportunity, as it saw its profits disappearing when the transaction costs of sharing music dropped precipitously. So, how did Steve Jobs get the record labels—which had been suing Napster and Kazaa—to sign up for the iTunes store to offer online, downloaded music?

Apple presented its proposal to the big four music companies— Universal, Sony BMG, EMI, and Warner—as a manageable risk. Apple's control of the iPod gave it the tools it needed to create enough digital rights management (DRM)—limiting music to five computers—to convince the companies that this was a brighter opportunity for them than the completely open MP3 files that users created when they imported music from CDs. Jobs was actually able to leverage Apple's small market share into a promising position:[2]

> Now, remember, it was initially just on the Mac, so one of the arguments that we used was, "If we're completely wrong and you completely screw up the entire music market for Mac owners, the sandbox is small enough that you really won't damage the overall music industry very much." That was one instance where Macintosh's [small] market share helped us.

Apple also played a key role in coordinating the pricing of songs among the big four music companies—99 cents a tune. This was a major step in weaning the music companies away from their high-priced retail distribution of prepackaged bundled digital goods—

---

[2] Steven Levy, "Q&A: Jobs on iPod's Cultural Impact," *Newsweek*, Oct. 16, 2006, *http://www.msnbc.msn.com/id/15262121/site/newsweek/print/1/displaymode/ 1098/*.

CDs—toward a digital distribution channel with a per-user/per-song revenue structure and potentially strong social-network effects. Downloads were also carefully priced to incentivize users who preferred having legal downloads and who trusted Apple and Steve Jobs to keep the price at that level despite the protests of the music labels.

After 18 months of negotiations, Apple was able to get started on its own platform, and later carry the DRM strategy to Windows. (One pleasant side effect for Apple of the DRM deal with the music companies is that it is difficult for Apple to license that DRM technology, preserving Apple's monopoly there.)

Apple provided the music companies with a revenue stream built on an approach that would let them compete with pirated music, although the companies aren't entirely excited about adapting to song-by-song models and the new distribution channels. However, EMI's decision in April 2007 to start selling premium versions of its music without DRM—still through the iTunes store but also through other sellers—suggests that there is more to come in this developing relationship. Ecosystems evolve, and business ecosystems often evolve beyond their creators' vision.

Working with the Carriers: Jajah

On September 15, 2005, the normally reserved *Economist*'s cover proclaimed, "How the internet killed the phone business." The article heralded the end of the world's trillion-dollar telecoms industry as Skype and other VoIP companies promised to make all phone calls free. Once Kazaa's founders had been blocked from p2p file-sharing in the highly copyrighted music digital download arena, they turned that powerful viral distribution engine toward the Internet phone business, and aimed to make it profitable with a freemium strategy of charging business users to support free PC-to-PC calling for everyone else. The *Economist* article stated that "It is now no longer a question of whether VoIP will wipe out traditional telephony, but a question of how quickly it will do so...perhaps only five years away."

Fast forward to a little more than two years later and the picture looks quite different. eBay has written off its acquisition of Skype, and Skype's dynamic cofounders and serial entrepreneurs have moved on to disrupting the business models of yet another profitable industry—the media and video advertising industry—with their startup Joost.

Enter Jajah, a Web 2.0 voice telephony startup that seems to have taken a page out of Apple iTunes strategy playbook. Jajah partners and revenue-shares with local carriers to offer high-quality long-distance everywhere, using existing landline phones or cellphones. Calls between registered Jajah users are free, while long-distance calls to anyone else are at amazingly low local rates. In fact, its new service, Jajah Direct, assigns local numbers to all the long distance phone numbers in your online telephone directory so that you can call your family, friends, and colleagues overseas for almost the same cost as dialing a next door neighbor. Jajah routes long-distance calls over their own "backbone" infrastructure, allowing higher-quality service than the public IP system.

Jajah is breaking new ground in the mobile advertising arena as well. The challenge here goes beyond the usual relevancy and behavioral targeting. Jajah has to shape customer expectations in the emerging mobile, audio, and cross-media advertising areas. It's easy to place Japan Air travel ads with callers who have a high volume of calls between the U.S. and Japan, but what does the ad say and when during the call? This is where the call-back system, described below, turns out to be an advertising opportunity. Phone callers don't mind hearing a short ad while waiting to be connected at a low rate. And follow-up information can be displayed on the user's account page, sent by SMS or opt-in to an email.

The User Experience

The Jajah calling experience is so convenient that 2 million users signed up for Jajah the first year, twice as many as Skype in its first year. There are more than 4 million users now worldwide. No special headset or phone equipment is required, and users are not tied to their computers or laptops. If you're a frequent business traveler, you may have had the somewhat awkward experience of trying to have a Skype PC-to-PC call enroute to your gate while balancing your laptop on your carry-on luggage or a tiny telephone shelf. Like Flickr and other Web 2.0 companies, active, frequent users and independent bloggers created a critical mass and triggered a bandwagon effect. Interestingly enough, doing so little of its own marketing and advertising gave Jajah enormous credibility with users, both in the U.S. and overseas.

Jajah offers free calling between Jajah users. This provides a clear incentive for viral marketing—and encourages new users to bring their whole rolodex of friends on to the system. Soon IM (instant messenger) "buddy lists" will join as well.

Most frequently, a user will visit the company's web site at *http:// www.jajah.com* and schedule a Jajah call online, as shown in Figure 5-6. In a few minutes, or at the scheduled time, the user will receive a phone call on her phone or cell phone. When she picks up, a voice will greet her and inform her that Jajah is connecting her call. The caller should then hear the destination phone start to ring. During this call-ringing wait time, she may hear an ad message. As soon as the party at the other end picks up, the call is connected—for free if the destination phone is a Jajah user; for a minimal local charge if the destination phone is located in any of the 27 countries Jajah serves.

The web page also provides three-way calling, web-conferencing services, and the Jajah Direct feature. Blackberry and mobile phone users with Internet/broadband connections can call long distance and access Jajah phone services directly from their phones. Jajah also offers business services for operations like call centers.

Alliances Make It Work

Rather than promising to turn the telecom world upside down, Jajah worked together with large industry players that had already invested huge amounts in infrastructure, ecosystems, and customer relationships. This nonthreatening *co-opetition* approach avoids the backlash that occurs when entrenched or incumbent interests feel threatened by industry turbulence and disruptive technology.

Like with Apple and the major music labels, Jajah generates a new source of revenue for local carriers, rather than threatening to cut them out of the loop entirely, as Skype threatened to do. Deutsche

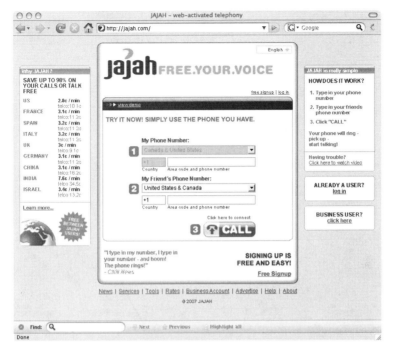

Figure 5-6. *Scheduling a call using Jajah's web interface*

Telekom, the owner of T-Mobile, has even invested capital in Jajah to grow and expand its Voice 2.0 services, along with Intel Capital.

More Recombinant Innovation: The iPhone

Lessons from both the iPod and Jajah fit well with Apple's latest innovation, the iPhone. Apple applied the lessons it had learned from managing the iPod and iTunes ecosystems to the much-heralded June 2007 release of the iPhone, combining its own technology reputation with a partnership in a new field. Cellular provider AT&T Mobility distributed and provided a set of new service features necessary to showcase the phone's unique user experience and touchscreen.

The iPhone itself is technically fascinating, combining updated iPod software with a new touchscreen and software that applies Apple's user interface experience to users who are familiar with the Web and earlier cell phone designs. It offers many features beyond cell phone service, including web browsing and email over wireless networks (avoiding cellular data charges when browsing in places with cheaper service), multimedia viewing and listening, and viewers for typical computer data formats such as Microsoft Word, Microsoft Excel, and PDFs.

When releasing the iPhone, Apple chose to partner with a single cellular carrier, a decision that allowed it to have more control over the iPhone user experience. It generated some controversy as well as many efforts, some successful, to hack the phone so it would work with other providers. Currently, Apple needs to reach 10 million users to achieve a 1% market share in the cellular market; in the first three months after its release, Apple managed to sell one million iPhones—though it took a price cut. AT&T Mobility's 63 million subscribers are a good market in which to achieve this goal, but a small share of possible cell phone users who might want an iPhone.

Of course, if the iPhone becomes usable over broadly-deployed Wi-Fi and WiMAX, a single cellular carrier might become a moot point. In September 2007, Apple released the iPod Touch, giving users the option of getting the iPhone's features minus cellular service. That doesn't do much for the cellular partnership side of this ecosystem story. However, it will certainly widen the reach of the iPod ecosystem—deepening its connections with the Web and with software developers who are willing to work through Apple's web-based mechanism for extending the devices' capabilities.

While AT&T Mobility will be the only U.S. service provider for the iPhone through 2009, Apple plans to announce availability in Canada and Europe in 2007, and in Asia and Australia in 2008. Although the famously secretive Apple hasn't released its plans yet, it's likely that it will work through partnerships again, leveraging the iPhone's prestige to ensure distribution. So far, it has fought hard against efforts in France and Germany to release the phone as an open device, limiting the openness of the device in France to French carriers and winning a court battle in Germany to keep the device locked to T-Mobile.

Given Apple's insistence on control, is the iPhone really a sign of Web 2.0? Perhaps not—Apple doesn't recognize that fighting the Internet is rarely a successful strategy—but at the same time, the iPhone experience demonstrates how a company can leverage its existing experience and brand, connect with allies, and make money while combining an old business (telephones) with a new one (handheld access to the Web).

Lessons Learned

Revolutions may bring success, but not every successful business leads a revolution. Established companies that have built infrastructure, reputations, and customer relationships can also make good alliances. They benefit from the growth that newcomers can create, while the newcomers can enjoy much of what the older firms have to offer.

Apple and Jajah offer softer alternatives than their crusading predecessors. Pioneers Napster and Kazaa had left record executives convinced that digital music was the enemy, while Skype's proclamations of the coming end of established phone networks left the telecom industry wondering what its future might look like. Apple offers the music industry a way to collect on its enormous library of recordings while joining the digital age; Jajah offers telephone companies a share of its revenue while shifting its customers away from regular long-distance service.

Both Jajah and Apple have depended on their users to grow their businesses, though Apple's key hardware component—the iPod and, later, the iPhone—makes its model a little more complicated. Jajah relies on word-of-mouth to spread the message of free phone calls, whereas Apple relies on word of mouth *and* the media to spread the message that the iPod and iPhone are cool and "must haves."

Apple's ecosystems are much more complicated than Jajah's, the result of the iPod's business model, which sprouts new connections to support the iPhone. Nonetheless, all of them rely to some degree on cooperation and take advantage of network effects where possible, or on more typical economies of scale where network effects aren't available.

The iPhone is still brand new, finding its place in a field in which Apple wasn't previously established, but its success or failure promises to illustrate how far this kind of collaborative ecosystem building can go and what impact it can have on an evolving field.

Questions to Ask

Your business may not mine gold, produce shiny iPods and iPhones, or handle telephone calls, but you are likely to have old practices that can grow by connecting to new ones—or new ideas that need to build a foundation on older businesses.

Strategic Questions

- What opportunities do you have for collaborative or recombinant innovation that could create a breakthrough possibility and opportunity?

- Is collaborative innovation relevant to both sides? Is a particular collaboration win-win and positive sum—or is one party contributing/taking away more than the other?

- What shared work or know-how will this collaborative innovation stimulate? What additional kinds of mind set shifts, conversations, and processes will this collaboration and the shared knowledge require among those involved?

- What assumptions or beliefs are embedded in the process of the way this innovation will take place? Will there be issues with NIH (Not Invented Here) or perceived "cannibalism" of existing products and services or channels?

- Is this collaborative innovation likely to generate forward out-of-the-box thinking, or is it likely to increase a focus on past problems and obstacles?

- Does this collaboration leave room for new and different ways to work together, especially with a larger group or ecosystem of partners?

- Consider how your business and industry currently works. To what degree have you opened up to "collaborative innovation," multiplying the ways that users inside and outside of your project, team, or organizational unit can easily leverage, aggregate, and spark collective work, knowledge, and systems?

- If you took the perspective of a CEO and strategic leader, how and when do you see Web 2.0-enabled collaborative innovation disrupting the current practices, business model, competitive advantages, and economics of your business and industry? What's the risk of being a leader or laggard? When should this become a board room agenda item?

- If you took the perspective of a CIO and program manager, how could you better benchmark, analyze, compare, and quantify the impact of shifts in collaborative innovation in key functional areas (e.g., marketing and sales, product and services development, customer support, inventory management, logistics and operations, recruitment and training, partner and supplier relations, and procurement)? How can this provide a new basis for enterprise and financial valuation?

Tactical Questions

- What existing businesses (or business units) are likely to feel threatened by your projects?

- What kind of support would you like for your projects from other businesses?

- Among your competitors, are there any areas where competition is less keenly felt?

- Can you find synergies among the network effects you create and your suppliers?

- Do you have a product or service that could complement an existing web service?

- How do you see your company diversifying or expanding opportunities?

- What are your online–offline opportunities?

- How can you maximize your online opportunities?

- Do you have a product(s) that could be "recombined"?

- How can you streamline processes or distribution?

CHAPTER SIX

Businesses Incorporate Strategies

YOU NOW HAVE ALL THE TOOLS YOU NEED TO APPLY WEB 2.0 STRATEGIC THINKING TO YOUR BUSINESS. The next step is to do it yourself. Reading about Web 2.0 in the previous chapters gives you the background you need to make it work, but getting there will require a lot more than reading. How can you get started?

Five Steps to Web 2.0

Here's a five-step action plan for embedding Web 2.0 business models into your decision-making and convincing others to join you. These actions flow roughly from the earlier chapters, and they are driven by a few key questions about how you can apply the examples to your own situation.

Build on Collective User Value

A key ingredient of many Web 2.0 projects is their ability to collect information from users and then share it in a form that people are willing to pay for. The users themselves, in the course of doing what they want for their own projects, contribute value to the larger system. Creating systems where users want to do this can be difficult, requiring a different kind of analysis then when creating systems that present information to purely consumer users.

Even if you're in the middle of a project or business that's been running for years, it may help to start from a blank slate, a *tabula rasa*, much like zero-based accounting. Take a fresh look at your project, program, or business from the viewpoint of an individual customer. Getting to a user's perspective and then carefully tracking that single user's cash inflows and outflows—as well as the value created, captured, or wasted by an individual user's actions and interactions—is a focusing lens that helps you better appreciate your most valuable, active, and creative contributors. You may want to change your cost structure and model so that you can spot ways to reward your top contributors, incentivize and support collective user value, and monetize this value to make it beneficial for you and your users as quickly as possible.

First, take a look at the cash inflows and outflows of your business from the perspective of a single user. It's important to evaluate your costs and opportunities when working with new users because there may be a few different kinds to consider and multiple sources of revenue—and costs. (If you haven't yet started your business, of course, you have an opportunity to plan how you'd like these flows to work.) It's important to understand the basic value and cost of your users.

Flickr had six key areas in which collective user value was important. You'll need to evaluate your own project to find the areas where collective user value can help you. Are there ways to maximize the creation of value by changing the relationships or interactions between your online users or even your offline partners? How could the creation of a community or ecosystem affect your business, revenue streams, revenue-sharing, or cost structure? Could collaboration; sharing; and shifts in frequency, loyalty, or multiple revenue streams be a sustainable competitive edge, measurable in individual customer profitability and lifetime value, and aggregated into a customer-facing total enterprise value?

Flickr gave its users instant gratification with easy-access digital photo storage and management, using its huge library of public photos to build a new kind of community. Depending on the nature of your project and business, centering your work on that kind of customer data may not work, but there may still be many ways for you to expand the information that users share with each other.

Experiment with making small changes immediately, and, if they work, see whether you can make them a default condition so that your system and business model are continuously and automatically increasing your system and user value.

Activate Network Effects

Network effects are the heart of Web 2.0, underlying all of the strategies presented here. Network effects come in a variety of flavors, however, and applying them well means seeking out and enabling their power.

The first step is to figure out what your offline and online network effects are and how you can measure their value. Where are all the likely and unlikely places and groups that could generate positive network effects—direct, indirect, demand-side, cross-network, and social? Can you identify and track the ones you leverage and capture more effectively than your competitors? (Can you identify possible effects that you haven't started to capture?)

Once you've inventoried the possibilities, it's time to examine how to combine them. How can you multiply and compound your online network effects, creating increasing returns, using powerful dynamic pricing demand-side effects, and developing n-sided cross-network effects? Free or highly subsidized services are often a key for such multiplication.

The more systematically you examine the influence of network effects on your project or business, the more opportunities you will find for creating and capturing both online and offline network effects. Because positive network effects grow exponentially, combining more than one type leads to multiplicative outcomes, not just simple incremental value-added.

Google's search-engine story demonstrated the hair-raising twists and turns in a highly fluid, complex, and time-sensitive competitive race. In the early race between Google and Overture/GoTo and Excite, having the right combination of network-effects strategies and monetization meant that Google could overcome its competitors' early lead.

However, in the Google advertising platform, the network effects helped many more players than Google. There have been a multitude of unexpected winners—all the small- and medium-size businesses, first-time advertisers, and online storefronts as well as bloggers—that became part of the fast-growing online advertising business because of its stellar returns with pay-per-click direct advertising. It isn't a zero-sum game: positive network effects can grow the entire pie and even proliferate thousands of little pies and tartlets. This makes it possible to redistribute the exponentially increaseing value more broadly throughout the Google ecosystem, resulting in a win-win-win-win....

You also need to consider how important network effects are in your efforts to grow your market share and the returns on that expansion. Are you in a close competitive race with a tippy market? Are there early- or late-mover advantages? How much should you be willing to pay for the dominant bandwagon and market share position in a tippy market? Who owns the swing votes in your industry?

Markets with strong network effects also tend to be "winner-take-all" or "winner-take-most." Even leading companies can be vulnerable to a swing vote of six or seven market-share points. It may seem like the tail wagging the dog, but AOL played a decisive role in the early race between Google and Overture, as well as in the tippy race between Google, Yahoo!, and Microsoft. It's important to accurately track, assess, and influence the impact and potential role of all players and complementors in close competitive races.

Your company may not resemble Google, but there are lots of tippy markets out there, and you want your business prepared to seize the day—and the market.

Work Through Social Networks

While you may think of social networking as a particular kind of Web 2.0 application, social networks permeate and enrich Web 2.0 projects even when they aren't the central focus. Social networks are a natural conduit for network effects and a key field for community-building that can strengthen your project's appeal. In addition to being a business of their own, social networks can help you reach a much larger audience and build stronger ties within your project's user community.

Have you mapped out the online social network structure of your target market? How do you currently identify, help activate, and reward the online connectors, mavens, and salesmen in your system? How about the most active 1 to 3% of uploaders?

Can you systematically identify ways to increase the viral, interactive, or social influence/referral factors of your business, especially during the critical-mass stage of the marketing bell curve? How can you trigger socially influenced viral distribution as well as classic viral marketing and buzz?

Note that answering these questions doesn't mean you need to build social networking software. You don't need to know the details of a social network's structure to make use of it. One extra line at the end of each Hotmail—"Get your private, free email at *http://www.hotmail.com*"—was the source of its phenomenal success through viral marketing. Infections and innovations with a higher spreading rate reach a larger population more quickly. Hotmail reminds us that free services have a high spreading rate because they reduce the perceived financial and social risks of adoption and the distribution costs to zero.

Social networking software can certainly highlight key issues for your projects. LinkedIn demonstrates how online social networks follow the principles predicated by network power laws and social-marketing bell curves, as they relate to critical mass and the 1 to 3% of users who are active contributors. Unlike the well-established 80/20 Pareto Principle where 80% of results comes from 20% of people, networks like the Web follow an even more extreme power law where 1 to 3% of users can form a critical mass triggering exponential growth.

We see this when a small number of web sites like Yahoo!, MySpace, YouTube, Wikipedia, and Digg generate significant traffic and viral buzz. Only about 1% of the 7.4 million users of Wikipedia add new content or make changes, with 1.8% of that 1% writing about 72% of the articles. According to Bradley Horowitz, Yahoo! vice president and blogger, 1% of the users start a group or thread; 10% interact with the content, remixing and synthesizing it; and 9.2 million Yahoo! group visitors benefit from these creators and synthesizers.

You might have been surprised to learn that 90% of LinkedIn members are first-degree relationship builders and 5% are networkers, with the final 5% being infrequent but highly intense-use contactors—salespeople, recruiters, and one-time hiring managers. But that is why it's smart to map and analyze your underlying online social network structure in as much detail as LinkedIn did. You too can act on this social network knowledge to develop the social networking aspects of your Web 2.0 business model and better customize your free, basic, and premium features, and incentive pricing to the right target groups in your n-sided market space. Like LinkedIn, you should also ask whether it would be in your interest to vary the services, products, and features you offer to different sides of the two-sided market.

You should also contemplate Facebook's twist on viral marketing: socially influenced viral distribution. It opened up hypergrowth in the college-age population to a whole new ecosystem of active users, contributors, and developers—not only from startups but from other Web 2.0-savvy marketers, such as Amazon, eBay, and Apple. No doubt, several of your current businesses or services could benefit from this kind of accelerated growth, traffic, and visibility.

Dynamically Syndicate Competence

Firms build their businesses on competences. Success depends on a business doing better than its competition. Can it produce something unique, something faster, something better, something cheaper? Web 2.0 may change the way you look at these competences, helping you find new ones (offered by other businesses) and letting you share your existing ones.

First, evaluate your strengths and weaknesses. Do you have shareable competences that are strong enough to sell? Do you have or can you build the organizational capability to dynamically mix and match internally and externally sourced competences and resources? Does your firm value dynamic capabilities—flexibly creating, connecting, and discarding competences as needed?

Web 2.0 competence syndication is a new kind of digital open remixing. Mashups and viral distribution of previously hoarded company secret recipes can turn competitors, ecosystem partners, and a broad range of small- and medium-size enterprises into your loyal, revenue-generating, revenue-sharing users, while increasing your economies of scale and global scope. Are you flexible enough to play the competence syndication game—adjusting to different competence syndication roles while figuring out the rules you need to optimize value creation and capture?

Online content syndication is a viral engine for the blogosphere. RSS feeds, hyperlinks, and ubiquitous news aggregators—such as MyYahoo! and Google—enable web syndication to accelerate the transfer of previously inaccessible personal and tacit knowledge and competences into publicly shared, extensively archived, and searchable web documents, images, podcasts, and video.

IBM, Amazon, and Google moved beyond content feeds to more sophisticated techniques for building dynamic capabilities and capturing value from syndicating competences and services. Each demonstrates a different path, one or more of which might fit your needs.

One option might be going global with your successful local business. IBM has applied Web 2.0 strategies of open systems, community-generated software development, and virtual mentoring to catalyze local network effects in software applications and web services that can be marketed and proliferated worldwide.

Alternately, you could syndicate your back-office skills like Amazon did and become a master at multiple service syndication roles. Syndicate and digitize multiple services and competences— not only customer-facing applications but a range of back-office, logistics, and supply-chain capabilities that were previously out of reach for small- and medium-size businesses.

Google's open APIs have spawned a wide range of consumer and company competence mashups. You'll probably want to evaluate the pros and cons of opening up your own APIs to third-party developers, as well as outsourced development services for non-tech and primarily offline partners in the mashup ecosystem.

Recombine Innovations

Web 2.0 promises great change, but not necessarily the kind of creative destruction that the prophets of the original dot-com boom had expected. Web 2.0 changes the rules of business, but it isn't a simple disintermediation play aimed at replacing earlier businesses with web-based businesses. New-style click-and-mortar, online-offline network partnerships focus on bridging and building new networks rather than replacing or disrupting the infrastructures of offline companies. There's plenty of opportunity for connecting innovations in both the online and the offline business worlds, and potential competitors are also potential partners.

There are many opportunities for Web 2.0-style online-offline cooperation besides competition in your relationships with customers, suppliers, competitors, and complementors. Who stands to gain if you bridge rather than disrupt the current cast of players in the industry? Who stands to lose? How can Web 2.0 redefine and transform the scope of business model innovation and collaboration in your industry, and across industries and geographies?

Recombinant innovation is a key component of emerging Web 2.0 businesses. Jajah's VoIP alliances with major global telecom carriers like Deutsche Telekom (the owner of T-Mobile) take a revenue-sharing approach to create an online-offline, win-win alliance and ecosystem. Apple's turnaround of the online music industry with the iPod and iTunes is very different from—and more successful than—the Napster and Kazaa approach. And Apple's latest major push, the iPhone, builds on its success with the music industry to partner with yet another industry, cellular phone service.

You may not be selling a product like the iPhone, but you should consider ways to integrate partners in your business. Web 2.0 technology makes building these connections easier, and you and your partners can benefit mutually from the network effects you create.

Building Web 2.0 Business Plans

Web 2.0 belongs in your business plan if you're an entrepreneur, in your portfolio if you're an investor or venture capitalist, and in your group's business case if you're in a large company or division. Web 2.0 changes the underlying dynamics that business plan creators and readers may expect, and a great Web 2.0 business plan has a realistic chance of reducing the risks to starting a profitable business. So, where does Web 2.0 show up in the business plan?

Let's start with a Table of Contents in a boilerplate business plan that has the following sections:

Executive Summary

I. Background, Business Concept, Objectives, and Funding Requirements

II. Market Analysis

III. Competitive Analysis

IV. Products and Services

V. Time Line and Milestones

VI. Management and Executive Team

VII. Governance, Ownership, and Control

VIII. Financials

The Executive Summary and Section I summarize what's in the rest of the plan. Web 2.0 ideas don't necessarily have to fit into all of these sections (notably section VII), but they apply in many other parts of the business plan.

Despite the immense amount of effort focused on business plans, most entrepreneurship professors and venture investors would agree that it's still hard to find a great business plan. Why? Because too little time is spent on the information that is most important to savvy investors. The numbers need to reflect a business model and cash flow analysis that show the team's deep and accurate understanding and experience with the drivers and risks of the venture or project's success or failure.

Is it different inside big companies? Are the acid tests for ventures and projects funded inside a company or corporation more systematic or disciplined than in the private funding arena? Not really, although the process is more politicized. The research seems to indicate that it's hard to find a great business plan inside or outside companies.

Market Analysis

Market analysis is all about *opportunity*—or as Steve Jurvetson, a well-known venture capitalist, once put it, "How high is up?" Choosing a large market space that was growing and structurally attractive to new entrants used to be a given. Of course, online marketing and the rapidly growing penetration of broadband, mobile, and digital devices have made consumer niches and long-tail markets more reachable.

The key questions still remain, though:

- What will it cost to reach the market?
- What is the likely customer response to a new product or service?
- How long will it take customers to try, adopt, and maybe influence others to do the same?

It's usually difficult to guess the market response—how much people will pay for something, and how quickly word will spread about a great product or service. But Web 2.0 business models shine at coming up with that information. You can often replace market analysis with real-time experimentation, do-it-yourself trials, and detailed web analytics. Just as Flickr or Craigslist or Digg did, you can throw something out there to see what works at a relatively low cost while you keep fine-tuning the parts that don't work. Real market data and performance metrics beat overly optimistic and wildly imaginative predictions any day.

On the key revenue and pricing question of how much people are willing to pay, Web 2.0 business models again offer a significant and somewhat hidden advantage over other approaches. For most offline products, especially consumer goods, there are well-recognized price points, and it is difficult to offer different prices to different customers. For a while, there was the $100 consumer electronics price point and the belief that consumer demand would explode only when you could get your DVD player, color printer, or new and improved technology gadget under that price point.

In Google's case, it was able to support dynamic pricing and what economists call "perfect price discrimination." In simpler terms, advertisers are charged almost exactly what they are willing to pay, and every keyword and keyword phrase has its price connected to its pay-per-click. Talk about the fundamentals of differential pricing—personalized pricing, versioning, and group pricing are all available instantaneously, dynamically, and on a one-to-one customer and per-click basis. Even in the relatively more static online subscription Web 2.0 businesses, personalized and individualized pricing, different versions of the service or product offering, as well as group and n-sided market pricing are a snap to implement and even to adjust on the fly.

In some cases, the very low cost of entry and capital investment in getting started with a Web 2.0 business might make pricing a decision to be reviewed and analyzed only after building up a critical mass of 1 to 3% active participants, viral growth, and a sustainable social network structure that has ongoing network effects value. Particularly in cases where there are strong network effects, a competitive race, and a two-sided market, building a critical mass of free customers might be valuable. Doing so will multiply cross-network and indirect effects, and trigger widespread social influence and bandwagon effects, as well as active and passive clickstream contributions to the collective user value of the business.

Web 2.0 business models bring a lot of marketing benefits not only to the entrepreneur team but to the investors. Each of the areas discussed above could either add to or reduce the risk and unpredictability of a new venture. A Web 2.0 business plan marketing section is more likely to be able to show real customers and have a web-analytics data-driven visualization of what works and what doesn't with a target market. Not surprisingly, this is a quantum leap ahead of the highly creative predictions often seen in business plans.

Competitive Analysis

The market analysis is important, but there's more going on in the world than just this one plan. Timing is critical in competitive race situations. The plan needs to answer questions such as the following:

- How long will it take users to try and adopt this new service or product and to influence others to do the same?
- What about expansion and multiple revenue streams?
- Which matters more—the number of users or the number of units?

These questions lead to a fundamental but nonetheless often difficult question:

- What is the business model?

This is the meat of the case, the place where it is critical to articulate explicitly that Web 2.0 business models are a different way of thinking about the business and the unit economics. For example, most products and services in the offline world will look at per-unit or per-labor/service hour economics, while most localized or geographically constrained products and services will look at the per-local-market economics. By contrast, the Web 2.0 online business models we looked at all had per-user and usage economics—Netflix had per-individual-subscriber economics; Google had per-unique visitor, per-query, and per-click economics. This kind of user-focused economics is crucial to capturing value in digital and online marketplaces. The increased traffic and the number of users exponentially increases the network value of the system while the costs of digitally available service and distribution remain zero after the fixed, one-time initial upfront cost of development.

If a project can already show hypergrowth comparative numbers and an innovative viral growth and distribution strategy, it probably doesn't need funding to break even and be profitable, so it's likely that venture capitalists will be lining up at the door.

Also, if the key drivers of Web 2.0 business models are fundamentally collaborative, you should consider adding a robust section on collaborative analysis to complement the section on competitive analysis. It could include detailed descriptions of how your business model creates, captures, and redistributes value from many of the following sources and linkages:

- Collective user value arising from valuable uploaded contributions
- Peer-to-peer interaction within open content and sharing communities

- Network effects arising from social networks
- Ecosystems that create indirect network effects generating complementary and third-party business-to-business partnerships and relationships

Understanding the competition is still important, but Web 2.0 adds emphasis on finding win-win collaborations.

Products and Services

Web 2.0 products and services may be digital, but they still need to be carefully defined, and they present challenges for standard analysis. User-generated content is especially difficult to forecast effectively, and first you'll need to figure out how to integrate it into the fundamentals of your business plan:

- How do you think about products and services—as cost-based or customer/user-based?
- How do you incorporate user contributions into the system?

There are also some questions you should consider early, rather than leave them to a possible breaking point at which you risk alienating your customers or damaging your business:

- How will user-generated content be licensed and distributed?
- What return, benefits (discounts), or revenue-sharing will users be given?
- How will long-tail communities and offerings be sustained so that there is no concern about "misappropriation" or abandonment?

These questions may be unfamiliar territory for businesses that are used to creating and directly owning what they sell, but they're essential for businesses that rely on their users to create content for them. Users need to trust a business before they are willing to donate their energies to it. The need for trust may vary depending on how much users feel they're giving away, but it's best to be prepared for these kinds of questions from users and investors.

Time Line and Milestones

Thanks to collective user contributions and the importance of open and third-party ecosystems, this section should look quite different from the typical employee and man-hour chart. There are a few key factors that may not be easily estimated:

- How much content users will generate, and how quickly
- How strongly possible collaborators will respond to opportunities
- How rapidly the application underlying the business will need to change

There will still be a business rollout, but many times Web 2.0 projects don't even start with a 1.0 release. Companies like Flickr and Google have done very well with open betas, letting thousands or millions of users work with software that's changing constantly, perhaps even hourly. The iterative nature of Web 2.0 projects gives them incredible flexibility but makes it difficult to create long-term predictions about what the time line and milestones will look like.

Management and Executive Team

Many venture capitalists and experienced investors will say that they "read the résumés first" when deciding whether to look more closely at a business plan or to toss it. Not surprisingly, they pay a lot of attention to what the team knows (relevant experience), who they know (relevant relationships and social networks, from customers to suppliers to partners to talent), and whether they are known (track record for execution and dealing with unexpected challenges).

Arthur Rock, a legendary venture capitalist who funded Apple, Intel, and others, stated, "I invest in people, not ideas." But what distinguishes a Web 2.0 entrepreneur? Maybe it's a style or an approach. In Web 2.0 businesses, the winning formula for a founding team seems to be quite different from what it was during the dot-com era. Collaborative skills such as listening, peer inter-action, and speedy responsiveness and innovativeness—all dynamic capabilities for orchestrating and catalyzing large online connected and interactive groups—are emerging as higher priorities than the shoot-from-the-hip, take-no-prisoners style that earlier high-tech entrepreneurs were known for.

Financials

In the end, it (almost) always comes down to the financials. So, in short, the challenge is to show that the financials, forecast, and time line are driven by some distinctive Web 2.0 economics, including:

Per-user economics

The basic math of customer acquisition and return is still important. Lifetime value of a customer can be estimated by looking at the acquisition cost (amount spent in marketing over the number of members acquired) and the lifetime margin (average tenure and margin).

Community value

The value of a community gives Web 2.0 plans much more power than their predecessors, thanks to the many benefits provided as users form communities. A sense of community, i.e., "It's where I talk with my friends," keeps users at a site and encourages them to invite more friends. The power of collaboration makes it more likely that a group of users will produce polished results that will attract new users. A large number of users in a community makes it possible to set up markets within that community, as Google's AdWords does. The different kinds of interactions among users may also produce additional value that can potentially be captured, as is probably most obvious in the social network cases discussed in Chapter 3.

Ecosystem value

The users, their community, and the business exist within a much larger world of related businesses and communities. Are there synergies that can help the community and the ecosystem? Looking around at related projects can sometimes reveal partners who can help with promotions, products, services, revenue sharing, or even investment.

One final point is worth remembering: many Web 2.0 projects can be low-investment projects with a large potential upside. Although Google, for example, took a big risk in developing and releasing Google Maps—because it depended on existing (and expensive) map data—many Web 2.0 projects can start with an idea and a site, and grow from there. If your plan shows good reason to spend a lot of money upfront, and if you can get that investment, it may be worthwhile, but don't start off thinking that your next web venture has to cost a fortune at the outset.

Look Around While Moving Forward

At this point, it should be pretty clear that Web 2.0 offers new opportunities to businesses that are willing to break the mold of conventional approaches. As you're developing your business plan or examining your strategy, you should consider these three key takeaways:

Online network effects are a powerful multiplying force

Network effects explain the rapid emergence, victories in close competitive races, and dominance of major players like Google and Facebook. They can also create opportunities for smaller projects, initially helping them reach the niches they serve and then supporting their rapid growth.

A few active uploaders can create online critical mass and community

Online platforms are a convenient shortcut for reaching the passionate, authentic, and interactive users—1 to 3% of the total—who can catalyze a social network and community, generating collective user value and raising average lifetime values exponentially. It's possible to do a lot with a little in Web 2.0.

Viral distribution and cooperative advantage can build ecosystems rapidly

The Web provides a mechanism for letting users spread the word about their new projects, as well as for syndicating the competences they already have and recombining innovations.

The Web is much more than an information distribution network—it's a place where users can talk about the new kinds of businesses that are relatively easy to assemble in this hugely productive virtual space.

Thinking about these components will help you move your business forward and focus on how to make your projects take off, without getting trapped in the "powerful anti-meeting spell" of endless contemplation about whether something is Web 1.0 or Web 2.0. The network effects and audiences are out there waiting, and they are not particularly concerned with how you categorize your project.

As you integrate these principles into your projects, you should also keep an eye out to see what other businesses are doing, and not just Web 2.0 companies like Flickr, Twitter, or even Google. Amazon, a classic dot-com pioneer, integrates Web 2.0 approaches into every page of its bookselling site and tests new possibilities constantly. Exploring Amazon, perhaps together with fellow members of your team, can be a good way to look for ideas that might work well for you. As Web 2.0 ideas spread, they adapt to new circumstances and situations to create more opportunities. They may not always be your opportunities, but this new field is churning out innovations as well as potential partners.

It's also important to remember that you don't have to use every feature covered in this book to create a successful Web 2.0 business. The low cost and high connectivity of the Web mean that you can experiment easily, building a starter application to find an initial audience, and then continue to build in the directions that you find (perhaps with the help of your user base) to accelerate growth. You may not be able to predict exactly what users want until they're interested in what you have, and once you provide it, they'll help promote your work, contribute to your project's value, and help you find the next big opportunity.

So why not get powered up? You're only a click away....

End Notes

THESE NOTES ARE SUPPLEMENTAL INFORMATION FOR THE CHAPTERS TO WHICH THEY BELONG. They are listed in the order the chapters follow, but aren't necessarily bound to specific sections.

Chapter 1

Prosumers and the Third Wave

Offline do-it-yourselfers are well known. One of my executive M.B.A. class members asked me whether online DIY uploaders were related to the prosumers talked about in Alvin Toffler's *Third Wave*. In the strategy field, W. Chan Kim and Renée Mauborgne (both of the business school INSEAD) have written the *Harvard Business Review* (*HBR*) article "Value Innovation: The Strategic Logic of High Growth," in which they discuss the customer becoming an integral part of the value chain, not just the receiver of an end product or service. Their *HBR* article discusses the impact on competitive strategy in a range of offline, consumer-focused businesses, from hospitality, to movie theaters, to retail furniture stores. These new user-producers, as in the case of IKEA, are willing to become coproducers and home-based constructors of home furnishings, contributing their valuable time and effort in return for company-offered service and brand features such as personalization, style, immediacy, and convenience.

Online DIY and the experience economy

B. Joseph Pine and James Gilmore's book *The Experience Economy: Work Is Theater & Every Business a Stage* (Harvard Business School Press), was an early prediction of a major shift in society and business markets toward active participation—experiencing, doing, seeing for yourself, and personalizing. Max Lenderman's book, *Experience the Message: How Experiential Marketing Is Changing the Brand World* (Carroll & Graf) looks at the implications of this social shift within marketing.

Uploaders

Kevin Kelly, author of the prescient *Out of Control* (Addison-Wesley) and the classic *New Rules for the New Economy* (Penguin), wrote a must-read article in *Wired* for the 10th anniversary of the Web, dating the Web from Netscape's IPO in 1995. In the article, "We are the Web" from *Wired* 13.08, he noted that we had reached a "crossover point" in 2005 at which there was more digital content being uploaded to the Web than downloaded. That implied that active uploaders—givers, creators, and contributors—were finally taking over from passive downloaders—takers, readers, and viewers.

Collective user value

In his book the *Wealth of Networks: How Social Production Transforms Markets and Freedom* (Yale University Press), Yochai Benkler, a Yale law professor, explores the social and economic implications of a "gift" economy, in which intangible and tangible monetary rewards influence our behavior. In a very similar vein, Steven Weber, professor of political science at U.C. Berkeley, examines the complex social, political, and economic interactions underlying open source communities in his book, *The Success of Open Source* (Harvard University Press).

With a very different framework and approach, Rick Levine et al.'s *The ClueTrain Manifesto: The End of Business as Usual* (Perseus) and Eric Raymond's *The Cathedral and the Bazaar: Musings on Linux and Open Source by an Accidental Revolutionary* (O'Reilly)—books that were themselves products of collaboration and interactive feedback online—argue that markets are not company-controlled seats, eyeballs, end users, or consumers—but human beings, individuals, equals with a voice, all conversing and interacting. And by doing so, they irreversibly scramble and remix the number and power of linkages away from the typical company-to-customer, buyer-seller business transaction and one-way communication.

Freemiums

The conversation that created the word "freemium" took place on venture capitalist Fred Wilson's blog (*http://avc.blogs.com/ a_vc/2006/03/my_favorite_bus.html*). Katherine Heires also wrote on related subjects in "Why It Pays to Give Away the Store," in the November 2006 issue of *Business 2.0* (*http:// money.cnn.com/magazines/business2/business2_archive/2006/ 10/01/8387115/index.htm*).

Public and open sharing of online digital content, trust, and communities of practice

Larry Lessig's framework presented in *The Future of Ideas: The Fate of the Commons in a Connected World* (Vintage) explains how the explosion of innovation on the Web relies on it being an open forum for ideas, and a community and ecosystem of knowledge creators, thinkers, and combiners. This is the basis for the movement behind Creative Commons.

The Semantic Web and metadata

Tim Berners-Lee in his book *Weaving the Web* (HarperCollins) writes about the Semantic Web as one of the paths toward "scaling intuition" (or allowing group intuition) because individual readers notice relevant relationships and create a shortcut link to record it so that creativity, feedback, and knowledge about any problem or idea can occur across larger and more diverse groups and be stored across time. Metadata, like hyperlinks, are a kind of human-added information shortcut, indexing, or annotation that allows information links and knowledge synapses to be integrated and multiplied.

Digital photo ecosystem and flickrized ecosystem

The linear value chain is compared to the value constellation or the more transient online value clickstream talked about by Nick Carr, former *Harvard Business Review* editor, in his blog (*http://www.roughtype.com/*). Of course, open APIs have a key role in supporting this system and will be discussed in later chapters.

Flickr's founders

Josh Quittner wrote "The Flickr Founders" for *TIME* (*http:// www.time.com/time/magazine/article/0,9171,1186931,00.html*).

Contexts for interaction

See John Musser's book *Web 2.0 Principles and Best Practices* (O'Reilly), page 72 and surrounding.

Business model analysis for the entrepreneur

After using several different textbooks and articles for teaching my M.B.A. classes in entrepreneurship and venture capitalism, I can highly recommend Richard Hamermesh's "Note on Business Model Analysis for the Entrepreneur" (Harvard Business School). It is the only business model framework that seems to work equally well in conveying the basics of how to analyze offline versus online as well as hybrid business models. It does a stellar job of focusing attention on the cash flow curve and individual customer profitability analysis rather than trying to generate a product-based balance sheet and pro forma. The two illustrative but brief cases he uses—the Grateful Dead and 7-Eleven in Japan—are always favorites.

Burn rate and J-curve cash flow analysis

As Figure 1-8 shows, the burn rate is the negative slope of the curve and the rate that investment dollars are flowing out or being "consumed" by the entrepreneurial bonfire per unit time. In my teaching, I tend to call the cash flow curve a J-curve—not only because of its distinctive shape, but also in honor of the well-known venture capitalist Steve Jurvetson's J-curve blog. Several of his classic venture capital investment insights are captured in the *HBR* article "Bringing Silicon

Valley Inside," in which he argues for the strategic borrowing of venture-capital-style thinking for managers in large corporations and multinationals.

Netflix financials and new customer acquisition cost

The HBS case *Netflix.com* is a gem because it was written for M.B.A.-level finance and accounting courses to illustrate how to calculate individual subscriber cash flow curves over time as well as customer retention (usually in percent of total retained at one month, three months, six months, and yearly) so that these calculations can be used to generate aggregated (over total subscriber/customer numbers) and discounted cash flows to come up with average customer lifetime values. I present only a simplified and nondiscounted calculation to show that the new customer acquisition cost can be estimated as the cost of 3 DVDs and shipping or $3 \times 20 = \$60$ of DVDs + $3 of shipping, but free customers bring in only $20/month if they stay past the first free month. The HBS case presents enough quantitative data and market information to calculate or perform *sensitivity analyses* for three or four strategic scenarios—dropping the free-month trial, raising the subscription fee, lowering the number of free DVDs from four to three to two, etc.

Single customer/subscriber cash flow analysis

Per user revenue, average lifetime value, customer profitability analysis, and brand equity are metrics used in individual subscriber economics and can be easily translated for use in online user economic analysis and profit and loss (P&L) business plan financials. See HBS notes *Customer Profitability and Lifetime Value* and *Subscriber Models* (Elie Ofek). The key importance of loyalty or customer retention in online customer-focused businesses is discussed in the *HBR* article, "E-Loyalty: Your Secret Weapon on the Web" (Frederick F. Reichheld and Phil Schefter). The *HBR* article "Diamonds in the Data Mine" (Gary W. Loveman) provides a compelling real-world example of how HBS professor-turned-CEO of Harrah's used individual customer analytics for both profitability and competitive advantage.

S-curve, new technology adoption, and crossing the chasm

S-curves and technology diffusion follow a similar path and have a similar shape as infectious or viral disease epidemics. New technology adoption is explained in Everett Rogers' classic work, *Diffusion of Innovation* (The Free Press), in which he first introduces the concept of different groups of the population having distinctive behaviors and attitudes toward technology—early adopters, mainstream users, laggards. A good summary is available in the HBS note *Note on Innovation Diffusion: Rogers' Five Factors* (John T. Gourville). But the original book is well worth reading in its entirety.

In his bestseller on high-tech marketing, *Crossing the Chasm* (HarperBusiness), Geoffrey Moore introduces the strategic concept of the "chasm." This gap in usage and expectations between early technology adopters and mainstream users turns out to be the downfall for many high-tech companies that look quite promising in their early stages but fail to "cross the chasm" to build and sustain a mainstream market.

There is much more on this subject in Chapter 3.

Company financial valuation methodologies

See William A. Sahlman's HBS note *Venture Capital Valuation Problem Set*; also see Michael Mauboussin's Legg Mason Analyst Report "Valuing Customer-Focused Businesses," available at *http://www.lmcm.com/search/default.aspx?qt=exhibit.*

Entrepreneur/founder's net worth at exit

Again, see William H. Sahlman's HBS note *Venture Capital Valuation Problem Set*, specifically the section on dilution and IPO value. There's clearly a significant structural shift in the venture investing and private equity environment due to large Internet players like Google and eBay snatching up YouTube and Skype at IPO-level public market valuations. The shift is also evidenced by Microsoft ratcheting up the value of Facebook, buying minority stakes at levels that would put the total market capitalization of Facebook at a lofty $15 billion (similar to an Intel or Oracle). This section doesn't include any inside information on the actual net worth of these different founders, but it does provide a perspective on the relative difficulty of IPO as an exit for online companies after the dot-com boom compared to the frothy and active acquisition market available for Web 2.0 companies.

The following HBS notes show how venture capitalists value their portfolio companies and the process of dilution through different stages of investment funding: *How Venture Capital Works* (Bob Zider); *The Process of "Going Public" in the United States* (Gregory Miller); *Introduction to Valuation Multiples* (Robin Greenwood and Lucy White); *A Method for Valuing High-Risk, Long-Term Investments: The Venture Capital Method* (William A. Sahlman and Daniel R. Scherlis); and *The Basic Venture Capital Formula* (William A. Sahlman and R. Matthew Willis). I haven't used the HBS note *Funding New Ventures: Valuation, Financing and Capitalization Tables* (Michael J. Roberts), but it sounds like it might actually provide a set of cap tables to use, so you don't have to calculate them out.

Funding requirements of Web 1.0 versus Web 2.0

For some background on venture financing, take a look at the James McNeill Stancill *HBR* article "How Much Money Does Your New Venture Need?"

Also see John Heilemann's article "Retooling the Entrepreneur," *Business 2.0*, November 1, 2005 (*http://money.cnn.com/ magazines/business2/business2_archive/2005/11/01/8362816/ index.htm*), for an interesting interview with Joe Kraus, cofounder of Excite (Web 1.0) and JotSpot (Web 2.0).

Chapter 2

Negative network effects and traffic congestion

As noted in the Wikipedia entry for network effects, after a certain point, most networks become either congested or saturated, preventing future uptake. Congestion occurs due to overuse. Another applicable analogy would be that of a telephone network. While the number of users is below the congestion point, each additional user adds more value to every other customer. However, at some point, the addition of an extra user (n+1 if n is the number of users) exceeds the capacity of the existing system. After that point, each additional user decreases the value obtained by every other user. In practical terms, each additional user increases the total system load, leading to busy signals, the inability to get a dial tone, and poor customer support. The n+1 person begins to decrease the value of a network if additional resources are not provided.

Congestion point and total market size

In the online Web 2.0 world, hypergrowth and scalability in the number of users and usage has a much higher limit because the congestion point may be larger than the total market size. Skype is an example of a peer-to-peer network that distributes its load among the user pool, allowing each user to add traffic capacity and routing management to the system. See the HBS case *Skype, Inc.* for background reading.

Network effects and network externalities

In economics, an externality is an impact (positive or negative) on anyone not party to a given economic transaction. Negative externalities include tragedy of the commons and secondhand smoke. Positive externalities include education and technology spillover. The key difference in the economic literature between network effects and network externalities is whether the value or impact of an additional user on other network users is internalized or captured. Another aspect of economic concern is how network effects value is internalized. Is the capture of the benefits or the distribution of multiplied network value private (by the provider of the network platform), public (available to the users of the network), individual (distributed or monetized by individual users), or social (actively distributed in the aggregate as in a community of practice)?

Internalizing externalities and the knowledge economy

This is why Web 2.0, with its strong network effects and interactivity, could accelerate the growth of a global knowledge economy and stimulate the online communities necessary to practice-based fields like education and increasingly interdisciplinary scientific domains like nanotechnology and biotechnology. Dominique Foray's comprehensive book *The Economics of Knowledge* (The MIT Press) points out that Ronald Coase, Nobel Prize winner in Economics and author of *The Firm, The Market, and the Law* (University of Chicago Press), also predicted that large-scale value capture of knowledge spillovers, information externalities, and consumer surplus would occur if the costs of collaboration—especially transaction costs between consortiums of firms—could be reduced.

Network value creation

Robert Metcalfe, the founder of Ethernet, used the term network effect to argue that a certain critical mass of Ethernet card customers was necessary for the network to create value—the cost of n nodes or users is proportional to the number of networking cards/units installed, but the value of the network is arguably proportionate to the number of 1–1 linkages that have been enabled in the network of n nodes, that is, $n \times (n-1)$ or approximately n squared. This algebraic relationship between the number of nodes and the number of two-party linkages is behind the notion that network value increases exponentially by a power of 2, rather than only incrementally or via a value-added process in physical goods markets. So, if the cost of a network card was $1, and the value of each network link was $1, a 10 member network would be worth $100 to each of the network members who had paid $1 to join; and a 100 member network would be worth $1,000 to each of the network members.

Bill Gross, founder of GoTo/Overture quotations

The story of GoTo/Overture and the comments of Bill Gross, its innovative founder, are detailed in John Battelle's fascinating and comprehensive book *The Search*. This chapter reinterprets the events of the competitive race between GoTo and Google with a network effects and two-sided market framework. In contrast, Bill Gross refers to his paid keyword strategy as an "arbitrage" strategy, the practice of taking advantage of a price differential between two or more markets and profiting from the difference in market prices or currencies. Without going into a great deal of theoretical detail, these are two very different explanatory models of why it might be worth 5 cents for a search engine to acquire a new search user to get advertisers to pay 1 cent or more for that search user's pay-per-click keyword advertising.

Performance-based online advertising, pay-per-click keyword advertising, pay-per click

Performance-based online advertising using pay-per-click allowed advertisers to measure the effectiveness of an online ad to change viewers' behaviors (to actively click compared to passively viewing an ad) and pay based on those measurable clickthroughs. At first, most Internet ads were banners and followed the media payment method of offline advertising called CPM, a payment or cost based on the number of impressions or viewings or "eyeballs" reached. However, in the HBS note *How Media Choices Are Changing Online Advertising*, its authors (Stephen Bradley and Nancy Bartlett) mention that in April 1996 it was the powerful Procter & Gamble that convinced Yahoo! to switch its online ads to PPC clickthroughs rather than CPM. By 2004, 41% of all online ads were performance-based.

For those readers unfamiliar with the traditional offline media and advertising world, good background reading is Harold Vogel's *Entertainment Industry Economics: A Guide for Financial Analysis* (Cambridge University Press), *Ogilvy on Advertising* (Vintage), and *Confessions of an Advertising Man* (Southbank Publishing), (the latter two by the advertising legend David Ogilvy). For those readers interested in the early rich media trends in online advertising, take a look at the 2003 HBS case *Eyeblaster: Enabling the Next Generation of Online Advertising* (Elie Ofek).

Paid keyword search and organic keyword search or SEO (search engine optimization)

Paid keyword search or PPC on Googles's AdWords or Yahoo!'s Search Marketing (formerly GoTo/Overture) results in a small text ad in the sponsored link section. However, as explained further in this chapter, the average cost per click for the top placement spots keeps rising due to advertiser "willingness to pay" demand—sometimes 15% or more per year, making it difficult to estimate a ROI for advertising spending or an online marketing campaign. The SEO process of trying to get a web site to the top of the listings for organic search results is a lengthier and much less straightforward process.

ROI metrics and web analytics

Pay for performance online advertising and PPC keyword advertising opens up a whole new world of immediate, real-time, quantitative clickstream data for marketing analysis, customer behavioral tracking, and data-mining. Online advertisers—whether individuals, small businesses, or large corporations—can measure and monitor their advertising ROI dollars or cents—on a minute-by-minute, hourly, or daily basis, as well as continually experiment with tweaking keywords, keyword combinations, pricing, and page positioning.

The web analytics and online marketing tools provided with a service like Google's AdWords are very powerful and sophisticated enough for the savvy marketer and allow even the smallest advertiser to become extremely cost-effective at targeting online advertising spending.

See the *HBR* article "Competing on Analytics" and the book *Competing on Analytics: The New Science of Winning* (Harvard Business School Press), authored by Thomas Davenport and Jeanne Harris. Although written primarily about offline quantitative analysis, it reminds us that real-time data can often give us insight and early warning into unexpected or invisible shifts in the business environment and marketplace, as well as test the validity of our previously successful recipes and ways of doing business.

U.S. and global advertising expenditures, specifically online advertising industry analysis and quantitative models

See Thomas Weisel Partner Christa Sober Quarles's September 2006 *Investment Analyst Report on Internet Services* and quarterly updates.

Critical mass, one-percenters, and uploaders

> See Chapter 3 end notes "Accidental influentials" and "Bass Diffusion Curve."

Compatibility and complementary products and service

> Ecosystems and indirect network effects arise from compatibility in standards and complementary products and services. One very well-known example comes from Professors Michael Katz and Carl Shapiro's economic brief during the court battles around Microsoft. It drew from upon their classic articles on indirect and complementary network effects. See their articles "Network Externalities, Competition, and Compatibility" and "Systems Competition and Network Effects." The economic analysis was later summarized in Richard J. Gilbert and Michael L. Katz's article "An Economist's Guide to U.S. v. Microsoft" in the *Journal of Economic Perspectives*.

N-sided markets and ecosystems

> Professor Marco Iansiti and Roy Levien's book *The Keystone Advantage: What the New Dynamics of Business Ecosystems Mean for Strategy, Innovation, and Sustainability* (Harvard Business School Press) looks at n-sided markets from the perspective of business ecosystems. It also discusses the strategic advantage gained from being a keystone, hub, platform provider, or orchestrator in connecting multiple businesses. They cite Visa, American Express, and Microsoft as well-known examples in the research literature.

N-sided markets and online networks

> See the *HBR* article "Strategies for Two-Sided Markets" by Professor Thomas Eisenmann et al. It provides an overview of the industrial economics approach. His examples emphasize the connection of n-sided markets to online and offline networks, using examples such as Google, Craigslist, and eBay, as well as open system hardware platforms, such as Linux supported by IBM, Sun, and HP.

N-sided markets and the value of a free customer

> "What is the value of a 'free' customer?" (*http://www.hbs. edu/research/pdf/07-035.pdf*), a working paper published for

comment on the Web by Sunil Gupta—a HBS marketing professor—looks at the connection between two-sided markets and online free services. (See *http://hbswk.hbs.edu/item.5595.html* for an interview in which Gupta explains the concepts in his working paper. Another interesting commentary is available on Nick Carr's blog at *http://www.roughtype.com/*). eBay and Monster are used as examples of profitable online transaction revenue model businesses through n-sided markets, although empirical analysis is done with data from a conventional offline auction site.

Synthetic worlds and two-sided networks

Edward Castronova's book *Synthetic Worlds: The Business and Culture of Online Games* (University of Chicago Press) explains the active digital macroeconomics of gaming worlds, like World of Warcraft, as primarily due to "arbitrage"—the fact that there's a difference in real-world versus digital-world economic systems regarding how labor is linked to the production of goods, pricing, and economic growth. Additionally, the utilities, preferences, and economic behavior of the online gamer is distinguishable in many ways from the average real-worlder. This also seems to apply to the macroeconomics of Linden Lab's Second Life—a virtual 3-D world entirely created by users (*http://secondlife.com/whatis/*).

Unfortunately, I could not find a similarly comprehensive economic overview and analysis of Second Life, although there are many business articles and several guide books, including Paul Carr and Graham Pond's *The Unofficial Tourists' Guide to Second Life* (St. Martin's Press), as well as Julian Dibbell's *Play Money: Or, How I Quit My Day Job and Made Millions Trading Virtual Loot* (Basic Books). However, arbitrage tends to be a chance to make money on price differentials due to temporary disequilibrium. My own microeconomic explanation would focus on two-sided markets and cross-network effects and argue that there is stable perfect price differentiation—where one group is willing to use an online service or good for free and contribute direct positive network effects, and another group is willing to pay or sponsor with a premium price because of dynamic pricing, high ROI, and/or cross-network and indirect network effects.

Increasing returns

Brian Arthur, a Stanford professor and external professor at the Santa Fe Institute, is the founding father of "increasing returns economics." His research was part of an influential white paper that helped block the Microsoft buyout of Intuit, arguing that increasing returns can stifle innovation in emerging markets by locking customers into inferior technical standards too quickly.

Demand-side driven scale economies

I first started to search for Mauboussin's investment reports after reading the fascinating comments and insights attributed to him in Nassim Taleb's book, *Fooled by Randomness: The Hidden Role of Chance in Life and in the Markets* (Random House). The willingness-to-pay diagram in this chapter was inspired by diagrams in Mauboussin's report, available on the Web *(http://www.lmcm.com/search/default.aspx?qt=exhibit)*. However, my explanation is modified to apply to online network business examples.

Power laws

Power laws on the Web and elsewhere are explained in Albert-László Barabási's book *Linked: How Everything Is Connected to Everything Else and What It Means* (Plume), along with a broad and fascinating look at the implication of networks in many fields from physics to social sciences and biology, as well as everyday life. Power laws, in particular, mean that most of our experience in statistics and our commonplace intuition about "normal" distributions actually mislead us when it comes to exponential curves and strong network effects.

Long tail

Chris Anderson's book *The Long Tail: Why the Future of Business Is Selling Less of More* (Hyperion) provides a focused look at the implications of power laws for businesses in all sorts of industries from entertainment and radio to retailing and online businesses. It is wonderful reading with great examples.

AdRank

Page listing rank placement due to an ad's popularity measured by clickthroughs, as explained in John Battelle's book *The Search* and subsequently discussed by a number of bloggers.

Wisdom of the crowd

The Wisdom of Crowds (Anchor) is the title of the best-selling book by James Surowiecki. Google's search algorithm tracks the clicks and choices people make on the Web—what links they follow, what sites they look at, and what links and words they use in their own sites—and uses that information to make a dynamically updated calculation and weighted aggregation of the crowd's collective judgment or "wisdom" about popularity, authority, timeliness, importance (the criteria for the results served up by Google, Yahoo!, and other search engines). So, in some way, Google is data-mining the wisdom of the crowd, running it through its algorithm, and then selling that newly aggregated wisdom back to advertisers in the form of targeted keyword advertising.

In his famous essay *What Is Web 2.0?*, Tim O'Reilly reminds us that this is not a matter of encouraging the active participation of web users and uploaders as in Flickr's collective user value, but more like collecting the "crumbs" of wisdom left as users journey through the hyperlinks of the Web. A fascinating discussion started by Om Malik's blog (*http://gigaom. com/2005/10/27/crowds-wisdom-who-owns-it/*) raises the controversial question, "Who owns the wisdom of the crowd?" Or to pose this same question with a more revenue model spin—"Who captures the value and monetization of the wisdom of the crowd?"

Arguably Google does and then turns around and redistributes the benefits to an ecosystem of new-to-online advertisers and highly popular bloggers.

Blogging for dollars

"Blogging for Dollars" was a catchy front page article by Paul Sloan and Paul Kaihla for *Business 2.0* (September 1, 2006). The article provided data on ad revenues of some of the most highly touted and widely read bloggers, as well as comparisons of the estimated revenue splits of Google's AdSense with their ecosystem of bloggers compared to Federated Media and others.

AdSense and blogging

AdSense is the advertising platform that Google uses to serve ads to bloggers' web sites and redistribute a portion of the advertising payments for clickthroughs to the bloggers. Robert Scoble and Shel Israel's book *Naked Conversations: How Blogs are Changing the Way Businesses Talk with Customers* (Wiley) is recommended reading on understanding the business implications of the blogosphere—especially from the perspective of a former Microsoft employee/blogger. Also, it explains the concept of Google "juice," how interactivity, frequent links, and RSS impact page rankings.

Competitive races

Good background reading on this subject is the HBS note by Thomas Eisenmann, *A Note on Racing to Acquire Customers.*

Winner-take-all tippy market diagram

See this diagram in the must-read classic on digital economics and business, *Information Rules* (Harvard Business School Press), written by Carl Shapiro and Hal Varian. (Hal Varian is currently chief economist at Google.)

VHS versus Beta

The videocassette recorder market is a well-known example of a competitive battle of high-tech consumer electronic companies and standards. Several different explanations are possible—VHS was a standard formed by JVC, which sought worldwide licensing, production, and distribution allies in Matsushita, GE, Phillips, and Thomson. Beta was a standard formed by Sony, which chose to keep its technology proprietary and did not have any licensing allies. Comparisons could be made to IBM PCs with Wintel (Microsoft Windows plus Intel microprocessors) versus integrated Apple Macintoshes. However, *Information Rules* highlights the important crossover point at 50%, arguing for the presence of a strong network effect causing a tippy market to occur.

The AOL-Google Story

The tippy market example involving Google, AOL, and Microsoft in 2005 is drawn from the HBS case *Google Inc.* by HBS Professor Thomas Eisenmann. There are definite parallels to be drawn to the 2008 Google, Yahoo!, and Microsoft takeover struggle. Although there are other business school cases written about Google, this is a must-read for its attention to competitive races in networked, winner-take-all markets. (The HBS explanatory notes on these specific topics are also authored by Professor Eisenmann.) The case provides the contextual details and quantitative information on why the analysts at the time believed that Google had paid about $100 million too much in the AOL deal.

Tippy market

The Google case data together with Christa Sober Quarles' *Investment Analyst Report on Internet Services*—reporting market shares of search engine players in 2005—gave me a significantly different perspective of the AOL deal as illustrative of a tippy market. The search market shares in 2005 reveal that Google was in a fairly vulnerable position because it was clearly in the battle zone for a tippy market, with AOL playing the swing vote.

Battle zone of a tippy market

Christa Sober Quarles's report and its detailed models of revenue per search for different competitors in the search market supported my hypothesis that the clearly dominant 50+ market share leader in a tippy and highly networked two-sided market, like the search market, could receive more than 2 times the average revenue per search query compared to search engines such as MSN or AskJeeves that were "one of the pack." This became the basis for my simplified number back-of-the-envelope analysis of the financial implications of losing 7% market share for Google in a tippy market.

Web 2.0 path to growth and the freemium strategy

I first heard the term "freemium" in a *Business 2.0* article more than a year back and only recently realized that it was Fred Wilson, the venture capitalist, who first used the term. The original freemium strategy was stated as:

> Give your service away for free, possibly ad supported but maybe not, acquire a lot of customers efficiently through word of mouth, referral networks, organic search marketing, etc., then offer premium priced value added services or an enhanced version of your service to your customer base.

But don't try it without Web 2.0—low capital investment, collective user value, network effects, n-sided markets, and long tail ad-monetization make this kind of freemium strategy work effectively now, but many pieces were missing before.

Chapter 3

Electronic communications and communities

The terms *electronic communications* and *electronic interactions* point to a much larger and richer body of work on *virtual communities*, *cyberspace identity*, and *educational and scientific online communications* that were not covered in this chapter. I suggest reading all of the books by Howard Rheingold, known as the First Citizen of the Internet, as he explores *The Virtual Community* (The MIT Press) in the late '80s, *Virtual Reality* (Simon & Schuster) in the '90s, and *Smart Mobs* (Basic Books) in the 2000s. Sherry Turkle explores the evolution of our electronic psyche and persona in cyberspace in the books *Second Self* (The MIT Press) and *Life on the Screen* (Simon & Schuster). Numerous academic articles analyze the collaboration and communication patterns of educational and scientific communities. Etienne Wenger's book on *Cultivating*

Communities of Practice (Harvard Business School Press) is considered a classic in the knowledge management field, with examples drawn from offline cases.

Local and social network effects

This chapter focuses on the socially mediated and socially influenced network structure of people connected or linked on the Web. This network structure or linkage pattern provides the basis for *local network effects*. In Malcolm Gladwell's popular book *The Tipping Point* (Back Bay Books), he provides many everyday and historical examples in which a small number of individuals were a *critical mass* or *threshold tipping point* in triggering exponentially large network effects. More business examples are available in the *HBR* article, "Tipping Point Leadership" (W. Kim Chan and Renée Mauborgne).

Social network effects, S-curves, emergence, and complex systems

We are all familiar with the surprisingly explosive growth of a virus, epidemic, or forest fire, but we're not used to thinking about them as exponential growth patterns or S-curves on a graph (see Chapter 1 end notes). Steven Johnson's book *Emergence: The Connected Lives of Ants, Brains, Cities, and Software* (Scribner) has many interesting examples of systems showing emergent properties, including unregulated exponential growth or free-scaling. The Wikipedia definition of emergence points out that the Web is a popular example of a decentralized system exhibiting emergent properties. There is no central organization allocating the number of links, yet the number of links pointing to each page follows a power law (see Chapter 2 end notes on power laws) in which a few pages are linked to many times and most pages are seldom linked to.

A related property of the network of links in the World Wide Web is that almost any pair of pages can be connected to each other through a relatively short chain of links, called *degrees of separation*. Although relatively well known now, this property was initially unexpected in an unregulated network. It is shared with many other types of networks called *small-world networks*. The study of complex systems looks at why very large decentralized and distributed systems with many independent actors (sometimes called agents or nodes) seem to act in a highly coordinated or organized fashion, although there is no apparent hierarchical leadership but ad hoc, intermittent, or limited inter-node communication and linkage.

The book *Complexity: The Emerging Science at the Edge of Order and Chaos* (Simon & Schuster) by Mitchell Waldrop is a great introduction to this area and shows the connection between Brian Arthur's economics work in *increasing returns* to this field, as well as the exciting interdisciplinary beginnings of the Santa Fe Institute.

Local network effects, clusters, and Silicon Valley

Local network effects are also a type of social network effect because certain nodes or users are influenced directly by a small subset of local nodes that it is connected to, typically via an underlying social or business or locally geographical cluster, grouping, community, or neighborhood. In these cases, structural factors—such as extent, interaction, density, and the strength of ties of clustering in the network, along with social influence and information access—shape diffusion and adoption patterns. Silicon Valley is a good example of this, whereas Route 128 in Boston is not, according to the classic book on this subject *Regional Advantage* (Harvard University Press), written by AnnaLee Saxenian (now Dean of the School of Information Systems at U.C. Berkeley).

Social network mapping

Figures 3-1 through 3-6 are examples of social network mapping where linkages designate person-to-person relationships between individuals or "nodes" on a spatial graph.

Figure 3-1 is redrawn and modified from a blog entry Dave Pollard posted on August 11, 2005 about social network analysis (sometimes abbreviated as SNA). The article was titled "How to Save the World" (*http://blogs.salon.com/0002007/2005/08/11.html*). Organizational theorists and sociologists have observed that these maps often reveal actual or informal networks and information/knowledge/power relationships, as distinct from formal or official organization charts. Small and large data-set social networks can be analyzed for attributes like degree centrality (the number of connections), between-ness centrality (the number of connections to the otherwise disconnected), and closeness centrality (the shortness of the average path to others). Connectors have a high betweenness centrality, for example.

Figure 3-2 is a social network map that illustrates the importance of hubs and highly connected nodes to the length of paths between you and a target destination. In Gladwell's recount of the Milgram experiment (p. 34–36 in *The Tipping Point*), he points out that in six degrees of separation, not all degrees are equal. Of the 24 letters that reached the stockbroker at his home, 16 were given to him by the same person, Mr. Jacobs. In fact, half of the responses that came back were delivered by the same three people: Jacobs, Jones, and Brown. Watts in his book *Six Degrees of Separation* (p. 133) also points out that a more careful analysis of Milgram's papers reveals that of the 300 starting letters, only 96 started in Omaha, Nebraska, and only 18 reached the target.

Figures 3-3, 3-5, and 3-6 are redrawn social network maps from the HBS case *Monster Networking*. They illustrate the point that not only high betweenness centrality is important, but so is the somewhat counterintuitive combination of weak and strong ties. It was Mark Granovetter in his 1973 article on "The Strength of Weak Ties: A Network Theory Revisited" who observed that most first-degree groups of friends tend to be close-knit, and circles of friends have a high degree of overlap. Hubs or brokers play the role of boundary-spanner or gatekeeper, connecting the internally cohesive group or circle of friends to a wider external network of relationships throughout the organization and environment. The importance of strong and weak ties in different social and organizational environments and communities is explored in Robert Putnam's *Bowling Alone—The Collapse and Renewal of American Community* (Simon & Schuster), and the article "Using Social Network Analysis to Improve Communities of Practice" in the *California Management Review*, by Cross et al.

Figure 3-4 is a redrawn social network map from the *HBR* article "How to Build Your Network" by Brian Uzzi and

Shannon Dunlap. The authors use it to explain how individuals and business professionals can carefully construct and map their own social networks and strategize to strengthen their own personal business networks and linkages.

Social network analysis

This is a process of painstakingly mapping the nodes, linkages, and types of interaction in people-connected networks and groups that has been used extensively in sociological and organizational business research. Again, see "Using Social Network Analysis to Improve Communities of Practice," and "Making Invisible Work Visible: Using Social Network Analysis to Support Strategic Collaboration," by Cross et al.

Connectors, mavens, and salesmen

Malcolm Gladwell's article in the *New Yorker* and best-selling book *The Tipping Point* split the well-researched social network broker/hub role into three distinct types that he calls connectors, mavens, and salesmen. His stories seem to indicate that tipping points, thresholds, or critical mass for social epidemics might require some level of interaction or interdependence between these different types of brokers, as recounted in the stories of Paul Revere and William Dawes.

A simplified summary might be that connectors are social glue, mavens are information brokers, and salesmen are catalysts to action. The collaboration or combination of all of these roles might be necessary to "trigger" a social epidemic. This is a fascinating "personification" of our theoretical understanding of the different factors necessary to innovation diffusion or the spread of disease—for example, with HIV, the presence of several highly socially and sexually active individuals, who are strongly contagious due to unsafe practices and who travel actively and extensively to many new areas and partners, can cause a local outbreak to explode into an epidemic.

Social epidemics, fads, viral marketing, buzz marketing, word-of-mouth marketing

The *HBR* article "The Buzz on Buzz" is a good overview of buzz marketing. It looks at the widespread applicability in offline markets as well as common misconceptions. Two articles on viral marketing that provide helpful background— although they are mostly focused on offline viral marketing— are "Controlled Infection! Spreading the Brand Message Through Viral Marketing," an article in *Business Horizons* by Angela Dobele et al., and the *HBR* article by Duncan Watts "Viral Marketing for the Real World."

Several marketing and branding books also look at this subject: Andy Sernovitz's book *Word of Mouth Marketing: How Smart Companies Get People Talking* (with Afterword by Guy Kawasaki) (Kaplan Publishing); *Brand Hijack: Marketing Without Marketing* (Penguin Group) by Alex Wipperfürth; *Buzz Marketing: Get People to Talk About Your Stuff* (Portfolio Hardcover) by Mark Hughes; *Citizen Marketers: When People Are the Message* (Kaplan Publishing) by Ben McConnell and Jackie Huba; and *Experience the Message* by Max Lenderman.

Online connectors, mavens, and salesmen, catalysts, and evangelists

The main question driving this chapter: how does the Web change social network patterns, particularly in viral marketing and diffusion, and small world network effects? So, those looking for ethnographic, anthropological treatments of the cyber-community will be disappointed and need to search elsewhere. The chapter looks at the mechanisms behind the tipping of word-of-mouth epidemics in the online world, better known as viral marketing or buzz marketing. Ori Brafman and Rod Beckstrom's book *The Starfish and the Spider: The Unstoppable Power of Leaderless Organizations* (Portfolio Hardcover) emphasizes the role of catalysts—active peers in our new decentralized un-organizations like the Web, Skype, or Napster—in triggering high-impact changes that ripple through the entire small-world group.

Ben McConnell's book *Creating Customer Evangelists: How Loyal Customers Become a Volunteer Sales Force* (Kaplan Publishing) considers the expansion and amplification of the traditional commercially oriented salesforce through online communities, especially in specialized areas that have passionately loyal and dedicated users, including religion, music, and the arts. Many of these business concepts were discussed during the Web 1.0 era, for example, John Hagel III and Arthur Armstrong's *Net Gain: Expanding Markets Through Virtual Communities* (Harvard Business School Press), but could not be realized as effectively without Web 2.0 and widespread broadband and mobile penetration.

Snailmail

Snailmail refers to regular U.S. postal service, seemingly moving at a snail's pace in the physical, offline world compared to almost instantaneous email service online. (Hotmail is the free email service that became the leading example of viral marketing.)

Small worlds and leapfrog links

Additionally but somewhat separately, I also discuss the emergence of small worlds and leapfrog links in cyberspace. This is a more targeted usage of the Web's interconnected linkages to shortcut geographical and social distance by finding the shortest social distance path (or friends of friends' degrees of separation) online between you and someone you want to connect to directly. Small worlds, despite the name, are not really sustaining communities; rather, they are the outcome of exponentially increasing linkages within online networks along with superhubs, allowing each of us to be much fewer than six degrees of separation away from any other node on the Web—which is why an email sent to China might take the same number of "hops" as an email to someone in the same neighborhood who has a different Internet provider and social network linkage structure. The key readings in this area are Duncan Watts' books, *Six Degrees: The Science of a Connected Age* (W. W. Norton & Company) and *Small Worlds: The Dynamics of Networks between Order and Randomness* (Princeton Studies in Complexity) (W. W. Norton & Company).

LinkedIn and beyond

Harvard Business School cases *LinkedIn (A)* and *LinkedIn (B)* were written by HBS Strategy professor Mikolaj Jan Piskorski to illustrate strategy for online search business and how to

monetize a 5-million-node business network. The same professor and Carin-Isabel Knoop also wrote HBS cases
Friendster (A) and *Friendster (B)*, which focus on the social
networking business and how Friendster tried to turn around
its first-generation social network.

The HBS case *Monster Networking* (David Vivero and Thomas
Eisenmann) looks at the challenges Monster.com—the success-
ful Web 1.0 online recruiting leader—faced trying to integrate
Web 2.0-style social and business networking into its services,
through acquisition and internal development. Also see *MIT
Tech Review* articles on social networking.

Stanford Case "Facebook"

This case is available through the Harvard Business School
case distribution service (*http://www.hbsp.harvard.edu/hbsp/
case_studies.jsp*).

*Viral marketing, viral distribution and referral marketing, social
and peer pressure*

The *HBR* article "The One Number You Need to Grow,"
written by Frederick Reichheld (also the author of the *HBR*
article "E-Loyalty: Your Secret Weapon on the Web"),
reminded me that tell-a-friend, referral marketing, and peer
pressure (Facebook tells you how many of your friends have
already signed up for a free Facebook application) are actually quite different from conventional viral or buzz marketing. One person doesn't broadcast or "infect" a large number
of people; instead, a small number of friends, a cluster, or critical mass acts as a mini-bandwagon, reducing the perceived
risk of experimenting with something new. Rather than transaction costs, you have invisible upfront "attention" or
"threshold time to download a trial" costs.

Accidental influentials

The term "accidental influentials" was coined by sociologist
Duncan Watts, now at Yahoo!, and publicized as part of the
HBR List: Breakthrough Ideas for 2007. His empirical work
on online networks using large-scale data set analysis has
shown that the popular notion of social epidemics being

driven by a few celebrities is inaccurate, although intuitively appealing. Instead, a critical mass of accidental influentials or ordinary people who act as sparks, catalysts, active uploaders, bloggers, or 1–3 percenters can trigger an exponential social epidemic or explosive uptake. Like a forest fire, the extent and range depend on the environmental conditions as well as the initiating spark.

Information propagation

Dan Gruhl, R. Guha, David Liben-Nowell, and Andrew Tomkins studied the dynamics of information propagation in environments of low-overhead personal publishing, using a large collection of weblogs over time as an example domain. They characterized and modeled this collection at both macroscopic and microscopic levels. Based only on information about which topics were covered by which authors at which times, they presented, validated, and employed an algorithm to induce the underlying propagation network, which learns three fundamental properties: the stickiness of each individual topic, the likelihood that one author will adopt a topic from another, and the frequency with which one author reads the content of another. See their article, "Information diffusion through Blogspace" (from the International World Wide Web Conference).

Ravi Kumar, Jasmine Novak, Prabhakar Raghavan, and Andrew Tomkins proposed two new tools to address the evolution of hyperlinked corpora (like Blogspace, the space of weblogs). First, they defined time graphs to extend the traditional notion of an evolving directed graph, thereby capturing link creation as a point phenomenon in time; second, they developed definitions and algorithms for time-dense community tracking to crystallize the notion of community evolution. They extend recent work of Kleinberg to discover dense periods of "bursty" intra-community link creation. See their article "On the bursty evolution of Blogspace" (also from the International World Wide Web Conference).

Bass Diffusion Curve

See *http://www.useit.com/alertbox/basscurves.html*.

The three curves in Figure 3-14 were generated using *http://andorraweb.com/bass/*. This web site allows users to enter predictive variables for industry, introduction date, degree of innovation, and degree of imitation to generate a Bass Diffusion Curve using the standard formula. Another web site shows that the curves as drawn are very similar to home PCs, new devices, and cell phones (*http://www.marketingnpv.com/tools/all/forecasting_market_size_for_a_unique_new_product*).

Chapter 4

Dynamic capabilities

This term was first introduced in a working paper that David Teece and I coauthored to be presented as the organizing theme of the Napa Valley Strategy Conference in 1989. The working paper was strongly influenced by my INSEAD collaborations and research—alliance processes (Doz and Shuen, 1989), competitive collaboration field studies (Hamel, Prahalad, and Doz), competence stocks and flows (Dierickx and Cool), and campus lunch discussions on firm-level resources with Edith Penrose (*The Theory of the Growth of the Firm* [Oxford University Press]) and Guy de Carmoy. David Teece's research influences included evolutionary economics and technological trajectories (*The Nature and Dynamics of Organizational Capabilities* [Oxford University Press]), absorptive capacity (Levinthal), and knowledge creation at the firm-level (*The Knowledge-Creating Company: How Japanese Companies Create the Dynamics of Innovation* [Oxford University Press] by Ikujiro Nonaka and Hirotaka Takeuchi).

Worldwide business transaction costs

Ronald Coase received the Nobel Memorial Prize in Economics for his work on transaction costs, as well as for highlighting the difficulties of internalizing network externalities effectively. In his work *The Economic Institutions Of Capitalism* (The Free Press), Oliver Williamson (a contemporary of Coase's) added two key concepts of transaction cost economics largely missing from Coase's work but critical for application of transaction costs to online networks. They are (1) *specialized assets* fundamentally transformed faceless transactions into relationships with different economic characteristics, and (2) the *risk of opportunism* required economic and/or legal safeguards, including price premiums; collateral, credible commitments or hostages; or building a pattern of trust or reputation through interactions over time in a social or cultural context.

Friction in the transaction cost system

These are extra costs generated by the one-time summation of contractual, procedural, search, and "ink" transaction costs. This also includes the systemic and continuing transaction costs of market failures such as *sticky, lumpy,* or *complex* knowledge, technology, or information goods that are difficult to price or efficiently transfer in an economic transaction. In short, within transaction cost economics, firms exist to avoid the transaction costs and market failures of transferring and managing complex information, knowledge, and experience goods.

Multi-network power, efficacy, and reach, many-to-many networks

An influential article "Interorganizational Collaboration and the Locus of Innovation: Networks of Learning in Biotechnology" by Powell et al. provides empirical evidence of multi-network power—an unexpected gain in value and an inherently positive network effect of coordinating large numbers of firms that counterbalance the largely negative coordinative costs predicted by transaction cost economics. However, this research was based on networks of business transactions, not connected online networks of businesses. The best-selling book *Blown to Bits* (Random House) by Philip Evans and Thomas Wurster, written in 2000 during the first generation of the Web, further argued that online networks allow efficiency, richness, and reach, whereas most previous businesses had to deal with tradeoffs between these dimensions because of transaction costs. They use the example of *Encyclopedia Britannica* versus Microsoft's Encarta.

Corporate strategy and innovation

Corporate strategy differs from plain old vanilla business strategy because it is defined as the strategy of multiple businesses, not just a single business. As such, there are tradeoffs as well as opportunities created by juggling a large number of businesses and strategic business units, each of them competing in a different industry and targeting different market segments and geographies. Corporate strategy must balance overall and individual business short- and long-term profitability, market share, and growth.

One well-known corporate strategy framework, the BCG Growth-Share Matrix—introduced by Bruce Henderson in the early '70s and applied by leaders like GE—categorizes businesses as stars, cash cows, dogs, or question markets, depending on their relative market share (cash generation) and market growth rate (cash usage). See HBS's *Note on the Boston Consulting Group Concept of Competitive Analysis and Corporate Strategy* (John S. Hammond III and Gerald B., Allan). Also see the *HBR* article "Competing on Capabilities: The New Rules of Corporate Strategy" (George Stalk Jr. et al.).

Strategic performance

As mentioned, there are two different but complementary views of the determinants of strategic performance. Structural industry analysis, Porter's five-forces analysis, and the research streams of industrial organizational economics are the basis for many M.B.A.-trained stock market analysts. The resource-based approach (see Wernfelt's article in the *RAND Journal of Economics*, "Umbrella Branding as a Signal of New Product Quality: An Example of Signalling by Posting a Bond") to strategy and the evolutionary and innovation economics view do a better job explaining performance in high-tech industries where distinctive, hard-to-imitate capabilities and intangible assets are linked to market valuation, growth, and profitability.

Good background to the academic research in this area can be found in *Resource-Based and Evolutionary Theories of the Firm: Toward a Synthesis*, edited by Cynthia Montgomery, and the article "Strategic Alliances and Interfirm Knowledge Transfer" by Mowery et al. in *Strategic Management Journal.*

How these two contrasting views might actually underlie overall patterns of national competitiveness is explored in Hamel and Prahalad's *HBR* article, "The Core Competence of the Corporation." In it, they discuss the differences between Japanese and U.S./Western firms; the former are described as following a primarily internal competence approach, and the latter are characterized by an externally focused strategy approach.

In my corporate strategy programs, I recommend reading Andy Grove's *Only the Paranoid Survive: How to Exploit the Crisis Points That Challenge Every Company* (Currency) as a practicing high-tech CEO's guide to Porter's five-force analysis. Grove, the well-known cofounder and former CEO of Intel, developed his perspective while coteaching (with Professor Robert Burgelmann) M.B.A. courses at Stanford Business School.

Grove adds two key concepts to Porter's five forces. Strategic inflection points are transition or fundamental changes in the ways of doing business. He also extends Porter's Five Forces of Competition model into a six-forces model with the addition of the complements force. For example, Microsoft Windows is an important complement to Intel's chips.

Recombinant innovation

This term was popularized by Andrew Hargadon's book, *How Breakthroughs Happen: The Surprising Truth About How Companies Innovate* (Harvard Business School Press). In this chapter, I expand the usage of his original term in two very specific ways to better cover the emerging styles of collaborative online innovation described in later sections. First, peer-to-peer collaboration of older, more established industry incumbents with newer startups is the primary focus (compared to the examples Hargadon cites, which seem to be more unidirectional), where established technologies generated by industry leaders are applied in new application areas by startups in a kind of "fusion" or technology arbitrage play. Second, the chapter's emphasis is on making the analogy of recombinant innovation to recombinant genetic engineering much stronger and clearer.

Recombinant genetic engineering is not just the simple mixing of independent skills or competences, as in a team or ecosystem. Instead, both organisms or organizations end up being changed in a fundamental way by the insertion of new DNA material: the newer organism is changed because it now has a more powerful infrastructure for viral replication and distribution, and the host organism is changed because it has received and accepted new DNA (that could not have been internally generated) into its system from an unlike organism.

Developing dynamic capabilities

The difficulty and economic costs of transferring complex technologies between companies are considerations in international technology transfer, technology appropriability, gains and hazards in make versus buy decisions, and virtual versus virtuous companies. One challenge is capturing individual skills, tacit knowledge, and know-how into organizational learning, processes, and "routines" (see *An Evolutionary Theory of Economic Change* [Belknap Press] by Richard Nelson and Sidney Winter). Another is the relative slowness of the diffusion process of learning-by-doing and know-how transfer, even within closely coupled technology collaborations. (For background on organizational learning, see the article "The Persistence and Transfer of Learning in Industrial Settings" in *Management Science* (Linda Argote et al.).

The seminal article "Organizational Learning and Communities-of-Practice: Toward a Unified View of Working, Learning, and Innovation" was published in 1991 in *Organization Science* (John Seely Brown and Paul Duguid). Thomas Stewart's *Fortune* articles from *The Invisible Key to Success* in 1996 and his book *Intellectual Capital: The New Wealth of Organizations* (Currency) provide a thoughtful and comprehensive look at the best practices in the knowledge management area.

Buying brains and acquiring competences

The *HBR* article "The Hollow Corporation" highlighted the poor performance of mergers and acquisitions of acquiring valuable competences and talent. A more recent multi-network example would be eBay's $2.6 billion acquisition of Skype in September 2005. The potential for a very powerful multi-network multiplier effect could explain this unusually high valuation. However, the implementation challenges of creating a seamless click-to-call advertising-based system, as well as Skype's founders' focus on their new venture Joost, likely hindered the realization of that potential. eBay took a $900 million write-down after two years. At the same time, Niklas Zennström, Skype's chief executive and cofounder, resigned.

Valuable intangible assets

Often brand, reputation, relationships, technology, and goodwill are included in a list of intangible assets. See *Mobilizing Invisible Assets* (Harvard University Press) by Hiroyuki Itami and Thomas Roehl and *Working Knowledge* (Harvard Business School Press) by Thomas Davenport and Laurence Prusak. This list includes a number of valuable, intangible assets generated specifically by Web 2.0 businesses: network effects, buzz or viral marketing and distribution, business models, ecosystems, and momentum.

Syndication and online publishing

Syndication is a business model well understood in the publishing and media world. Thanks to a lunch arranged by David Irons (who at the time was the director of communications at Haas and later cofounder of Ascribe, an online research news feed) Assistant Dean Paul Grabowicz at U.C. Berkeley's Graduate School of Journalism and I developed and cotaught an interdisciplinary course titled New Media Business Models. We brought in exciting speakers and thought leaders in the converging space of new media, digital economics, and online publishing (Haas NewsWire April 5, 1999), including Kevin Kelly (*New Rules for the New Economy*) and Hal Varian

(*Information Rules*), Kara Swisher (*Wall Street Journal*), John Battelle (*The Search*). Many others helped initiate the New Media program at U.C. Berkeley, including Patricia Dunn (then vice chairman of Barclays Global Investors), John Gage at Sun Microsystems, Dan Gillmor (then of *San Jose Mercury News*, now of Grassroots Media and author of *We the Media: Grassroots Journalism By the People, For the People* [O'Reilly]), and Paul Saffo at the Institute for the Future.

Online syndication

See the outstanding *HBR* article, "Syndication: The Emerging Model for Business in the Internet Era," written by Kevin Werbach in 2000, now a professor at Wharton and founder of the Supernova conferences. The article was prescient in highlighting the business and strategic implications of syndication business models on the Web, as it was written well before the advent of Web 2.0 technologies and business models, including RSS, blogging, podcasting, videostreaming, social networks, and viral distribution via software as a service.

Software as a service and web services

See John Hagel III's *Out of the Box: Strategies for Achieving Profits Today & Growth Tomorrow Through Web Services*, with a foreword by John Seely Brown (Harvard Business School Press). See also *Harvard Management Update*'s article "Web Services: Technology as a Catalyst for Strategic Thinking." Another perspective on SaaS is offered in Andrew McAfee's *MIT Sloan Management Review* (*SMR*) article "Will Web Services Really Transform Collaboration?," as well as his following article "Enterprise 2.0: The Dawn of Emergent Collaboration." Background and overview of the implications for the industry are in the HBS case, *The Global Software Industry in 2006*.

Salesforce.com

See the HBS case *Oracle vs. Salesforce.com*.

IBM and Dynamic Capabilities

See the *CMR* article "Dynamic Capabilities at IBM: Driving Strategy into Action," coauthored by IBM's head of strategy, Bruce Harreld. Also see the HBS case, *Emerging Business Opportunities at IBM (A)*; Louis Gerstner's book *Who Says Elephants Can't Dance?: Leading a Great Enterprise Through Dramatic Change* (Collins); and *Wikinomics: How Mass Collaboration Changes Everything* (Portfolio Hardcover) by Don Tapscott and Anthony Williams.

Global knowledge economy and the flat world

See the following books: *The World Is Flat: A Brief History of the Twenty-first Century* (Farrar, Straus and Giroux) by Thomas Friedman; *Six Billion Minds: Managing Outsourcing in the Global Knowledge Economy* (Aspatore Books) by Mark Minevich et al.; *India and the Knowledge Economy: Leveraging Strengths and Opportunities* (World Bank Publications) by Carl Dahlman and Anuja Utz; and *Bottom of the Pyramid* (Wharton School Publishing) by C.K. Prahalad.

Amazon: Giving Away the Store

This is the title of an article in *Business 2.0* that made me see that Amazon was an ideal example of competence syndication (*http://www.technologyreview.com/Biztech/14089/*). More details about the development of the Amazon infrastructure and system can be found in the 2000 HBS case *Amazon.com: Exploiting the Value of Digital Business Infrastructure* (Lynda M. Applegate and Meredith Collura).

Give to get strategy

Give something away for free but do it in such a way that it ends up expanding the business or producing cross-network effects in an n-sided market, in which one group will be willing to pay more.

Competence mashups

This is a tinker toys connection of different proprietary databases. My emphasis is first on the localized and real-time know-how that is embedded in the data that is collected, which makes it valuable; and second, on the APIs, or sections of interface code, that allow outsiders a view of how the data and information is architected within a company's system.

Chapter 5

Schumpeter's creative winds of destruction

Joseph Schumpeter, an Austrian economist, wrote in 1932 about the "creative gales of destruction" and described them as clusters of innovation that could change the whole economy along with social and cultural practices.

Disruptive innovation

Clayton Christensen characterizes disruptive innovation as primarily disruptive technologies in his best-selling book: *The Innovator's Dilemma: The Revolutionary Book that Will Change the Way You Do Business* (HarperBusiness). Also see the *HBR* article "Disruptive Technologies: Catching the Wave." This is somewhat unexpected when contrasted to the classic approaches in the management of innovation literature (for example Utterback's *Mastering the Dynamics of Innovation* [Harvard Business School Press] or Foster's *Innovation: The Attacker's Advantage* [Simon & Schuster]) that looked at innovation rates and their interdependencies in products and/or related production processes. A focus on strictly disruptive technologies, while critical for industrial hardware-oriented industries, would seem to give short shrift to many significant business innovations in solutions, services, organizations, processes, and customer-focused businesses. One book that provides a collection of classic management of innovation and technology papers on this topic is Tushman and Anderson (eds.) *Managing Strategic Innovation and Change: A Collection of Readings* (Oxford University Press).

For example Andy Grove's own list of strategic inflection points or industry discontinuities mainly consists of business, organizational, or system-wide innovations such as container shipping that revolutionized the logistics, physical goods distribution, and transportation industries. His list also contains lean manufacturing and just-in-time supply chains that completely shifted the cost structure, timing, organization, and interactions of man, machine, and inventory in the modern factory (rather than changing the technologies of the capital equipment purchased) (see his book *Only the Paranoid Survive*). A classic worth reading on this subject is *Winning Through Innovation: A Practical Guide to Leading Organizational Change and Renewal* (Harvard Business School Press), by Michael Tushman and Charles O'Reilly.

Disruptive business models

I like to use the inclusive term *disruptive business models* to describe business, organizational, and system-wide innovations that cause strategic inflection points or industry discontinuities. In Chapter 2, we saw in the case of Web 2.0 that collective user value and n-sided markets in digital networked markets can shift cost structures and generate increasing returns and demand side economies. Digital and online networked technologies are creating an increasingly connected online mobile broadband user base, where different business models and growth patterns are emerging.

Flat world and the global knowledge economy

Thomas Friedman's book *The World Is Flat* was the talk of the World Economic Forum at Davos in 2006, echoing the concern of CEOs, Wall Street, policymakers, and political figures that the balance of economic power was shifting toward the emerging geographies of BRIC: Brazil, Russia, India, and China. The term "flat world" emphasized the increasing connectedness and speed of communication available through technology, shortcutting geographic distance and time. In a previous endnote on global competence syndication, I mentioned the impact of this free flow and spillover of knowledge for the global knowledge economy. Friedman also highlights the importance of individual uploaders and Web 2.0 technologies like blogging, podcasting, and Wikipedia in bringing individual local experiences available globally.

Peer-to-peer architecture and Skype

Many people heard about peer-to-peer file-sharing for the first time in connection with Napster, which used a distributed file-sharing system and peer-to-peer web connections to allow online, real-time, and ad hoc downloading of music files from one node or peer's hard drive to another's. See *The Starfish and the Spider* for an interesting account. Unfortunately, the legal battles that ensued around this particular application may have given most people an unnecessarily negative impression of the technology of peer-to-peer architectures and file-sharing, intrinsically a very powerful and elegant solution to large-scale computing problems, ad hoc point-to-point, or multi-hop connectivity and system resource management.

The founders of Kazaa developed a very powerful peer-to-peer architecture for ad hoc distribution of digital bits from one connected and identified node to another—this system is considered illegal in the music-sharing context. However, it was worth $2.7 billion in market valuation to eBay when they applied their architecture (with the company name Skype) to the VoIP telephone industry. In this system, a user's laptop can become the routing hub or path for her own international calling rolodex, saving capital investment in infrastructure, just like SETI or grid computing applications.

Incremental innovation

Incremental innovation is typically a continuous and competence-enhancing improvement along an existing technology trajectory or between generations of related products or services.

Radical innovation

Radical innovation is typically a discontinuous and competence-destroying introduction of a breakthrough or entirely novel product, system, or business model requiring greater risk and considerable change in basic technologies, processes, and organization. However, the advantage is that radical innovators break past the mainstream industry and existing paradigms. See *Blue*

Ocean Strategy: How to Create Uncontested Market Space and Make Competition Irrelevant (Harvard Business School Press) by W. Chan Kim and Renée Mauborgne.

Architectural innovation

See the article "Architectural Innovation: The Reconfiguration of Existing Product Technologies and the Failure of Established Firms," by Rebecca Henderson with Kim Clark, in *Administrative Science Quarterly*. In the article, they say:

> Architectural innovation is the reconfiguration of an established system to link together existing components in a new way. The important point is that the core design concept behind each component—and the associated scientific and engineering knowledge—remain the same.

Competitive or collaborative innovation, co-opetition

The historical examples of the videocassette recorder industry and the Citibank ATM come from the book *Co-opetition: A Revolutionary Mindset That Combines Competition* and *Cooperation: The Game Theory Strategy That's Changing the Game of Business* (Currency) by Adam Brandenburger and Barry Nalebuff.

User-led or democratized innovation

See MIT Professor Eric von Hippel's book, *Democratizing Innovation* (The MIT Press) and his earlier classic *The Sources of Innovation* (The Oxford University Press).

Crowdsourcing or crowdcatching

In his book *Wikinomics*, Don Tapscott uses Wikipedia as the classic example of mass collaboration or crowdsourcing. Also see the *HBR* article "Connect and Develop: Inside Procter & Gamble's New Model of Innovation" (Larry Huston and Nabil Sakkab) and the *SMR* article, "The New Principles of a Swarm Business" (Peter Gloor and Scott M. Cooper) for more good examples.

Open source, ecosystem, and platform innovation

See Henry Chesbrough's most recent book *Open Business Models: How to Thrive in the New Innovation Landscape* and his *HBR* article "The New Business Logic of Open Innovation."

Also see Annabelle Gawer and Michael Cusumano's book *Platform Leadership: How Intel, Microsoft and Cisco Drive Industry Innovation*, and the HBS note, "Platform-Mediated Networks: Definitions and Core Concepts."

The iPod as a mobile platform for entertainment versus communication

See the following HBS cases: *The Music Industry and the Internet* (Bharat N. Anand and Estelle S. Cantillon); its sequel *Update: The Music Industry in 2006* (John R. Wells and Elizabeth A. Raabe); *Apple Computer, Inc: iPod and iTunes* (Mary M. Crossan and Ken Mark); *and iPod vs. Cell Phone: A Mobile Music Revolution* (David B. Yoffie and Michael Slind).

Platform innovation ecosystem #4

User-provided metadata and Berkeley-based (but internationally known) Gracenote's CDDB technology and open software standards demonstrate that a company doesn't have to be an IBM, Red Hat, or Linux to cocreate value.

Click and mortar, brick and click, offline-online

These are different terms used to describe hybrid offline-online partnerships. The *HBR* article "Get the Right Mix of Bricks and Clicks" by Ranjay Gulati and Jason Garino, written before the advent of Web 2.0, provides an early overview.

Jajah and VoIP

See the *HBR* article "Using VoIP to Compete," by Kevin Werbach. Also see the presentation entitled "Jajah" given by Michel Veys, COO of Jajah, at the Chalmers-Berkeley program in June 2007 held at Standford University .

iPhone—Wi-Fi compatibility

The iPhone and its Wi-Fi compatibility has implications on the open standards use of the iPhone browser and the emergence of open developer and application ecosystems. It also might explain its early, exclusive partnership with AT&T—which performed a significant amount of technology development—but AT&T might not enjoy exclusivity for long.

Chapter 6

Web 2.0 business plan

Be sure to read the classic article "How to Write a Great Business Plan" by William A. Sahlman in the *Harvard Business Review*. You can find a summary of some of the key questions addressed in the article at *http://hbswk.hbs.edu/archive/565.html*.

Bibliography

Anderson, Chris. *The Long Tail: Why the Future of Business is Selling Less of More.* Hyperion, 2006.

Argote, Linda et al., "The Persistence and Transfer of Learning in Industrial Settings," *Management Science* 36, no. 2 (1990): 140–154.

Axelrod, Robert. *The Complexity of Cooperation: Agent-Based Models of Competition and Collaboration.* Princeton University Press, 1997.

Banks, Drew, and Kim Daus. *Customer Community: Unleashing the Power of Your Customer Base.* Jossey-Bass, 2002.

Barabási, Albert-László. *Linked: How Everything Is Connected to Everything Else and What It Means for Business, Science, and Everyday Life.* Plume, 2003.

Bass, Frank, "A New Growth Model Product for Consumer Durables," *Management Science* 15, no. 5 (1969): 215–227.

Battelle, John. *The Search: How Google and Its Rivals Rewrote the Rules of Business and Transformed Our Culture.* Portfolio Trade, 2006.

Benkler, Yochai. *The Wealth of Networks: How Social Production Transforms Markets and Freedom.* Yale University Press, 2007.

Berners-Lee, Tim, with Mark Fischetti. *Weaving the Web: The Original Design and Ultimate Destiny of the World Wide Web.* Harper Collins, 2000.

Bhide, Amar et al. *Harvard Business Review on Entrepreneurship* (Harvard Business Review Paperback Series). Harvard Business School Press, 1999.

Brafman, Ori, and Rod Beckstrom. *The Starfish and the Spider: The Unstoppable Power of Leaderless Organizations.* Portfolio Hardcover, 2006.

Brandenburger, Adam, and Barry Nalebuff. *Co-opetition: A Revolutionary Mindset That Combines Competition and Cooperation: The Game Theory Strategy That's Changing the Game of Business.* Currency, 1997.

Bremmer, Ian. *The J Curve: A New Way to Understand Why Nations Rise and Fall.* Simon & Schuster. 2007.

Brown, John Seely, and Paul Duguid. *The Social Life of Information.* Harvard Business School Press, 2002.

Brown, John Seely, and Paul Duguid, "Organizational Learning and Communities-of-Practice: Toward a Unified View of Working, Learning, and Innovation," *Organization Science* 2, no. 1 (1991): 40–57.

Brown, Shona L., and Kathleen M. Eisenhardt. *Competing on the Edge: Strategy as Structured Chaos.* Harvard Business School Press, 1998.

Buchanan, Mark. *Nexus: Small Worlds and the Groundbreaking Theory of Networks.* W. W. Norton & Company, 2003.

Burgelman, Robert. *Strategy Is Destiny: How Strategy-Making Shapes a Company's Future.* The Free Press, 2001.

Burgelman, Robert et al. *Strategic Dynamics: Concepts and Cases.* McGraw-Hill/Irwin, 2005.

Burgelman, Robert et al. *Strategic Management of Technology and Innovation.* McGraw-Hill/Irwin, 2003.

Carr, Paul, and Graham Pond. *The Unofficial Tourists' Guide to Second Life: The Essential Guide to an Amazing Virtual World—with Millions of Users.* St. Martin's Press, 2007.

Castronova, Edward. *Synthetic Worlds: The Business and Culture of Online Games.* University of Chicago Press, 2006.

Chesbrough, Henry. *Open Business Models: How to Thrive in the New Innovation Landscape.* Harvard Business School Press, 2006.

Christensen, Clayton M. *The Innovator's Dilemma: The Revolutionary Book that Will Change the Way You Do Business.* HarperBusiness, 2003.

Coase, Ronald. *The Firm, the Market, and the Law.* University of Chicago Press, 1990.

Coase, Ronald, "The Problem of Social Cost," *Journal of Law and Economics* 3 (1960): 1–44.

Cohen, Wesley, M., and Daniel A. Levinthal, "Absorptive Capacity: A New Perspective on Learning and Innovation," *Administrative Science Quarterly* 35, no. 1 (1990): 128–152.

Dahlman, Carl, and Anuja Utz. *India and the Knowledge Economy: Leveraging Strengths and Opportunities.* World Bank Publications, 2005.

Davenport, Thomas H., and Laurence Prusak. *Working Knowledge.* Harvard Business School Press, 2000.

Davenport, Thomas H., and Jeanne G. Harris. *Competing on Analytics: The New Science of Winning.* Harvard Business School Press, 2007.

Deare, Steven, "Cisco CEO sings praises of Web 2.0 future." ZDNet Australia, April 27, 2007, *http://www.zdnet.com.au/news/software/soa/Cisco-CEO-sings-praises-of-Web-2-0-future/0,130061733,339275139,00.htm.*

DeVany, Arthur. *Hollywood Economics: How Extreme Uncertainty Shapes the Film Industry.* Routledge, 2003.

Dibbell, Julian. *Play Money: Or, How I Quit My Day Job and Made Millions Trading Virtual Loot.* Basic Books, 2006.

Dierickx, Ingemar, and Karel Cool, "Asset Stock Accumulation and Sustainability of Competitive Advantage," *Management Science 35,* no. 12 (1989): 1504–1511.

Dosi, Giovanni et al., eds., *The Nature and Dynamics of Organizational Capabilities.* Oxford University Press, 2001.

Doz, Yves L., and Gary Hamel. *Alliance Advantage: The Art of Creating Value Through Partnering.* Harvard Business School Press, September 1998.

Doz, Yves L., "The Evolution of Cooperation in Strategic Alliances: Initial Conditions or Learning Processes?," *Strategic Management Journal* 17 (Summer Special Issue) (1996): 55–83.

Doz, Yves L., and Shuen, Amy. From Intent to Outcome: A Process Framework for Partnerships. Unpublished INSEAD Working Papers no. 88/46, 1988.

Evans, Philip, and Thomas S. Wurster. *Blown To Bits: How the New Economics of Information Transforms Strategy.* Random House, 2000.

Fast Company 50 interview with Stewart Butterfield, "Reinventing the a category whose flashbulb burnt out," *http://www. fastcompany.com/magazine/archives/2005.*

Fensel Dieter, James A. Hendler, Henry Lieberman, and Wolfgang Wahlster. *Spinning the Semantic Web: Bringing the World Wide Web to Its Full Potential.* The MIT Press, 2005.

Fitzgerald, Michael, "Internetworking: new social networking startups aim to mine digital connections to help people find jobs and close deals," *MIT Technology Review,* April 2004, *http://www.technologyreview.com/Infotech/13526/page1/ ?a=f.*

Foray, Dominique. *The Economics of Knowledge.* The MIT Press, 2006.

Friedman, Thomas. *The World Is Flat: A Brief History of the Twenty-First Century.* Farrar, Straus and Giroux, 2006.

Foster, Richard. *Innovation: The Attacker's Advantage.* Simon & Schuster, 1988.

Garud, Raghu et al. *Managing in the Modular Age: Architectures, Networks, and Organizations.* Blackwell Publishing Ltd., 2002.

Gawer, Annabelle and Michael Cusumano. *Platform Leadership: How Intel, Microsoft, and Cisco Drive Industry Innovation.* Harvard Business School Press, 2002.

Gerstner, Louis V. *Who Says Elephants Can't Dance?: Leading a Great Enterprise through Dramatic Change.* Collins, 2004.

Gilbert, Richard J., and Michael L. Katz, "An Economist's Guide to U.S. v. Microsoft," *Journal of Economic Perspectives* 15, no. 2 (2001): 25-44.

Gillmor, Dan. *We the Media: Grassroots Journalism by the People, for the People.* O'Reilly, 2006.

Gladwell, Malcolm. *The Tipping Point: How Little Things Can Make a Big Difference.* Back Bay Books, 2002.

Godin, Seth. *Small Is the New Big: and 183 Other Riffs, Rants, and Remarkable Business Ideas.* Portfolio Hardcover, 2006.

Granovetter, Mark, "The Strength of Weak Ties: A Network Theory Revisited," *Sociological Theory* 1 (1983): 201–233.

Grove, Andrew S. *Only the Paranoid Survive: How to Exploit the Crisis Points That Challenge Every Company.* Currency, 1999.

Gruhl, Daniel et al., "Information diffusion through Blogspace," *WWW 2004*: 491–501.

Hagel, John, III, and Arthur Armstrong. *Net Gain: Expanding Markets Through Virtual Communities.* Harvard Business School Press, 1997.

Hagel, John, III. *Out of the Box: Strategies for Achieving Profits Today and Growth Tomorrow Through Web Services.* Harvard Business School Press, 2002.

Hamel, Gary, with Bill Breen. *The Future of Management.* Harvard Business School Press, 2007.

Hamel, Gary, and C. K. Prahalad. *Competing for the Future.* Harvard Business School Press, 1996.

Hamner, Susanna, and Tom McNichol. "Ripping up the rules of management," *Business 2.0*, May 21, 2007, *http://money.cnn.com/galleries/2007/biz2/0705/gallery.contrarians.biz2/2.html.*

Hargadon, Andrew. *How Breakthroughs Happen: The Surprising Truth About How Companies Innovate.* Harvard Business School Press, 2003.

Heires, Katherine, "Why It Pays to Give Away the Store," *Business 2.0*, *http://money.cnn.com/magazines/business2/business2_archive/2006/10/01/8387115/index.htm.*

Helfat, Constance et al. *Dynamic Capabilities: Understanding Strategic Change in Organizations.* Blackwell Publishing Ltd., 2007.

Henderson, Rebecca, with Kim Clark. "Architectural Innovation: The Reconfiguration of Existing Product Technologies and The Failure of Established Firms," *Administrative Science Quarterly* 35, no. 1 (1990): 9–30.

Hippel, Eric von. *Democratizing Innovation.* The MIT Press, 2006.

Hippel, Eric von. *The Sources of Innovation.* Oxford University Press, 1994.

Hof, Robert, "Web 2.0 Has Corporate America Spinning," *BusinessWeek*, June 5, 2006, *http://www.businessweek.com/technology/content/jun2006/tc20060605_424102.htm.*

Hof, Robert, "Mix, Match, and Mutate," *BusinessWeek*, July 25, 2005, *http://www.businessweek.com/magazine/content/05_30/b3944108_mz063.htm.*

Hoover, J. Nicholas. "At Procter & Gamble, The Good and Bad of Web 2.0 Tools," *Information Week*, June 23, 2007, *http://www.informationweek.com/story/showArticle.jhtml?articleID=200000229.*

Hughes, Mark. *Buzzmarketing: Get People to Talk About Your Stuff.* Portfolio Hardcover, 2005.

Iansiti, Marco, and Roy Levien. *The Keystone Advantage: What the New Dynamics of Business Ecosystems Mean for Strategy, Innovation, and Sustainability.* Harvard Business School Press, 2004.

Indvik, Kurt, "Rev-Share Still Lives," Rentrak News online, Sept. 16, 2005, *http://www.rentrakonline.ca/content/news/news_09-16-05.html.*

Itami, Hiroyuki, with Thomas Roehl. *Mobilizing Invisible Assets.* Harvard University Press, 1991.

Johnson, Steven. *Emergence: The Connected Lives of Ants, Brains, Cities, and Software.* Scribner, 2002.

Katz, Michael, and Carl Shapiro, "Network Externalities, Competition, and Compatibility," *The American Economic Review* 75, no. 3 (1985): 424–440.

Katz, Michael, and Carl Shapiro, "Systems Competition and Network Effects," *Journal of Economic Perspectives* 8, no. 2 (1994): 93–115.

Kelly, Kevin. *New Rules for the New Economy: 10 Radical Strategies for a Connected World.* Penguin, 1999.

Kelly, Kevin. *Out Of Control: The New Biology of Machines, Social Systems, & the Economic World.* Addison-Wesley, 1995.

Kim, W. Chan, and Renée Mauborgne. *Blue Ocean Strategy: How to Create Uncontested Market Space and Make Competition Irrelevant.* Harvard Business School Press, 2005.

Krogh, Georg et al. *Enabling Knowledge Creation: How to Unlock the Mystery of Tacit Knowledge and Release the Power of Innovation.* Oxford University Press, 2000.

Kumar, Ravi et al. "On the bursty evolution of blogspace," WWW2003: 568–576.

Lenderman, Max. *Experience the Message: How Experiential Marketing Is Changing the Brand World*. Carroll & Graf, 2006.

Lessig, Lawrence. *The Future of Ideas: The Fate of the Commons in a Connected World*. Vintage, 2002.

Levine, Rick et al. *The ClueTrain Manifesto: The End of Business as Usual*. Perseus Publishing, 2001.

Levy, Steven, "Q&A: Jobs on iPod's Cultural Impact," *Newsweek*, October 16, 2006, *http://www.msnbc.msn.com/id/15262121/site/newsweek/print/1/displaymode/1098/*.

Liebowitz, Stan. *Re-Thinking the Network Economy: The True Forces That Drive the Digital Marketplace*. AMACOM/American Management Association, 2002.

Mauboussin, Michael. *More Than You Know: Finding Financial Wisdom in Unconventional Places*. Columbia University Press, 2006.

McConnell, Ben, and Jackie Huba. *Citizen Marketers: When People Are the Message*. Kaplan Publishing, 2006.

McConnell, Ben, and Jackie Huba. *Creating Customer Evangelists: How Loyal Customers Become a Volunteer Sales Force*. Kaplan Publishing, 2007.

Minevich, Mark et al. *Six Billion Minds: Managing Outsourcing in the Global Knowledge Economy*. Aspatore Books, 2006.

Montgomery, Cynthia, ed. *Resource-Based and Evolutionary Theories of the Firm: Toward a Synthesis*. Kluwer Academic Publishers, 1995.

Moore, Geoffrey A. *Dealing with Darwin: How Great Companies Innovate at Every Phase of Their Evolution*. Portfolio Hardcover, 2005.

Moore, Geoffrey. *Crossing the Chasm: Marketing and Selling High-Tech Products to Mainstream Customers*. HarperBusiness, 2002.

Mowery, David C., Joanne E. Oxley, and Brian S. Silverman, "Strategic Alliances and Interfirm Knowledge Transfer," *Strategic Management Journal* 17 (1996): 77–91.

Musser, John, with Tim O'Reilly. *Web 2.0 Principles and Best Practices*. O'Reilly Media, 2006.

Nelson, Richard R., and Sidney G. Winter. *An Evolutionary Theory of Economic Change*. Belknap Press, 2006.

"NetFlix Signs Revenue-sharing Pacts with Warner, Columbia," *Ultimate AV* magazine online. (December 17, 2000) *http:// ultimateavmag.com/news/10893/*.

"Netflix announces agreements with major motion picture distributors," Netflix press release (December 6, 2000) *http://www. netflix.com/MediaCenter?id=1024*.

Nonaka, Ikujiro, and Hirotaka Takeuchi. *The Knowledge-Creating Company: How Japanese Companies Create the Dynamics of Innovation*, Oxford University Press, 1995.

Ogilvy, David. *Confessions of an Advertising Man*. Southbank Publishing, 2004.

Ogilvy, David. *Ogilvy on Advertising*. Vintage, 1985.

Penrose, Edith. *The Theory of the Growth of the Firm*. Oxford University Press, 1995.

Perez, Juan Carlos, "Q&A: Vint Cerf on Google's Challenges Aspirations," *Computerworld,* (November 25, 2005) *http:// www.computerworld.com/developmenttopics/development/ story/0,10801,106535,00.html*.

Pine, B. Joseph, II, and James H. Gilmore. *The Experience Economy: Work is Theater and Every Business a Stage*. Harvard Business School Press, 1999.

Polanyi, Michael. *Personal Knowledge: Towards a Post-Critical Philosophy*. Revised edition. University of Chicago Press, 1974.

Pool, John Charles, and M. La Roe. *The Instant Economist*. Basic Books, 1986.

Porter, Michael. *Competitive Strategy*. The Free Press, 1980.

Porter, Michael. *Competitive Advantage: Creating and Sustaining Superior Performance*. The Free Press, 1985.

Powell, Walter W. et al., "Interorganizational Collaboration and the Locus of Innovation: Networks of Learning in Biotechnology," *Administrative Science Quarterly* 41, no. 1 (1996): 116–145.

Putnam, Robert D. *Bowling Alone: The Collapse and Revival of American Community*. Simon & Schuster, 2001.

Quarles, Christa Sober, September 2006 Thomas Weisel Partner *Investment Analyst Report on Internet Services*.

Raymond, Eric S. *The Cathedral & the Bazaar: Musings on Linux and Open Source by an Accidental Revolutionary*. O'Reilly, 2001.

Rheingold, Howard. *Virtual Reality: The Revolutionary Technology of Computer-Generated Artificial Worlds—and How It Promises to Transform Society*. Simon & Schuster, 1992.

Rheingold, Howard. *The Virtual Community: Homesteading on the Electronic Frontier*. The MIT Press, 2000.

Rheingold, Howard. *Smart Mobs: The Next Social Revolution*. Basic Books, 2003.

Rogers, Everett. *Diffusion of Innovations*. Fifth edition. The Free Press, 2003.

Rosenberg, David. *Cloning Silicon Valley: The Next Generation High-Tech Hotspots*. Financial Times/Prentice Hall, 2001.

Rymaszewski, Michael, Wagner James Au, Cory Ondrejka, and Richard Platel. *Second Life: The Official Guide*. Sybex, 2007.

Saxenian, AnnaLee. *Regional Advantage: Culture and Competition in Silicon Valley and Route 128*. Harvard University Press, 1996.

Scoble, Robert, and Shel Israel. *Naked Conversations: How Blogs are Changing the Way Businesses Talk with Customers.* Wiley, 2006.

Sernovitz, Andy. *Word of Mouth Marketing: How Smart Companies Get People Talking.* Kaplan Publishing, 2006.

Shapiro, Carl, and Hal Varian. *Information Rules: A Strategic Guide to the Network Economy.* Harvard Business School Press, 1998.

Shneiderman, Ben. *Leonardo's Laptop: Human Needs and the New Computing Technologies.* The MIT Press, 2003.

Shreeve, James. *The Genome War: How Craig Venter Tried to Capture the Code of Life and Save the World.* Ballantine Books, 2005.

Shy, Oz. *The Economics of Network Industries.* Cambridge University Press, 2001.

Sloan, Paul, and Paul Kaihla. "Blogging for Dollars," *Business 2.0,* October 2, 2006.

Stephens, R. Todd, comment on "P&G Web 2.0 Success Story," Forrester report cited on Collaborage: Enterprise 2.0 Implementation Overview blog, comment posted on Nov. 27, 2007, *http://www.rtodd.com/collaborage/2007/11/pg_web_20_success_story.html.*

Stewart, Thomas A. *Intellectual Capital: The New Wealth of Organizations.* Currency, 1998.

Surowiecki, James. *The Wisdom of Crowds: Why the Many Are Smarter Than the Few and How Collective Wisdom Shapes Business, Economies, Societies, and Nations.* Anchor, 2005.

Taleb, Nassim Nicholas. *Fooled by Randomness: The Hidden Role of Chance in Life and in the Markets.* Random House Trade Paperbacks, 2005.

Tapscott, Don, and Anthony Williams. *Wikinomics: How Mass Collaboration Changes Everything.* Portfolio Hardcover, 2006.

Teece, David J. et al. "Dynamic Capabilities and Strategic Management," *Strategic Management Journal* 18, no. 7 (1997): 509–533.

Terdiman, Daniel. "Folksonomies Tap People Power," Wired. com, Feb. 1, 2005, *http://www.wired.com/science/discoveries/news/2005/02/66456?currentPage=all*.

Turkle, Sherry. *Life on the Screen: Identity in the Age of the Internet*. Simon & Schuster, 1997.

Turkle, Sherry. *The Second Self: Computers and the Human Spirit*. The MIT Press, 2005.

Tushman, Michael L., and Philip Andersen, eds. *Managing Strategic Innovation and Change: A Collection of Readings*. Oxford University Press, 2004.

Tushman, Michael L., and Charles O'Reilly III. *Winning Through Innovation: A Practical Guide to Leading Organizational Change and Renewal*. Harvard Business School Press, 2002.

Utterback, James M. *Mastering the Dynamics of Innovation*. Harvard Business School Press, 1996.

Varian, Hal R, "An iPod Has Global Value. Ask the (Many) Countries That Make It," *New York Times*, June 28, 2007, *http://people.ischool.berkeley.edu/~hal/people/hal/NYTimes/2007-06-28.html*.

Varian, Hal et al. *The Economics of Information Technology: An Introduction*. Cambridge University Press, 2005.

Vogel, Harold L. *Entertainment Industry Economics: A Guide for Financial Analysis*. Cambridge University Press, 2007.

Waldrop, Mitchell M. *Complexity: The Emerging Science at the Edge of Order and Chaos*. Simon & Schuster, 1992.

Watts, Duncan. *Six Degrees: The Science of a Connected Age*. W. W. Norton & Company, 2004.

Watts, Duncan J. *Small Worlds: The Dynamics of Networks Between Order and Randomness*. Princeton University Press, 2003.

Weber, Steven. *The Success of Open Source.* Harvard University Press, 2005.

Wenger, Etienne et al. *Cultivating Communities of Practice.* Harvard Business School Press, 2002.

Wernerfelt, Birger, "Umbrella Branding as a Signal of New Product Quality: An Example of Signalling by Posting a Bond," *The RAND Journal of Economics* 19, no. 3 (1988): 458–466.

Williamson, Oliver E. *The Economic Institutions of Capitalism.* The Free Press, 1998.

Wilson, Fred. "A VC: The Freemium Business Model," Fred Wilson's blog, comment posted on March 23, 2006, *http://avc. blogs.com/a_vc/2006/03/the_freemium_bu.html.*

Wipperfürth, Alex. *Brand Hijack: Marketing Without Marketing.* Portfolio Trade, 2006.

Harvard Business School Materials

All of the cases, articles, notes, and other materials listed below are available at *http://harvardbusinessonline.hbsp.harvard.edu/.*

Adner, Ron, "Match Your Innovation Strategy to Your Innovation Ecosystem," *Harvard Business Review,* April 2006.

Anand, Bharat N., and Estelle S. Cantillon, *The Music Industry and the Internet,* Case (Library), April 2003.

Applegate, Lynda M. et al., *IBM's Decade of Transformation (A): The Turnaround,* Case (Library), April 2005.

Applegate, Lynda M. et al., *Overview of E-Business Pricing Models,* Supplement, September 2000.

Applegate, Lynda M., and Meredith Collura, *Amazon.com: Exploiting the Value of Digital Business Infrastructure,* Case (Library) and Teaching Note, June 2000.

Applegate, Lynda M., *Amazon.com Valuation Exercise,* Exercise, June 2000.

Austin, James E., and Liz Kind, *AOL, Cisco, Yahoo!: Building the Internet Commons,* Case (Field), March 2002.

Austin, Robert D., and Richard L. Nolan, *IBM Corp. Turn-around*, Case (Field), March 2000.

Bagley, Constance E., and Reed Martin, *Warner Bros. and Bit-Torrent*, Case (Field), September 2006.

Barber, Felix, and Michael Goold, "The Strategic Secret of Private Equity," *Harvard Business Review*, September 2007.

Barnett, William P. et al., *Facebook*, Case (Field), May 2006.

Beverland, Michael, and Michael Ewing, "Slowing the Adoption and Diffusion Process to Enhance Brand Repositioning: The Consumer Driven Repositioning of Dunlop Volley," *Business Horizons*, September 2005.

Birkinshaw, Julian et al., "Finding, Forming, and Performing: Creating Networks for Discontinuous Innovation," *California Management Review*, May 2007.

Bower, Joseph L., and Clayton M. Christensen, "Disruptive Technologies: Catching the Wave," *Harvard Business Review*, January 1995, and Teaching Note, December 1998.

Bradley, Stephen P., and Nancy Bartlett, *How Media Choices are Changing Online Advertising*, Note, October 2006.

Burgelman, Robert, and Steve Chung, *CDNetworks, Inc.*, Case (Field), July 2007.

Chesbrough, Henry W., "Why Companies Should Have Open Business Models," *Sloan Management Review*, January 2007.

Chesbrough, Henry W., "The New Business Logic of Open Innovation," *Strategy & Innovation*, July 2003.

Chesbrough, Henry W., and David J. Teece, "Organizing for Innovation: When Is Virtual Virtuous?" (*HBR* Classic), *Harvard Business Review*, August 2002.

Coyne, Kevin P., and Renee Dye, "The Competitive Dynamics of Network-Based Businesses," *Harvard Business Review*, January 1998.

Cross, Rob et al., "Using Social Network Analysis to Improve Communities of Practice," *California Management Review*, November 2006.

Cross, Rob, Jeanne Liedtka, and Leigh Weiss, "A Practical Guide to Social Networks," *Harvard Business Review*, March 2005.

Cross, Rob, Stephen P. Borgatti, and Andrew Parker, "Making Invisible Work Visible: Using Social Network Analysis to Support Strategic Collaboration," *California Management Review*, January 2002.

Crossan, Mary M., and Ken Mark, *Apple Computer, Inc.: iPods and iTunes*, Case (Field), July 2005.

Daugherty, Patricia J. et al., "Is Collaboration Paying Off for Firms?" *Business Horizons*, January 2006.

Davenport, Thomas H., "Competing on Analytics," *Harvard Business Review*, January 2006.

Davenport, Thomas H., "The Coming Commoditization of Processes," *Harvard Business Review*, June 2005.

Desai, Mihir A. et al., *Subscriber Models*, Note, December 2004.

Dobele, Angela et al., "Why Pass on Viral Messages? Because They Connect Emotionally," *Business Horizons*, July 2007.

Dobele, Angela et al., "Controlled Infection! Spreading the Brand Message Through Viral Marketing," *Business Horizons*, March 2005.

Dye, Renee, "The Buzz on Buzz," *Harvard Business Review*, November 2000.

Eisenmann, Thomas R., and Andrei Hagiu, *Staging Two-Sided Platforms*, Note, July 2007.

Eisenmann, Thomas R. et al., "Strategies for Two-Sided Markets," *Harvard Business Review*, October 2006.

Eisenmann, Thomas R., *Platform-Mediated Networks: Definitions and Core Concepts*, Instructor's Module Note, September 2006.

Eisenmann, Thomas R., and Lauren Barley, *PayPal Merchant Services*, Case (Library), April 2006.

Eisenmann, Thomas R., *Skype*, Case (Compilation), March 2006.

Eisenmann, Thomas R., *Winner-Take-All in Networked Markets*, Note, February 2006.

Eisenmann, Thomas R., *A Note on Racing to Acquire Customers*, Note, January 2003.

Eisenmann, Thomas R., and Alastair Brown, *Online Content Providers*, Note, November 2000.

Farhoomand, Ali F., and Samuel Tsang, *The Global Software Industry in 2006*, Case (Field), June 2006.

Farhoomand, Ali F., and Samuel Tsang, *IBM's On Demand Business Strategy*, Case (Field), September 2005.

Farrell, Diana, "The Real New Economy," *Harvard Business Review*, October 2003.

Frey, Sherman C., Jr., *Cash Flow and the Time Value of Money*, Note, August 1976.

Garvin, David A., and Lynne C. Levesque, *Emerging Business Opportunities at IBM (A)*, Case (Field), March 2004.

Gloor, Peter, and Scott M. Cooper, "The New Principles of a Swarm Business," *Sloan Management Review*, April 2007.

Gourville, John T., *Note on Innovation Diffusion: Rogers' Five Factors*, Note, May 2005.

Greenwood, Robin, and Lucy White, *Introduction to Valuation Multiples*, Note, February 2006.

Greenwood, Robin, and David Scharfstein, *Calculating Free Cash Flows*, Note, October 2005.

Gulati, Ranjay, and Jason Garino, "Get the Right Mix of Bricks and Clicks," *Harvard Business Review*, May 2000.

Hagel John, III, "Web Services: Technology as a Catalyst for Strategic Thinking," *Harvard Management Update*, January 2000.

Hamel, Gary, "Bringing Silicon Valley Inside," *Harvard Business Review*, September 1999.

Hamermesh, Richard G. et al., *Note on Business Model Analysis for the Entrepreneur*, Note, January 2002.

Hammond, John S., III, and Gerald B., Allan, *Note on the Boston Consulting Group Concept of Competitive Analysis and Corporate Strategy*, Note, February 1975.

Hansen, Morten T., and Julian Birkinshaw, "The Innovation Value Chain," *Harvard Business Review*, June 2007.

Harreld, J. Bruce, Charles A. O'Reilly III, and Michael L. Tushman, "Dynamic Capabilities at IBM: Driving Strategy into Action," *California Management Review*, August 2007.

Herman, Kerry, and Thomas R. Eisenmann, *Google, Inc.*, Case (Library), January 2006.

Hicks, Christian, and Dessislava Pachamanova, "Back-Propagation of User Innovations: The Open Source Compatibility Edge," *Business Horizons*, July 2007.

Holloway, Charles A., and Pratap Mukherjee, *Hotmail Corp.*, Case (Field), April 1999.

Huston, Larry, and Nabil Sakkab, "Connect and Develop: Inside Procter & Gamble's New Model for Innovation," *Harvard Business Review*, March 2006.

Iansiti, Marco, and Alan MacCormack. *Living on Internet Time: Product Development at Netscape, Yahoo!, NetDynamics, and Microsoft*, Case (Library), November 1996.

Interactive Marketing: New Channel, New Challenge. November 2005. HBS Press Chapter.

Kaikati, Jack G., and Andrew M. Kaikati, "Stealth Marketing: How to Reach Consumers Surreptitiously," *California Management Review*, August 2004.

Kim, W. Chan, and Renée Mauborgne, "Blue Ocean Strategy," *Harvard Business Review*, October 2004.

Kim, W. Chan, and Renée Mauborgne, "Value Innovation: The Strategic Logic of High Growth" (*HBR* Classic), *Harvard Business Review*, July 2004.

Kim, W. Chan, and Renée Mauborgne, "Tipping Point Leadership," *Harvard Business Review*, April 2003.

Kim, W. Chan, and Renée Mauborgne, "Fair Process: Managing in the Knowledge Economy" (*HBR* Classic), *Harvard Business Review*, January 2003.

Kim, W. Chan, and Renée Mauborgne, "Creating New Market Space," *Harvard Business Review*, January 1999.

Knoop, Carin-Isabel, and Mikolaj Jan Piskorski, *Friendster (A)*, Case (Field), September 2006.

Knoop, Carin-Isabel, and Mikolaj Jan Piskorski, *Friendster (B)*, Supplement (Field), September 2006.

Kuemmerle, Walter, and William J. Coughlin, *VacationSpot.com & Rent-A-Holiday: Negotiating a Trans-Atlantic Merger of Start-Ups*. Case (Field), March 2000, and Teaching Note, October 2002.

Kuemmerle, Walter, and William J. Coughlin, *TixToGo: Financing a Silicon Valley Start-Up*, Case (Field), April 2000.

Lakhani, Karim R., and Lars Bo Jeppesen, "Getting Unusual Suspects to Solve R&D Puzzles," *Harvard Business Review*, May 2007.

Lerner, Josh, *A Note on the Initial Public Offering Process*, Note, October 1999.

Lerner, Josh, and John Willinge, *Note on Valuation in Private Equity Settings*, Note, October 1996.

Leschly, Stig et al., *Amazon.com—2002*, Case (Field), November 2002.

Loveman, Gary W., "Diamonds in the Data Mine," *Harvard Business Review*, May 2003.

MacCormack, Alan, and Kerry Herman, *Red Hat and the Linux Revolution*, Case (Field), November 1999, and Teaching Note, March 2002.

Mangelsdorf, Martha E., "The Future of the Web," *Sloan Management Review*, April 2007.

Mayfield, E. Scott, *NetFlix.com, Inc.*, Case (Field), September 2000, Spreadsheet, October 2000, and Teaching Note, October 2001.

McAfee, Andrew, "Will Web Services Really Transform Collaboration?," *Sloan Management Review*, January 2005.

McFarland, Jennifer, "Instant Messaging," *Harvard Management Communication Letter*, August 2001.

Meister, Darren, and Ken Mark, *Google Inc.: Launching Gmail*, Case (Field), August 2004.

Meyer, Christopher, and Andre Schwager, "Understanding Customer Experience," *Harvard Business Review*, February 2007.

Miller, Gregory S., *The Process of "Going Public" in the United States*, Note, August 2004.

Moon, Youngme, and David Chen, *Google Advertising*, Case (Library), October 2006.

Nambisan, Satish, and Mohanbir Sawhney, "Meet the Innovation Capitalist," *Harvard Business Review*, March 2007.

Nambisan, Satish et al., "Innovating from the Outside In," 2nd Edition, *HBR OnPoint*, June 2007.

Nolop, Bruce, "Rules to Acquire By," *Harvard Business Review*, September 2007.

Ofek, Elie, *Forecasting the Adoption of a New Product*, Note, February 2005.

Ofek, Elie, *Eyeblaster: Enabling the Next Generation of Online Advertising*, Case (Field), September 2003, and Teaching Note, April 2004.

Ofek, Elie, *Customer Profitability and Lifetime Value*, Note, August 2002.

Palepu, Krishna G., and Amy P. Hutton, *America Online, Inc.*, Case (Library) February 1996 and Teaching Note, April 1999.

Pine, B. Joseph, and James Gilmore, "Welcome to the Experience Economy," *Harvard Business Review*, July 1998.

Piskorski, Mikolaj Jan, *Choosing Corporate and Global Scope*, Note, January 2007.

Piskorski, Mikolaj Jan, *LinkedIn (A)*, Case (Field), July 2006.

Piskorski, Mikolaj Jan, *LinkedIn (B)*, Supplement (Field), July 2006.

Porter, Michael, "How Competitive Forces Shape Strategy," *Harvard Business Review*, March/April 1979.

Prahalad, C. K., and Gary Hamel, "The Core Competence of the Corporation," *Harvard Business Review*, May 1990.

Prandelli, Emanuela et al., "Diffusion of Web-Based Product Innovation," *California Management Review*, August 2006.

Rachleff, Andrew, and Bethany Coates, *IMVU*, Case (Field), March 2007.

Reichheld, Frederick F., "The One Number You Need to Grow," *Harvard Business Review*, December 2003.

Reichheld, Frederick F., and Phil Schefter, "Put a New Lens on Loyalty—to Magnify Profitability," *HBR OnPoint*, July 2001.

Reichheld, Frederick F., and Phil Schefter. "E-Loyalty: Your Secret Weapon on the Web," *Harvard Business Review*, July 2000.

Rivkin, Jan W., and Jay Girotto, *Yahoo!: Business on Internet Time*, Case (Field), July 1999, and Teaching Note, January 2000.

Roberts, Michael J., and Howard H. Stevenson, *Deal Structure and Deal Terms*, Note, November 2005.

Roberts, Michael J., *Funding New Ventures: Valuation, Financing and Capitalization Tables*, Note, October 2005.

Roberts, Michael J., and Lauren Barley, *How Venture Capitalists Evaluate Potential Venture Opportunities*, Case (Field), July 2004.

Roberts, Michael J., and Shripriya Mahesh, *Hotmail*, Case (Field), February 1999, and Teaching Note, May 1999.

Sahlman, William A., *The Venture Capital Valuation Problem Set*, Exercise, August 2006.

Sahlman, William A., and R. Matthew Willis, *The Basic Venture Capital Formula*, Note, August 2003.

Sahlman, William A., "How to Write a Great Business Plan," *Harvard Business Review*, July 1997.

Sahlman, William A., *Note on Free Cash Flow Valuation Models*, Note, October 1987.

Sahlman, William A., and Daniel R. Scherlis, *A Method for Valuing High-Risk, Long-Term Investments: The Venture Capital Method*, Note, July 1987.

Schneberger, Scott, and Ken Mark, *DoubleClick, Inc.: Gathering Customer Intelligence*, Case (Field), February 2001.

Selden, Larry, and Ian C. MacMillan, "Manage Customer-Centric Innovation—Systematically," *Harvard Business Review*, April 2006.

Shih, Willy et al., *Netflix*, Case (Field), May 2007, and Teaching Note.

Silk, Alvin J., *Brand Valuation Methodology: A Simple Example*, Note, January 1996.

Stalk Jr., George et al., "Competing on Capabilities: The New Rules of Corporate Strategy," *Harvard Business Review*, March 1992.

Stancill, James McNeill, "How Much Money Does Your New Venture Need?" *Harvard Business Review*, May 1986.

Stevenson, Howard H., and Michael J. Roberts, *New Venture Financing*, Note, January 2002.

Vivero, David Andrew, and Thomas R. Eisenmann, *Monster Networking*, Case (Field).

Wagonfeld, Alison Berkley, and Thomas R. Eisenmann, *Yahoo! Messenger: Network Integration*, Case (Field), April 2005.

Watson Richard T. et al., "Attractors: Building Mountains in the Flat Landscape of the World Wide Web," *California Management Review*, January 1998.

Watts, Duncan J., and Jonah Peretti, "Viral Marketing for the Real World," *Harvard Business Review*, May 2007.

Wells, John R., and Elizabeth A. Raabe, *Update: The Music Industry in 2006*, Case (Library), February 2007.

Werbach, Kevin, "Using VoIP to Compete," *Harvard Business Review*, September 2005.

Werbach, Kevin, *Syndication: The Emerging Model for Business in the Internet Era*, HBR OnPoint, September 2000.

Yoffie, David B., and Michael Slind, *iPhone vs. Cell Phone*, Case (Library), October 2007.

Yoffie, David B. et al., *Brightcove and the Future of Internet Television*, Case (Field), January 2007, and Teaching Note, May 2007.

Yoffie, David B. et al., *iPod vs. Cell Phone: A Mobile Music Revolution?*, Case (Library), August 2006.

Yoffie, David B. and Michael Slind, *Apple Computer, 2006*, Case (Library), April 2006.

Yoffie, David B., and Alison Berkley Wagonfeld, *Oracle vs. Salesforce.com*, Case (Library), June 2005.

Yoffie, David B., and Debbie Freier, *Instant Messaging*, Case (Library), May 2004.

Yoffie, David B., and Mary Kwak, *AOL Europe vs. Freeserve (B)*, Teaching Note, December 2002.

Yoffie, David B., and Mary Kwak, *AOL Europe vs. Freeserve (A)*, Case (Library), August 2002.

Yoffie, David B., and Mary Kwak, *AOL Europe vs. Freeserve (C)*, Supplement (Library), August 2002.

Yoffie, David B., *Microsoft Goes Online: MSN—1996*, Case (Field), November 1997, and Teaching Note, December 1997.

Zider, Bob, "How Venture Capital Works," *Harvard Business Review*, November 1998.

Index

The O'Reilly Advantage

Stay Current and Save Money

Order books online:
www.oreilly.com/order_new

Questions about our products or your order:
order@oreilly.com

Join our email lists: Sign up to get topic specific email announcements or new books, conferences, special offers and technology news
elists@oreilly.com

For book content technical questions:
booktech@oreilly.com

To submit new book proposals to our editors:
proposals@oreilly.com

Contact us:
O'Reilly Media, Inc.
1005 Gravenstein Highway N.
Sebastopol, CA U.S.A. 95472
707-827-7000 or
800-998-9938
www.oreilly.com

Did you know that if you register your O'Reilly books, you'll get automatic notification and upgrade discounts on new editions?

And that's not all! Once you've registered your books you can:

» Win free books, T-shirts and O'Reilly Gear

» Get special offers available only to registered O'Reilly customers

» Get free catalogs announcing all our new titles (US and UK Only)

Registering is easy! Just go to www.oreilly.com/go/register

O'REILLY®

Try the online edition free for 45 days

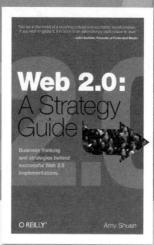

Get the information you need when you need it, with Safari Books Online. Safari Books Online contains the complete version of the print book in your hands plus thousands of titles from the best technical publishers, with sample code ready to cut and paste into your applications.

Safari is designed for people in a hurry to get the answers they need so they can get the job done. You can find what you need in the morning, and put it to work in the afternoon. As simple as cut, paste, and program.

To try out Safari and the online edition of the Subject To Change: Creating Great Products & Services for an Uncertain World FREE for 45 days, go to www.oreilly.com/go/safarienabled and enter the coupon code FRWKPWA.

To see the complete Safari Library visit:
safari.oreilly.com

3 1143 00730 5882